THE EROTIC IN SPORTS

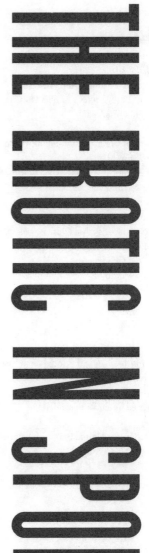

THE EROTIC IN SPORTS

ALLEN GUTTMANN

COLUMBIA UNIVERSITY PRESS

NEW YORK

Columbia University Press
Publishers since 1893
New York   Chichester, West Sussex
Copyright (c) 1996 Columbia University Press
All rights reserved

Library of Congress Cataloging-in-Publication Data
Guttmann, Allen.
  The Erotic in sports / Allen Guttmann.
    p. cm.
  Includes bibliographical references and index.
  ISBN 0-231-10556-8 (alk. paper)
    1. Sports—Psychological aspects. 2. Erotica. 3. Sexual
excitement. I. Title.
GV706.4.G88 1996
796'.01—dc20   96-15878
                                                      CIP

Casebound editions of Columbia University Press books
are Smyth-sewn and printed on permanent and
durable acid-free paper.

Designed by Linda Secondari

Printed in the United States of America
c 10 9 8 7 6 5 4 3 2 1

To Steven and Gridth Ablon

OTHER BOOKS ON SPORTS BY ALLEN GUTTMANN

From Ritual to Record: The Nature of Modern Sports.
New York: Columbia University Press, 1978.

*The Games Must Go On: Avery Brundage and the Olympic
Movement.* New York: Columbia University Press, 1984.

Sports Spectators. New York: Columbia University Press, 1986.

A Whole New Ball Game: An Interpretation of American Sports.
Chapel Hill: University of North Carolina Press, 1988.

Women's Sports: A History.
New York: Columbia University Press, 1991.

The Olympics: A History of the Modern Games.
Urbana: University of Illinois Press, 1992.

Games and Empires: Modern Sports and Cultural Imperialism.
New York: Columbia University Press, 1994.

CONTENTS

ACKNOWLEDGMENTS

Convention dictates that one acknowledge the help that one has received and repress the temptation to name the scoundrels who failed to answer letters, refused permission to reproduce images, and did their imaginative best to frustrate one's efforts. Meekly, I follow the convention.

John A. Cameron introduced me to the study of eros. Kim Townsend guided me into the field of men's studies. I am indebted to several scholars who invited me to speak on the topic of eros and sports: Alan Tomlinson, Donald Kyle, William Baker, and Hans Ulrich Gumbrecht. At various stages of my research, Thomas Scanlon and Andrew Doyle kindly sent me unpublished essays that proved to be quite useful. For help in the procurement of photographs, I am especially grateful to Jan and Terry Todd and to Gertrud Pfister. Deans Ronald Rosbottom and Lisa Raskin both provided funds to assist me in this project. Doris Bargen, Leslie Bialler, and Kate Wittenberg offered encouragement when it was most needed.

A number of paragraphs in the present work appeared, in different form, in previous books that I have published with Columbia University Press.

THE EROTIC IN SPORTS

Defenceless under the night
Our world in stupor lies;
Yet, dotted everywhere,
Ironic points of light
Flash out wherever the just
Exchange their messages:
May I, composed like them
Of Eros and of dust,
Beleaguered by the same
Negation and despair,
Show an affirming flame.

W. H. AUDEN
"September 1, 1939"

Introduction: Candor, Euphemism, and Denial

Idolatry is the mother of all games.
—Novatian, "De Spectaculus"

When Greek men and boys journeyed to Olympia to compete in the great panhellenic festival that honored Zeus, when Greek girls ran races at the same site for an olive branch and a portion of a sacrificial cow, everyone seems to have understood that physically trained bodies, observed in motion or at rest, can be sexually attractive. Most of the ancients acknowledged and celebrated the erotic element of sports. In modern times that same element has been observed by those who feared and deprecated it. Critics of sports have deplored their sensuality and their ability to entice, excite, and sexually arouse participants and spectators alike. In the Victorian era, a number of medical experts complained that the craze for the newly invented bicycle was a thinly disguised desire for the illicit pleasures of masturbation. It was charged that the bicycle seat induced "priapism."[1] The presidents of evangelical colleges warned ominously that football games were orgiastic affairs more fit for pagan haunts than the groves of academe. In 1892, the *Wesleyan Christian Advocate* complained that the violent game unleashed "the lower impulses of the physical man" and allowed young males to "find their pleasure in mere sensual energy."[2]

When Senda Berenson introduced basketball to the young women of Smith College, in Northampton, Massachusetts, the only man allowed in the gymnasium was the president of the college, a man whose age and dignity were thought to neutralize any danger that he might be erotically aroused. When the Australian press reported positively, in October 1907, on "the brown skinned specimens of manhood" and the "bronze Venuses" that were to be seen on the beaches and in the surf, there were immediate protests against "heaps of sprawling men and lads, naked, but for a nondescript rag around the middle."[3] In 1933, Sunny Lowry swam the English Channel and was berated as a "harlot" because she exposed her bare knees.[4] A year later, Cardinal Rodrigue Villeneuve of Quebec, condemning the "pagan" cult of the body as manifested in sports, bemoaned the rampant concern for "hysterical strength, sensual pleasure, and the development of the human animal." Meanwhile, his European colleagues thundered episcopal anathemas against female gymnasts who performed before mixed audiences.[5]

In response to the recurrent charge that sports are a sensual if not a satanic indulgence, most athletes and spectators have defended their passion as if the pleasure they derived from sports had no connection whatsoever with human sexuality. As one says in today's "postmodernist discourse," eros was "erased from the athletic text." In reply to heated allegations of sensuality, ingenuous lovers of sports have offered cool denial. Whenever outraged religious traditionalists have called attention to the erotic appeal of the human body at play, high-minded progressive reformers have blandly expatiated on the benefits of sunlight, fresh air, and unencumbered movement. In 1921 the journal *Die Freie Turnerin* showed off its new logo—a youthful nude. The editors of the periodical dedicated to women's gymnastics meant her to represent "a free maiden, with a joyful sense of her strength and her trained body, whose nakedness is unashamed because it is natural."[6] When confronted with clerical accusations of pornographic intent, German physical educators professed injured surprise: "For us," wrote the editors of the *Arbeiter-Turnzeitung*, "nudity is beauty, joy, and purity." This kind of nudity was *not*, they emphasized, erotic.[7] Countering similar allegations of prurience, a contributor to *Sport im Bild* announced in 1928 that sports participation actually dissipated "the mists of the erotic" that had enveloped German women. Thanks to sports, women were "cleaner, more free, fresher."[8]

YMCA workers, physical educators, and coaches have gone beyond mere self-deceptive denial. In response to the critics' exasperated insistence that sports can quite obviously be an occasion for erotic play, enthusiasts have propagated the modern myth that a heated contest and a cold shower divert or diminish adolescent sexuality. At best, they may even extinguish it. In response to charges of voyeurism, spectators enamoured of sports have proclaimed their chaste appreciation of "thrills and spills" and "all the moves" (except the erotic ones). When sports historian Richard Mandell mentioned to a group of Olympic coaches that there was "a suggestion of the erotic" in men's and women's gymnastics, they became as nervous as ninth graders viewing a film on sexually transmitted diseases.[9]

Scholarly specialists in sports studies appear to have joined the fans and the coaches in a conspiracy to suppress all mention of an erotic element in sports. Numerous studies have demonstrated that exercise programs result in an improved body image, but the sexual implications of this well-established finding are seldom explored. Sharp-eyed European and American experts have identified a vast array of motivations for sports participation, including an aesthetic dimension, but most have managed to overlook the fact that "fitness" and "to be in shape" are often euphemisms for the desire to be sexually attractive. Although the study of gender seems to have become a prerequisite for academic advancement, researchers in sports psychology rarely show more than a flicker of interest in sexuality. One looks, with scarcely more success, for references to sports in the voluminous psychological literature on sexuality. There is research indicating that men who exercise strenuously are more likely than their couch-potato peers to acknowledge a desire to date and kiss the attractive females whose photographs they are shown, but the psychologists who reported these experiments seem not to have raised questions about the erotic appeal of the exercisers.[10]

When an erotic element is too blatantly present to be overlooked, the customary reaction of the proponents of sports is promptly to condemn it. In an essay sharply critical of "the sexualization of female athletes in sport media," Donald Sabo and Michael Messner emphatically denied that men perceive *real* athletes—as opposed to television's fantastic fare—"in traditionally erotic terms." On the contrary, Real women

> athletes are too busy competing to pose; too caught up in the physical and mental demands of the game to engage in sexual innuendo; too independent, animated, and obviously three-dimensional for men to reduce them readily to sex objects. It is simple brain work for a traditional male to sexually objectify a wiggling cheerleader; a fully extended female smashing a volleyball does not erotically compute.[11]

Very recently, however, at least a few scholars have begun to ask some candid questions and to challenge some orthodox views. Why, wonder historians Elliott Gorn and Michael Oriard, are sports ignored in the academic debate over the history and social significance of the human body? After all, "power and eroticism meet most conspicuously in the athletic body—Florence Griffith-Joyner's, Greg Louganis's, or Michael Jordan's."[12] Why have historians "tended to retreat nervously from the erotic attractions of the male body"?[13] Why have those who are in love with sports been reluctant to examine their passion? The answer, presumably, is that the admission of simple facts acknowledged thousands of years ago is now blocked because the topic of eros and sports is obviously, for many if not for most modern coaches, athletes, and spectators, a taboo. To mention the topic is to cause them embarrassment. Like the timid lover in T. S. Eliot's "Love-Song of J. Alfred Prufrock," coaches, athletes, and spectators murmur, "That is not it at all, / That is not what I meant at all."

When nineteenth-century Anglicans touted "muscular Christianity," when YMCA workers invented basketball (1891) and volleyball (1895), when Pope Pius XII decided in 1945 to affirm the value of modern sports, critics became proponents, but there was no sudden acceptance of an erotic element in sports. Protestant and Catholic converts to sports seemed suddenly to become blind to the sexual dimensions that were anathema to their clerical predecessors (and to many of their contemporaries).

Ironically, once the mainstream churches took to celebrations of the joy of sports, to the construction of basketball courts, and to the establishment of church-related sports leagues, a number of secular critics, mostly neo-Marxists, began to deplore the "sexualization" of sports by capitalist society. Some of the more ascetic critics seem to have resurrected Tertullian's indictments of the Roman arena as the site of idolatry and perversion. Drawing on Freud as well as Marx, they blame sports, defined as "the capitalistically deformed form of play,"[14] for the psychological "castration" of the male athlete and for the deflection of his sexuality into sadism, masochism, narcissism, exhibitionism, and homosexuality. Critics have also condemned sports because they enhance a female athlete's heterosexual attractiveness and thus increase her "erotic exchange-value."[15] (The greater the value in the sexual marketplace, the more extreme the exploitation.) A number of radical feminists have added their charges to the indictment. While admitting that some women have benefited from sports and from the fitness fad, Nancy Theberge nonetheless alleges that programs promising enhanced attractiveness represent "not the liberation of women in sport, but their continued oppression through the sexualization of physical activity."[16] For Theberge as for Sabo and Messner (for whom female athletes did not "erotically compute"), the assumption behind the charge of sexualization is that the physical activity in question is not inherently sexual.

The reticulation of assertion and denial has recently become even more bizarrely tangled as Brian Pronger, Birgit Palzkill, and a number of other homosexual writers have decided to come out of the closet and head for the locker room. The International Gay Games celebrated in New York in 1994 must have caused cognitive dissonance in the ranks of two normally antagonistic groups: those on the political right who see athletes as the paladins of "family values" and those on the left who condemn athletes as the shock troops of "compulsory heterosexuality."

In short, the more or less unproblematic recognition of athletic eroticism by the pagan cultures of classical antiquity stands in sharp contrast to the hostile comments, the "erasure," and the confused obfuscation that have characterized most modern discussions of the phenomenon. Why has this been so? Why has this topic been a taboo among lovers of sports? Whatever may have been the case two hundred years ago, when industrialization imposed a new spatial and temporal discipline upon factory workers, I doubt that modern hypocrisy about human sexuality is the result of capitalism's alleged need continually to repress, sublimate, and exploit the instinctual self. The contrast between ancient openness and modern reticence has much more to do with the Protestant ethic than with the spirit of capitalism. As Pierre de Coubertin pointed out in an essay entitled "De la volupté sportive" (1913), "It is infinitely probable that the animosity the early Christians unleashed against athleticism was due precisely to the fleshly satisfaction which sport represented as well as that 'pride in life' pursued by sportsmen and denounced by the Holy Writ."[17] A moment's thought should convince anyone that Coubertin was correct. Today's emergent realization of an erotic element in sports is related to twentieth-century Christianity's relative loss of cultural influence rather than to a faltering in the expansion of the multinational corporation. If capitalism *were* the explanation for the suppression of eros, as Herbert Marcuse averred in *Eros and Civilization* (1955), we should now feel the taboo more intensely than ever. In fact, what we have witnessed in the last quarter century is capitalism's eager exploitation of the economic potential of eros in sports as in every other sector of our increasingly hedonistic culture. As Alphonso Lingis remarks in *Foreign Bodies* (1994), late capitalism depends on bodies "whose cupidity is heated up by advertising [to] serve as the pyres upon which an excess production of industrial commodities is destroyed."[18]

All this is most emphatically *not* to say that every sports performance has an erotic element or that all athletes are sexually attractive or that eros is the most important aspect of any particular sport. Obviously, not everyone finds athletes physically attractive. Indeed, there are undoubtedly athletes whom almost no one finds physically attractive. Mere physical attractiveness is certainly not the main reason why most spectators admire their athletic heroes and heroines. The heady rediscovery of an erotic component in sports need not impel one to assert that the "presentation of female athletes is . . . always eroticized by the fact that . . . any movement of the female body is erotic."[19] The sad truth is that some men and women will consider some male and female athletes, whether observed in motion or at rest, to be unattractive or even repulsive. *Chacun a son gout.*

Consider, for a moment, Western civilization in the late nineteenth century. There were young men who were excited by the prospect of the "Gibson Girl," tennis racquet in one hand, bicycle gripped in the other, and there were portly Victorian entrepreneurs who were sexually aroused by the thought of female invalidism. Some turn-of-the-century women swooned, literally, at the sight of Eugen Sandow's amazingly muscular body while the *beau idéal* of others was the decadent poet of the *rive gauche*, whose most strenuous activity was to lift not barbells but glasses of absinthe. Extreme cases, no doubt, but all of them have their counterparts in the gamut of actuality.

As this quite limited set of examples suggests, variations in the response to the erotic possibilities of sports are so myriad as to render the quest for constants quixotic. Accordingly, in my efforts to fathom the depths of eros and sports, I have been wary of essentialism's ever-present undertow. As David Halperin has forcefully insisted, "sexual experiences and forms of erotic life are culturally specific."[20] Thomas Laqueur has also warned of the need for caution: "Attempts to isolate [sexuality] from its discursive, socially determined milieu are as doomed to failure as the *philosophe's* search for a truly wild child or the modern anthropologist's efforts to filter out the cultural so as to leave a residue of essential humanity."[21] True enough, but Sander Gilman cautions, in the introduction to another book that stresses the historical mutability of sexual response, that the "social constructionists" can go too far in their indignation at those who misperceive the cultural as the natural. "There are social constructs that can exist separately from aspects of the physical world. Sexuality does not happen to be one of them."[22] Chris Schilling's sociological analysis of the body is informed by the same reasonable conviction: "Human bodies are taken up and transformed as a result of living in society, but they remain material, physical and biological entities."[23] The common physical basis of human sexuality implies that some sexual responses are, if not inevitable, at least more likely than others.

Although no cultural absolutes dictate the ideal masculine body, the muscularity of the Greek athlete, celebrated in antiquity by hundreds of sculptors and thousands of vase painters, is a norm from which the mathematical "standard deviation" has been rather small. That body seems functionally related to what were, until recently, the all-but-universal, taken-for-granted male roles of physically active protector and provider. Although there is considerable agreement about what may be termed the standard mesomorphic male body, cultural ideals for women have varied across a much wider range—from the sinewy bodies of Spartan girls to the soft debility of foot-bound Chinese brides unable to walk, much less run, on their mutilated feet. There is no agreement about a central tendency. Some scholars see a pattern cut by the determined scissors of patriarchal power:

> With the possible exception of the current athletic look, all images of feminine desirability over the ages share certain characteristics: they stress, from one angle or another, feminine helplessness and passivity, however this is to be achieved, whether because the woman is pregnant, or weak, dependent and sickly, or fat and slowed by her girth. Male beauty, as depicted in art, seldom if ever suggests weakness or dependency; idealized women almost always do.[24]

Other scholars see quite a different pattern. They suggest that focus on exotic extremes, like the Karen women of Burma, whose stretched and weakened necks require the support of twenty-four brass rings, draws attention from the nearly universal consensus that the ideal—at least for a young woman—is "roundness rather than angularity," a firm rather than a flabby body, health rather than sickness.[25]

Consideration of non-Western civilizations complicates one's speculations about physical ideals. Asian analogues to Mars and Venus do not look much like these deities as they were painted, for instance, by Sandro Botticelli. "The human body in traditional China," writes Mark Elvin, "was not seen as having its own intrinsic physical glory. One will look in vain in the Chinese arts for anything remotely approaching classical Greek statues of young unclothed male athletes."[26] Images of the Buddha enthroned upon a lotus leaf are liable to seem effeminate to European and American museum-goers. As Kenneth Dutton remarks, "the mesomorphic torso conveys a Western predilection for externality and activism which stands in sharp contrast to the stylized interiority of Eastern religious art."[27] The gates to Japanese temples are often flanked by larger-than-life carved figures—the *niô* —whose hypermuscularity and weaponry symbolizes their role as threatening guardians, but these are lesser deities whose bodies mark their inferior status in the heavenly order. In the eyes of the Japanese elite, the ideal masculine body was decidedly unathletic. I suspect, however, that the Asian glorification of the cerebral or the mystic can best be understood as an attempt to transcend the physical, whose presence and power is acknowledged by the determined—can one say by the "unnatural"?—effort at its suppression. Asceticism is the bitter tribute that mind pays to body.

There may be physiological clues that point to an intrinsically erotic element in sports. By definition, sports are competitions that require at least a modicum of controlled aggressiveness, and the relationship between aggression and sexuality has been closely studied. Twentieth-century scientists have discovered that the neurological centers governing sexuality and aggression are in such close proximity within the human brain that arousal of one influences arousal of the other. Within the hormonal system, there is a similar phenomenon; testosterone facilitates both sexual and aggressive arousal.[28] (In its synthetic form, as an anabolic steroid, testosterone has become the bane of modern sports.)

Quite apart from the association of aggression and sexuality, there are other clues that suggest a physical basis for the erotic element in sports. Among the hormones secreted by the human body are the pheromones, "chemical messengers" whose presence in perspiration has been identified as a (mild) aphrodisiac.[29] At the level of motor behavior, the rhythm of human movement is also suggestive. What Margaret Morse says about aerobics is probably true of sports as well: "The 'aerobic curve' of activity in a typical class bears a resemblance to an erotic curve of sexual excitement and release."[30] And then there is the simple fact—is it too embarrassingly obvious to mention?—that some sports involve the body in muscular exertions similar to those of sexual intercourse. I am intrigued by all of these facts but nonetheless content to leave physiological speculation to the physiologists. Although I am inclined to believe that there is an *inherent* erotic element in doing and watching sports, it should suffice for now if I can demonstrate that many men and women, from classical antiquity to modern times, have responded to sports as if they *were* inherently erotic. Cultural facts are no less interesting than natural ones.

In order to dispel the murk that surrounds the discussion of eros and sports, we need to consider the responses of both the participants and the spectators. One way to clarify matters is to offer a series of analytically organized chapters that deal first with the responses of the athletes and then with those of the spectators (whose responses can be divided between those aroused by the athletes' *activity* and those aroused by the activity as inscribed upon the athletes' *bodies*). I set off, originally, down this neatly marked organizational path, but I soon concluded that it led me away from the dense complexity of the phenomenon I wanted to understand. I have chosen, instead, to follow this introductory chapter with four chapters that investigate some of the historical evidence of an association between eros and sports in Europe and North America. These chapters move from Plato's dialogues to today's popular culture. A sixth chapter explores the theme as it is dramatized in a number of twentieth-century novels and films. This exploration of "eros imagined" leads to a commentary, in the seventh chapter, on some sociological and psychological contributions to the study of masculinity, femininity, physical attractiveness, and the sexuality implicit in sports. My eighth and last chapter is an argument for the acceptance of eros as *one* component, and only one, of the joy of sports.

My approach is eclectic and my evidence comes from many sources, ranging from the rhapsodic verses of ancient poets to the quantified and graphed conclusions of modern social scientists. I am aware that one cannot simply generalize from a poem or from a laboratory experiment, neither of which offers an unmediated or entirely objective glimpse of reality (whatever reality is).[31] Nonetheless, when signals derived from many different sources seem to point in the same direction, one should take them seriously. Wallace Stevens has a poem entitled "Thirteen Ways of Looking at a Blackbird." There's only one blackbird.

one

·

HISTORICAL
VICISSITUDES

RIGHT: Archaic Greek bronze statue of a running girl, probably Spartan.
Courtesy, Trustees of the British Museum.

BELOW: Gymnasium scene. Attic red-figure vase (ca. 480 B.C.).
Courtesy, Museum of Fine Arts, Boston.

Wrestling and hunting.
Attic black-figure vase (ca 550 B.C.)
Antikensammlung, Munich.

Knights and their admirers.
Manessa codex (ca. 1300).
Universitätsbibliothek Heidelberg.

Marco Dente DaRavenna, *Boxing Match Between Dares and Entellus* (16th century).

Graphische Sammlung Albertina, Vienna.

ABOVE: Guido Reni, *Atalanta and Hippomenes* (1620).
Museo Nazionale di Capodimonte, Naples.

BELOW: Chrispyn DePasse the Younger, *Baroque ring-tournament* (1623)
Bildarchiv des Schweizerischen Sportmuseums.

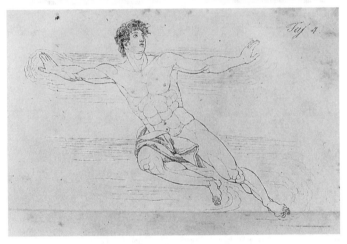

ABOVE: Michael Sweerts, *Roman Wrestlers* (ca. 1650).
Staatliche Kunsthalle, Karlsruhe.

BELOW: Christian Müller, *Swimmer* (1793).
Peter Kühnst Collection, Cologne.

J. Jackson, *Tom Cribb, Champion of England*,
engraved by J. Moore (1842).

Author's Collection

Jacques Joseph Tissot, *Croquet* (ca. 1878).
The Art Gallery of Hamilton (Ontario)

ABOVE: Jean Frédéric Bazille, *Summer Scene* (1869).
Harvard University Art Museums.

BELOW: Edgar Degas, *Spartan Girls Challenging the Boys
to Wrestle* (1860).
National Gallery (London).

ABOVE LEFT: Thomas Eakins, *Wrestlers* (1899).
Philadelphia Museum of Art, Bequest of Fiske and Marie Kimball.

BELOW LEFT: Eugen Sandow, photographed by Napoleon Sarony (1893).
From the collection of David Chapman, Seattle.

ABOVE RIGHT: Kate Roberts as "Vulcana" (from the cover of La *Santé par les Sport*, 1907.
Todd-McLean Collection, Austin.

Poster for a Six-Day Bicycle Race (1910).
Museum für Kunst und Gewerbe, Hamburg.

Suzanne Lenglen (1926).
AP/Wide World Photos.

Poster for Alpine Skiing (1931).
Museum für Gestaltung, Zurich.

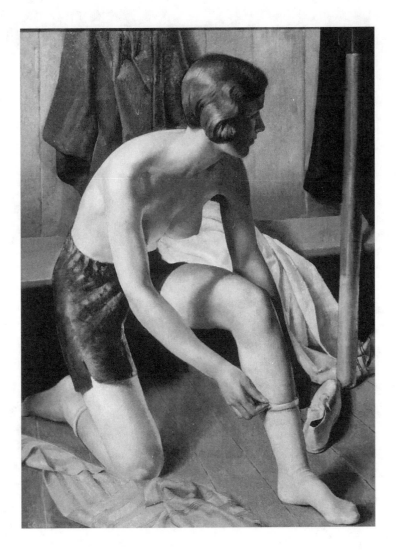

Lancelot Glasson, *The Young Rower* (1932).
Rochdale Art Gallery.

Работать, строить
и не ныть!
Нам к новой жизни
путь указан.
Атлетом можешь
ты не быть,
Но физкультурником—
обязан.

Alexander Deineka, *Work, Build, and Don't Complain* (1933).
Peter Kühnst Collection, Cologne.

2

Antiquity

*Bring water, bring wine, boy, bring us blossoming
garlands, bring them, so that I can box with Eros*
—ANACREON

GREECE

Despite the dauntingly vast amount of research published in the last
twenty years, neither the history of sexuality nor the history of
sports is detailed enough to allow anything more than an episodic
commentary on how men and women—at various times, in various
places—experienced (or failed to experience) the erotic element in
sports.[1] The historical data are sufficiently available for ancient
Greece and for the nineteenth and twentieth centuries in Europe
and North America, but they are seldom adequate for other times
and other places. As Arthur Brittan observed in *Masculinity and
Power* (1989), it is difficult to reconstruct conceptions of gender
before the modern era.[2] One way to deal with lacunae in the historical record is to construct a mosaic that is one part fact (Amenophis
III was depicted as an archer) and three parts conjecture (his skill
with the composite bow must have made him a icon of masculinity).
A better way to deal with the problem of inadequate evidence is to
be tentative and selective, to concentrate on those periods that *have*

been studied with relative thoroughness by sports historians (the laggards) as well as by historians of sexuality (the leaders).

While I am not averse to speculation, I think it important to have an evidentiary base from which to take flight. I have therefore decided to restrict my historical survey to Western civilization. I have discussed at some length the erotic aspects of ancient and medieval sports. My comments on the Renaissance and early modern times are briefer and more tentative. Those on the nineteenth and twentieth centuries are—no surprise—the most detailed.[3]

Greek sports may or may not have evolved from the rituals of primitive hunters, as David Sansone has maintained,[4] but religious ritual was unquestionably an intrinsic part of the great athletic festivals of the archaic, classical, and Hellenistic periods. This may be difficult for us to imagine, accustomed as we are to wholly secularized sports, but the evidence is incontestable. (Locker-room prayers before the contest and expressions of gratitude to Jesus after it may be common, but they are not an intrinsic part of the sports event.) From the eighth century B.C. to the end of the fourth century A.D., the Olympic Games institutionalized sports as cult. These grand quadrennial panhellenic athletic festivals were held at Olympia on a site that some archeologists believe was originally sacred to Gaia, goddess of the earth. By the legendary date of 776 B.C., Zeus was the main recipient of the athlete's homage.

Among the various stories told by the ancients in their attempts to account for the origin of the games, those of Pelops and of Herakles are prominent. Both founding myths involve a suitor's race. The first myth traces the games back to a chariot race in which Pelops vanquished the father of Hippodamia and thereby won the right to marry her; the second myth derives the athletic festival from a footrace won by Herakles, who then celebrated his marriage to Demeter Chamyne on a litter of olive branches. Common to both myths is the association of athletic prowess and sexual fulfillment. Herakles, who deflowered fifty virgins in a single night, was "the paradigm of the Greek athlete."[5]

Sports and religion merge with warfare in the earliest literary representation of Greek athletics: the funeral games for the slain Patroclus in Book XXIII of Homer's *Iliad*. For the Greeks, the warrior's role and the athlete's were necessarily related because both required considerable physical prowess. "Certainly," says the Athenian who is Plato's spokesman in *The Laws*, "the most military of all qualities is general activity of body, whether of foot or hand. For escaping or for capturing an enemy, quickness of foot is required; but hand-to-hand conflict and combat need vigour and strength."[6] The gymnasium, a prominent institution in every Greek *polis* worthy of the name, was one place where men trained for this requisite vigor and strength.

The confluence of military and athletic motives guaranteed that masculinity for most Greeks meant active physicality. The race in armor that was introduced into the Olympic Games in 520 B.C. "reminded the spectators that the soldier and the athlete were one and the same person."[7] The athletic male body was unquestionably a cultural ideal. From the visual evidence of our museums, where hundreds of statues and thousands of vases have been preserved, a composite image of that cultural ideal can readily be reconstructed. "Down to the middle of the fifth century," writes K. J. Dover, "the most striking and consistent ingredients of the 'approved' male figure are: broad shoulders, a deep chest, big pectoral muscles, big muscles above the hips, a slim waist, jutting buttocks and stout thighs and calves."[8] The pectoral muscles, referred to by modern scholars as the *cuirasse esthétique* because they were mimicked by the bronze breastplates worn by Greek warriors, were "the basis for the classical male nude's sex appeal."[9] The ideal was a soldier's body, an athlete's body.

And, it seems, a lover's body. Although it is an exaggeration to maintain that most Greek men preferred homosexual to heterosexual love, there is no reason to doubt the existence of homosexual relationships between an *erastes* ("lover"), who was usually a mature man, and an *eromenos* ("beloved"), who was usually a youth. Such relationships were socially acceptable as long as the older man took the more active part.

In the dynamics of desire, sports energized the relationship between the lover and the beloved. Cicero, Plutarch, Galen, and other sources from late antiquity indicate a widespread patrician dislike of the boxer's and the wrestler's heavy muscularity,[10] but athleticism was hardly a disincentive in the classical and Hellenistic periods. Quite the contrary: "The Greek ideal [was] the young but fully grown body, molded by gymnastics to the peak of its power."[11] The "lithe, taut and symmetrical body"[12] formed by years of sports participation was most erotically charged when in motion, and the gymnasium was an obvious place for athletic motion. There was even an untranslatable special term—*palaestrita*—to describe "boys, youths or young men who were adept at the exercises of the gymnasium and whose bodily beauty and grace of movement marked them . . . as shining examples of the physical ideal at which the gymnasium . . . aimed."[13]

Dover, the recognized authority on Greek homosexuality, comments on the gymnasium as a place that "provided opportunities for looking at naked boys, bringing oneself discreetly to a boy's notice in the hope of eventually speaking to him (for the gymnasium functioned as a social centre for males who could afford leisure), and even touching a boy in a suggestive way, as if by accident, while wrestling with him."[14] Appropriately, Eros joined Hermes as one of the gymnasium's tutelary deities. At Nemea, site of one of the four great panhellenic sports festivals, graffiti scratched into the walls of the "locker room" provide homely evidence of erotic interest. After the names of athletes, archeologists have found the word *kalos*—"beautiful." In the stadium at Aphrodisias in Asia Minor, a suggestive graffito reads simply *Topos Erotos*—"the place of love."[15]

The erotic ambiance of the gymnasium was a frequent motif for vase painters. A red-figured vase from the Louvre shows a gymnasium scene in which a youth embraces a responsive boy.

That it is indeed a gymnasium scene is indicated by an adjacent youth holding a discus. On another red-figured vase, this one in Oxford, a mature man fingers the penis of a responsive boy. On the wall behind them are a sponge and a scraper, sure signs of an athletic milieu.[16]

The polymath literary critic Northrop Frye has commented on hunting as another erotic activity: "The hunt is normally an image of the masculine erotic, a movement of pursuit and linear thrust, in which there are sexual overtones."[17] After an extensive study of the iconography of the hunt as it was depicted in Greek vase painting, Alain Schnapp's conclusions are similar to Frye's (and to Dover's): "The imagery . . . shows us . . . young men at the gymnasium, on the hunt, engaged in various games in which the erotic has a large role. The world of the young . . . creates a place for exercise of the body, athleticism, but also for seduction, for advances, for a complex and diversified eroticism."[18] The association of eros and hunting can be seen on a black-figured vase in Munich's *Antikensammlung*. Next to a hunter with a deer slung over his shoulder stands a man fondling a youth's penis. The shoulder of the vase has a wrestling scene.

Literary evidence supports the iconographical argument. In *Peace*, for instance, the comic playwright Aristophanes has a member of the chorus comment offhandedly that he "didn't tour round the wrestling-schools and make passes at boys."[19] The remark, of course, implies that others did. The famous orator Aeschines was among them. Speaking *Against Timarchos*, he admitted that he "made a nuisance of himself" at the gymnasium because he was erotically stimulated by the movements of beautiful young men running races or throwing the discus.[20] The poet Theognis of Megara managed to postpone sexual gratification until after his workout: "Happy the lover," he sang, "who exercises, then / Goes home to sleep all day with a handsome boy."[21]

The best examples of the erotic ambiance of the gymnasium come, not unexpectedly, from Plato's dialogues. Generations of scholars have debated, inconclusively, what Plato meant by the concept of eros in *Phaedrus* and *The Symposium*.[22] Fortunately, one can observe and comment upon some fairly simple interactions without having to venture into the philosophical debates.

In *Phaedrus*, Socrates comments that the lover will embrace his beloved "in gymnastic exercises and at other times of meeting."[23] In another dialogue, *Charmides*, Socrates marvels at the beauty of the young eponym, whom he first saw when he entered the gymnasium. "At that moment, when I saw him coming in, I confess that I was quite astonished at his beauty and stature; all the world seemed to be enamoured of him; amazement and confusion reigned when he entered; and a troop of lovers followed him." A moment later, the mood changes from astonishment to amusement. When the handsome youth walked over to a bench to take a seat, his excited admirers pushed "with might and main . . . in order to make a place for him next to themselves, until at the two ends of the row one had to get up and the other was rolled over sideways."[24]

An episode from *The Symposium* is an especially apt illustration of the erotic aspect of the gymnasium. The appropriateness of the source is suggested by Freud's comment, in the preface to the fourth edition of the *Three Essays* [1920], that "the *eros* of the divine Plato" approached "the extended sexuality of psychoanalysis."[25] In fact, Freud remarked a year later, in *Group Psychology and the Analysis of the Ego*, that Plato's use of the concept of eros was "completely congruent" with the term "libido" as used in psychoanalysis.[26] In *The Symposium*—a work to which Freud referred on many occasions[27]—Alcibiades complains to the group that his ardent love for Socrates has been unrequited:

> Well, he and I were alone together, and I thought that when there was nobody with us, I should hear him speak the language which lovers use to their loves when they are by themselves, and I was delighted. Nothing of the sort; he conversed as usual, and spent the day with me and then went away. Afterwards I challenged him to

the palaestra; and he wrestled and closed with me several times when there was no one present; I fancied that I might succeed in this manner. Not a bit; I made no way with him.[28]

To object that Alcibiades' motives are purely erotic and not at all athletic is to miss the point. Alcibiades expected Socrates to be as sexually aroused by their carnal grapple as he was.

The erotic element in sports made them—then as now—an ideal metaphor for sexual encounters. From the comedies of Aristophanes, we can reasonably infer that demotic Greek had many ingenious idioms with which to spice the gossip about amorously inept men, who in our lingo never get to first base. And there was, of course, more than one way to score in the game of love. Consider a comic scene from *Peace*, where some lascivious citizens are offered a slave girl named "Showtime":

> And *then*, now you've got her, first thing tomorrow you'll be able to hold a splendid athletic meeting—to wrestle on the ground, to stand her on all fours, to anoint yourselves and fight lustily in the free-style, knocking and gouging with fist and prick at once. After that, the day after tomorrow, you'll hold the equestrian events, in which jockey will outjockey jockey, while their chariots crash one on top of another, and thrust themselves together puffing and panting, and other charioteers will be lying with their cocks skinned, having come unstuck in the bends and twists.[29]

Implicit here is that sexual encounters were especially satisfying when they included, as sports do, the element of physical competition. The same implication can be discerned, centuries later, when the eponymous hero of *Daphnis and Chloe* is introduced by an older woman into the mysteries of sexuality. She likens lovers to wrestlers.[30] Another example comes from the poet Dioscorides, who imagined a sexual encounter in which Doris performed "the marathon of Venus" (after which she "was spread loose with limbs relaxed").[31]

If successful lovers were likened to athletes, then it should not be surprising that the inverse was also true: "athletic success seems to have been a powerful stimulus to . . . potential lovers."[32] Since most of the odes written by Greek poets to celebrate athletic victories "are more concerned with the mythological origin of the victor's family and the glories of his native city than with the details of his athletic prowess,"[33] they reveal very little about the association of eros and sports, but Pindar's 10th Pythian ode, celebrating the victory of Hippokleas of Thessaly in 498 B.C., is an exception. The poet seems confident that

> this music for his crowns
> will make Hippokleas
> still more admired
> among his peers and elders and keep him
> in the thoughts of young maidens.[34]

Xenophon's *Symposium* also documents this attractiveness when Socrates and the other guests at the banquet are stunned by the beauty of young Autolycus, who has just won the pankration at the Panathenaic Games.[35] A much more graphic instance of erotic response to youthful athleticism occurs in an anonymous poem from the *Palatine Anthology*. The presumably male poet expresses his delight in kissing a blood-spattered youth who has just won a boxing match.[36]

Pindar's reference to the maidens' interest in young Hippokleas raises a question: Did ancient Greek women respond as men did to the erotic element in men's sports? Since we have virtually no direct evidence on what Greek women thought on any topic, "We can only speculate about the reaction of Greek women to the persistent, insistent idealizing of the male body."[37] Anthropological evidence drawn from a vast array of preliterate societies suggests that Greek women were, indeed, attracted by the demonstration of athletic excellence. Among the Mehinaku of central Brazil, "The women say the wrestling champion is beautiful (*awitsiri*), and he is in demand as a paramour and husband. . . . Mehinaku sexual norms provide for the tacit approval of the wife who cuckolds a poor wrestler."[38] Pokot women squeal with pleasure at the sight of "tall and well-muscled men from their own and neighboring tribes."[39] Despite the paucity of direct evidence, we can heed Rudyard Kipling and conjecture that the Mehinaku, the Pokot, and the women of ancient Greece were—like Mrs. O'Grady and the colonel's lady—"sisters under the skin."

After all, if Greek women relied on their fathers, brothers, and sons for protection in time of war, as all but the mythical Amazons did, then it seems only reasonable to expect them to have admired the physical prowess that was the basis for military success. Beyond that, it seems equally reasonable to conjecture that women shared men's admiration of the stalwart athletic body. After all, women lived as men did among a profusion of visual images celebrating the beauty of male athletes. They too spent their lives surrounded by statues and vases that pictured men and gods as runners and jumpers, as throwers of the javelin and the discus, as boxers, wrestlers, and charioteers. Women must surely have been influenced by men's cultural preferences.

There is written evidence to support the conjecture that women shared men's response to athletic bodies. When homeward-bound Odysseus was shipwrecked and washed ashore in the land of the Phaiakians, Athena pitied him and "drifted a magical grace about his head and his shoulders, / and made him taller for the eye to behold, and thicker, / so that he might be loved by all the Phaiakians, and to them / might be wonderful and respected, and might accomplish many / trials of strength by which the Phaiakians tested Odysseus." When put to the test by his Phaiakian hosts, he amazed the men with his athletic prowess. Later, after the maids had bathed him, anointed him with oil, and put "a lovely mantle and a tunic about him," Nausikaa, daughter of King Alkinoös, "stood beside the pillar that supported the roof with its joinery, / and gazed upon Odysseus with all her eyes and admired him."[40]

After Homer, one turns (once again) to Plato. In *The Republic*, Socrates prescribes gymnastic exercises as part of the extensive education of the ideal state's male and female guardian elite. He suggests to Glaucon that an ancillary benefit of these exercises is that they will help bond the men and the women: "None of them will have anything specially his or her own; they will be together, and will be brought up together, and will associate at gymnastic exercises. And so they will be drawn by a necessity of their natures to have intercourse with each other—necessity is not too strong a word, I think?" Glaucon understands what Socrates means. He observes that the necessity in question here is "not geometrical" but rather "another sort of necessity which lovers know." Since Glaucon and Socrates then discuss marriages and how they "can . . . be made most beneficial," it seems clear enough that "intercourse" in this context refers not to the sexual act per se but to erotically suffused relationships—including gymnastics—that lead to marriages among men and women who are in the "prime of physical as well as intellectual vigour."[41]

When Plato returned to the question of the ideal state in *The Laws*, the anonymous Athenian who is his spokesman continues to assert the importance of athletic contests for girls as well as boys, but now the emphasis has shifted from what it was in *The Republic*. Love of the body comes in a poor second to love of the soul. The sexual feelings occasioned by sports are no longer affirmed as a stimulating prelude to a eugenic marriage. In *The Laws* they are deprecated as socially disruptive. Although the Athenian advocates sports contests for young men and women, both competing in the nude, he worries aloud about the dangers of concupiscence aroused by "young men and maidens holding friendly intercourse with one another." He reassures himself, sounding very much like a befuddled Victorian schoolmaster, that a man is "more likely to abstain from the pleasures of love . . . when his body is in a good condition." For women, temptation seems to be less of a problem, but they too are expected to be chastely abstinent until properly married.[42]

"Chaste" is hardly the word to characterize Simaitha, the lovelorn speaker of a poem by the Hellenistic poet Theocritus (who flourished a century after the death of Plato). Simaitha orders her servant to prepare a charm so that "I can tie him down, that man so hard on me." Where is Delphis, the man for whom Simaitha lusts? She spied him recently with his friend Eudamippos:

> Their beards were creamier than helichryse [a yellow flower],
> their breasts far brighter than you, O Moon,
> since they'd just left the gym's sweet exercise.

Simaitha surmises that Delphis is probably at the gymnasium now, which is where he seems to spend most of his time, and she wants him back.

> O Eros, torturer, why do you drain the dark blood
> from my skin, like a leech of the marsh?

When he does arrive at last, Delphis claims that Simaitha's summons "outpaced me by no more than I / the other day did Philinos in the race." Since Philinos of Kos was a famous runner who won victories at all four of the panhellenic games, Delphis—if his boast can be credited—was clearly quite an athlete.[43]

There is no reason to think that Simaitha's love of the athletic Delphis was eccentric or unusual, but there is a scholarly consensus that Greek men did not care for athletic women. It was certainly the rule for women to be sequestered in the home and for the gymnasium and the stadium, like the battlefield and the agora, to be reserved for men, but doubts about the consensus have been raised by an unusual red-figured Attic vase painting, now in the Museo Civico of Bari. Claude Bérard has interpreted the painting as a gymnasium scene. Three young women are shown "after their exercise. The one on the left, with a very athletic body, is in the process of cleaning her back with a strigil [to remove oil, sweat, and dust]; above her on the right, one sees the sponge and oil flacon."[44] Although Bérard admitted in an earlier article that the scene is never "explicitly marked as from a gymnasium,"[45] he suggests that young women may indeed have been frequenters of gymnasia.

The women shown on this vase are not the only ones to be depicted with athletic bodies. Statues of Aphrodite almost always present the goddess of love as voluptuous, but vase painters endowed their female figures with broad shoulders and deep chests. Dover notes that "women may be represented as having the characteristically male bulge of muscle above the hip-bone." Ceramic artists sometimes observed "the differences of configuration of hip, abdomen and groin," but they also, quite frequently, painted "male and female bodies . . . distinguishable only by the presence or absence of the breasts and the external genitals."[46] Margaret Walters agrees about Greek artistic conventions: "Young girls have hard muscular bodies, broad shoulders and narrow hips, with firm full buttocks. Their breasts often seem an afterthought."[47] More specifically, according to iconographic convention, depiction of the "abdominal muscles in a woman seem[s] to indicate a *hetaira*."[48] Like the Japanese geisha, the *hetaira*—a courtesan rather than a prostitute—was expected to be present at the symposium (as wives were not) and to contribute to the symposium's witty conversation, artistic ambiance, and erotic play.

Do these pictorial conventions merely underline men's habitual acceptance of their own masculine bodies as the human norm? Perhaps not. There is good reason to suspect that these female bodies may be more than mere projections of the overweening male ego. Recent excavations at the temple of Artemis at Brauron near Athens have unearthed direct visual evidence of sports for girls if not for grown women. A number of shards depict races run by naked adolescent maidens in the course of what most scholars take to be a prenuptial initiation into mature womanhood. The evidence is quite fragmentary—in addition to the shards there is a mysterious reference in the *Lysistrata* of Aristophanes—and scholars have differed in their interpretation of the ritual, but Lilly Kahil's conclusions seem plausible. Girls as young as nine or ten, dressed in tunics, "performed rites in honor of Artemis, either races or dances; when they attained the age of puberty, in a true *rite de passage*, they performed the same religious acts, entirely nude, for the last time."[49] At least one of the older runners has the long stride and the muscular physique of a modern sprinter.[50] If small girls appeared clothed while older, more physically developed maidens ran naked, then Athenian practice reversed modern conventions, which accept public nudity in prepubescent children more readily than in adolescents, but Kahil's interpretation makes perfect sense if the race was, indeed, a premarital rite. Artemis was, after all, the goddess of procreation as well as the goddess of the hunt. Athletic ability presaged fecundity—and may also have promised erotic pleasure.

There is even stronger evidence of men's acceptance (if not encouragement) of female athleticism. Although the Olympic Games were limited to men and boys, with women excluded even from the spectator's role, the Greeks celebrated a quadrennial athletic festival in honor of the goddess Hera, consort to Zeus. At this event, which took place at Olympia in the spring of the year, approximately a month before the men's festival, girls competed in footraces. Almost all our information about the Heraia comes from Pausanias, whose *Description of Greece*, written in the second century A.D., is also our best literary source for the Olympic Games.

> The games consist of foot-races for maidens. These are not all of the same age. The first to run are youngest; after them come the next in age, and the last to run are the oldest of the maidens. They run in the following way: their hair hangs down, a tunic reaches to a little above the knee, and they bare the right shoulder as far as the breast. . . . To the winning maidens they give crowns of olive and a portion of the cow sacrificed to Hera.[51]

It may be that we have visual evidence of these runners. An archaic bronze statuette from Sparta shows a running girl in a short tunic, with her right breast bare.

At Sparta, there were other rituals that attest to the association of eros and sports. Fragments from a *partheneion* (chorus for girls) by the archaic poet Alcman describe a Spartan initiation ceremony similar to the *rite de passage* at Brauron. The ritual included a race.[52] Some eight hundred years later, during his visit to second-century A.D. Sparta, Pausanias learned of a race run by eleven girls as part of the annual Festival of Dionysus Colonatas. Giampiera Arrigoni interprets this race as a device enabling the Spartans to select the priestesses of Dionysus, but Thomas Scanlon has argued forcefully that the contest was "a prenuptial initiatory trial."[53] Here too there is an implied association between eros and sports.

An even closer association appears in the sports that constituted an important part of the Spartan girl's secular regimen. These sports were notorious in the eyes of other Greeks because girls as well as boys were required regularly to train as athletes and to compete in public. The motivation was political and eugenic—to produce vigorous mothers and thus to engender the healthy boys required by a military state. (The similarity of Spartan practice to the utopian arrangements described in Plato's *Republic* was not accidental. Plato was known for his admiration of Sparta.[54])

The historian Xenophon, who seems to have approved wholeheartedly of women's sports and of Sparta's garrison state, credited the law-giver Lycurgus with the inauguration of sports for girls:

> Believing that the highest function of a free woman was the bearing of children, in the first place he insisted on the training of the body as incumbent no less on the female than the male; and in pursuit of the same idea instituted rival contests in running and feats of strength for women as [well as] for men. His belief was that where both parents were strong their progeny would be found to be more vigorous.[55]

Plutarch, writing five centuries later, added a number of details (which may or may not be authentic). Lycurgus "ordered the maidens to exercise themselves with wrestling, running, throwing, the discus, and casting the javelin, to the end that the fruit they conceived might, in strong and healthy bodies, take firmer root and find better growth." Thanks to their rigorous regimen, the Spartan girls were "more able to undergo the pains of childbearing."[56]

When engaged in sports (and when performing their dances and appearing in processions), the girls were naked. This nudity scandalized Xenophon's contemporary, the Athenian dramatist Euripides, who wrote in *Andromache* that

> No Spartan girl
> could ever live clean if she wanted.
> They're always out on the street in scanty outfits,
> Making a great display of naked limbs.
> In those they race and wrestle with the boys too—
> Abominable's the word.[57]

Plutarch, on the other hand, seems thoroughly to have approved of Spartan practices.

> Nor was there any thing shameful in this nakedness of the young
> women; modesty attended them, and all wantonness was excluded.
> It taught them simplicity and a care for good health, and gave them
> some taste of higher feelings, admitted as they thus were to the field
> of noble action and glory.

That the girls appeared naked was also a socially useful incitement to marriage. Plutarch was convinced that the naked appearances of the young women—in sports, in dances, in processions—operated "upon the young [men] with the rigor and certainty, as Plato says, of love if not of mathematics."[58] Commenting on the physical regimen of Spartan girls, a modern classicist—Giampiera Arrigoni— agrees that one function of the races was erotic; they demonstrated the eugenic fitness of the adolescent girls and acted "to stimulate the young [male] spectators to matrimony."[59]

ROME

Centuries later, the Roman poet Propertius (50 B.C.-ca. 2 A.D.), famed for his erotic verses, was unrestrained and almost absurdly lyrical about these Spartan girls:

> I much admire the Spartan wrestling schools,
> but most of all I like the women's rules:
> for girls and men can wrestle in the nude
> (the Spartans think such exercise is good);
> naked they throw the ball too fast to catch,
> and steer the creaking hoop in the bowling match,
> stand waiting, grimed with dust, for the starting gun,
> and bear the brunt of the Pancration,
> put boxing gloves on hands so soft and fair,
> and whirl the heavy discus through the air,
> gallop the circuit, helmets on their brow,
> buckling a sword to thighs as white as snow;
> with hoar-frost on their hair, they join the chase
> as the hounds of Sparta climb Taygetus,
> like Amazons, breasts naked to the fray,
> who bathed in Pontic streams at the end of day,
> like Helen training on Eurotas' sands
> with nipples bare and weapons in her hands,
> while boxer, horseman, champions to be,
> her brothers watched, and did not blush to see.[60]

Needless to say, Propertius relied more on his febrile imagination than upon the historical record, but who is to say that his was the only Roman imagination overheated by the contemplation of nubile, muscular, bellicose, competitive, female physicality? In fact, others seem to have shared similar fantasies.[61]

Although Ovid was another Roman poet famed for his erotic verses, his most vivid portrayal of an athletic woman appears in his *Metamorphoses* rather than in *The Art of Love*. When the mythical

Atalanta races against a youth whom she will marry only if he can defeat her, she is even more beautiful than when she is motionless:

> Her running redoubled her beauty.
> The ribbon-ties at her ankles
> Were the wing-tips of swallows.
> The ribbon-ties at her knees
> Were the wing-tips of swifts.
>
> Her hair blazed above her oiled shoulders
> And the flush on her slender body
> Was ivory tinted
> By rays that glow
> Through a crimson curtain.[62]

Atalanta sprints through Ovid's fantastic poem, where anything is possible. The degree to which Roman girls and women indulged in historically attested sports is uncertain. At some of the athletic festivals, such as the Capitoline Games in Rome and the Augustalia celebrated at Naples, girls competed in footraces. The famous "Bikini Mosaic" of the Piazza Armerina in Sicily shows ten lightly clad young women whose activities have been variously described as dancing, doing calisthenics, or participating in sports.[63] The location of the Piazza Armerina—in a region where Greek culture persisted into Roman times—suggests that these young women really were engaged in athletics. How typical they were of the age is, of course, uncertain. How Roman men responded to athletic women is still another question, one to which we have the satirist Juvenal's jaundiced answer. Writing late in the first century A.D. about adults rather than adolescent girls, he satirized Roman matrons who defied convention and indulged in "athletic workouts." He lampooned the women who sought additional countercultural thrills by dressing themselves as gladiators and slashing with swords at wooden dummies. These women, grunting and groaning, sweating and panting, were a more repulsive sight in Juvenal's eyes than the "gladiator's wench" or the "striptease broad."[64]

What about the gladiators whose deadly combats these pathetic women imitated? Odd as it may seem to us, the gladiator who entered the arena and risked his life in armed combat was sexually attractive, an "erotically charged figure"[65] whose physical presence excited women of every social class (which may explain the pathetic imitation that outraged Juvenal). The word *gladius* ("sword") was often used as a slang term for the penis. Describing the bloodshed of the Roman arena, the poet Ovid wrote, in *The Art of Love*, that "on that sorrowful sand Venus has often contested."[66] The man with the sword or trident, not the orator and certainly not the poet, was the hero of "the Roman romance with death, unendurably intensified and concentrated."[67] The men whose lives were at stake in this "temple of a decadent Venus"[68] faced death, and the presence of death seems to have been a crucial factor in the gladiator's erotic appeal. Keith Hopkins remarks that even "the dead gladiator had something sexually portentous about him. It was customary for a new bride to have her hair parted with a spear, at best one which had been dipped 'in the body of a defeated and killed gladiator.' "[69] (Hopkins is quoting from the poet Festus.)

Gladiators may have been legally *infama*, but Roman women responded nonetheless (and perhaps all the more) to their erotic attraction. Graffiti found in Pompeii announced that the gladiator Celadus was *"suspirium puellarum,"* which might be freely translated as "the heart-throb of all the girls." His colleague Crescens was allegedly the *"puparum dominus"* ("the master of the girls").[70] Chrysis, a servant, explains in the *Satyricon* of Petronius that there were respectable matrons who developed "a hankering for gladiators."[71] There is archeological evidence that at least one of them was ready to risk her aristocratic reputation for the sake of sexual adventure. In the courtyard of the building in which Pompeii's gladiators were housed, excavators found the "skeleton of a woman richly adorned with gold jewelry—a necklace of emeralds, two armbands, rings, and other ornaments—and carrying a cameo in a small casket."[72] Did she allow the love ignited by a gladiator to overcome her fears of an erupting volcano?

Juvenal had something to say about women like her. He was acerbic about aristocratic women who found male athletes sexually irresistible. What hope was there for Rome when a senator's wife is said to have thought that gladiators "look better than any Adonis"? Eppia abandoned her family and followed her gladiator lover from Rome to Alexandria. "This is what she preferred to children, country, and sister, / This to her husband." With a flourish of conventional sexually suggestive imagery, Juvenal concluded about these excited women, "The sword is what they dote on."[73]

Archeological evidence adds details to Juvenal's picture of Roman sexual customs. In 295 B.C., a temple to Venus was dedicated within the Circus Maximus (the site of chariot races). When the facilities for spectators were improved, brothels were constructed in the arcades beneath the seats—for the convenience of prostitutes who found customers at the races.[74] There were linguistic as well as architectural associations. In Latin as in Greek (and probably in every other language), metaphor linked eros to sports. The Romans were neither the first nor the last to notice that the physical positions, tensed muscles, and heavy breathing of a sexual encounter resemble those of an athletic contest. In this respect, Apuleius, the second-century fabulist, was less imaginative in his *Metamorphoses* than Aristophanes had been in *Peace*, but he too enlivened his popular philosophical narrative of supernatural adventure with some "gladiatorial games of Venus."[75]

Male homosexual relationships were far less common in Roman than in Greek culture, but they did exist and athleticism was a factor in them—at least for some men. An epigram attributed to Strato of Sardis succinctly expressed the writer's dislike of boys with fashionable ringlets and his preference for young wrestlers whose tanned and sinewy bodies were still covered with the arena's powdery dust.[76] Of course, not every ancient lover found hard bodies attractive. Since Roman slave owners sometimes castrated the boys whom they selected for their personal sexual gratification, the ideal of an epicenely soft male body was also widespread—at least among aristocrats with homosexual propensities. The poet Martial sang the praises of a boy who was "smooth and soft all over." Postpubescent youths lost their erotic appeal in the eyes of older men.[77]

Early in the sixth century A.D., when gladiatorial games were only a memory, when the Byzantine empire ruled by Justinian was at the peak of its glory, the most widely admired man in Constantinople was probably Porphyrius the charioteer. His place and date of birth are uncertain; he may have been born in Libya in about 480. His father may also have been a charioteer. What is certain is that his victories with the *quadriga*—the four-horse chariot—were celebrated from one end of the empire to the other. Partisans of the "Blues" and partisans of the "Greens"—the two "circus factions" whose rivalry disturbed the domestic tranquility of the empire with innumerable riots[78]—both erected monuments to him. Epigrams were written in his honor, thirty-two of which were preserved in manuscript anthologies that survived into the Middle Ages. When Porphyrius entered the hippodrome in Constantinople, the crowd greeted him with shouts of *tu vincas!* ("May you win!"). The very same formulaic words marked the entrance of the emperor. Alan Cameron, whose *Porphyrius the Charioteer* (1976) is my source, notes that "the parallelism between victorious charioteer and victorious Emperor is further emphasized by the fact that the Porphyrius stelae are plainly modelled on the base of Theodosius' obelisk, itself erected to commemorate a real imperial victory."[79] Neither the iconography of the phallic monuments erected to Porphyrius nor the images of the epigrams that celebrate his victories prove that there was an erotic component to the adoration of the "circus factions," but the carved figures and the verbal portraits do suggest that the charioteer, not the emperor and certainly not the Patriarch of the Greek Orthodox Church, was Constantinople's most potent symbol of masculinity.

Porphyrius was the idol of an officially Christian empire, but athleticism was idealized neither by the Greek Orthodox nor by the Roman Catholic faithful. In the years following Constantine's conversion, "the athlete of classical sculpture [changed] into the ascetic of the Byzantine icons."[80] Christian opposition put an end to both the Olympic Games (at the end of the fourth century or the beginning of the fifth) and the Roman gladiatorial contests (at about the same time). In their hostility to these events Christian spokesmen and activists were probably motivated more by their horror at pagan rituals than by the real and imagined lasciviousness of Roman sports, but patristic rhetoric certainly betrayed a frenzied fear of sensual indulgence. Augustine's language, describing the lamentable apostasy of Alypius, was typically agitated. His disciple had foolishly succumbed to the lure of a gladiatorial spectacle:

> For so soon as he saw that blood, he therewith drunk down savageness; nor turned away, but fixed his eye, drinking in frenzy, unawares, and was delighted with that guilty fight, and intoxicated with the bloody pastime.[81]

The Fathers of the Church employed exactly this sort of language when they exhorted the faithful to overcome the temptations of the flesh. Augustine's disappointment with his lapsed disciple was surely intensified by his awareness that on this same bloody ground, Christian martyrs were thrown to wild beasts.

The mortal bodies mangled in the arena were, of course, less prized by the faithful than were the immortal souls they housed. In fact, "house" is too weak a metaphor to express the asceticism that was unquestionably part of Christian piety. References to the human body as a prison, a charnel house, a grave, or a sink of corruption were ubiquitous in the religious literature of late antiquity and the Middle Ages as ascetic men and women were inspired to join the ranks of "those who have made themselves eunuchs for the sake of the Kingdom of Heaven" (Matthew 19:2). "The free abandonment of sexuality," writes Peter Brown, "was thought to have brought a halt to the chill contagion of the grave."[82] Simeon Stylites, who died only a few years before the birth of Porphyrius the charioteer, glorified God by spending thirty physically inactive years atop a sixty-foot-high Byzantine pillar. He was, like hundreds of others who mortified their flesh, canonized. In response to the death of a beautiful woman who had tempted him, one monk—praised as an example—"dippled his coat in her decomposed body and lived with this smell to help him fight his constant thoughts of beauty."[83] Clement of Alexandria was more moderate. He managed to accept the sacrament of marriage as a concession to the weakness of the flesh, but he was anything but enthusiastic about the carnality involved in human reproduction. "Our idea of self-control," he taught, "is freedom from desire."[84] In Clement's Egypt, asceticism replaced the pagan fertility rites that had once brought an overflow of water to the valley of the Nile. Peter Brown ends his magisterial study of *The Body and Society* with remarks about the disappearance, in early Christianity, of the exemplary body of the athlete. "No longer were the body's taut musculature and its refined poise, signs of the athlete and the potential warrior, put on display . . . as marks of upper-class status." Brown comments wryly on the change in attitudes: "Egyptian Christians now believed that the shriveled, sterile bodies of monks and virgins caused the valley to turn green every year."[85]

3

From the Middle Ages to the Renaissance

Iconographically, depictions of Christ's crucified body in medieval altarpieces, contrast pitiably with those of the robust physiques of the Roman soldiers shown mocking him and nailing him to the cross. Even in the early sixteenth century, when Matthäus Grünewald executed the Isenheim altar, he followed iconographic tradition and portrayed Christ on the Cross as a physically crippled sacrificial victim. "His skin is a greenish pallor, and is covered all over with cuts and bruises. He is twisted into a grotesque, almost inhuman shape; the feet are swollen from the nails and the fingers locked into a rigid cramp."[1] Christian hagiography did make room for doughty warriors like Saint Michael, but medieval artists tended to portray a meeker, less martial version of masculinity. Virile images of Michael, armed for battle against the rebellious angels, occurred less frequently than the sadomasochistic portraits of handsome young Saint Sebastian, stripped to a loin-clothed minimum, roped to a tree, and "swooning in a state between pain and ecstasy as the arrows pierce his flesh."[2] Carved and painted images of Sebastian's

martyrdom were so common and so sexually suggestive that the rid-
dled saint has been called "a glorified pinup of the pious."[3]

In medieval theology, eros was thought to be the opposite of
agape—the selfless love of God for His creation. Accordingly,
monastic rules called for austere asceticism and monastic practice
included the mortification of the flesh. Aelred of Rievaulx was lam-
entably typical when he rejoiced "that the weakness of the body is
an opportunity for spiritual elevation."[4] The ideals that inspired
men to welcome physical torment also animated convent life.
Jacques de Vitry, one of the most notable of thirteenth-century
preachers, praised ascetic women for their triumph over the temptations of the flesh: "They melted altogether in wondrous love for
God until it seemed that they bowed under the burden of desire and
for many years did not leave their beds except on rare occasions. . . .
Resting in tranquility with the master, they became deformed in
body but comforted and made strong in spirit." Vitry wrote with
special enthusiasm of Mary of Oignies (1177–1213). The contemplation of Christ induced her to cut off pieces of her own body and
to bury them in the earth.[5]

In contrast to the valorization of the mutilated body, there was
clerical denigration of the voluptuous female body. Posed like an
image of Aphrodite, the seductively lovely young woman carved in
the lintel of the "Last Judgment" tympanum of the cathedral of
Bourges was meant to admonish rather than to attract. She "stands
in a grave awakened by the sound of the last trumpet." The sculptor placed her "on the side of the damned, the sinister side of the
sinners who will burn in Hell for ever."[6]

The haggard monk and the anorexic nun were not, however, the
only exemplars of medieval life. They comprised only one of the
"three orders" who cooperated to maintain society by their pray-
ing, their laboring, and their fighting.[7] The Middle Ages were peo-
pled by arrogant warriors and sturdy footpads as well as by emaci-
ated clerics meekly devoted to the *Imitatio Christi*. The men who
struck down the infidel Saracen (or the insurgent peasant) with

heavy two-handed swords were obviously not puny specimens. To prevail in combat—and to excel at his favorite sport—the armored knight had to be a man of considerable physical strength.

Jo Ann McNamara, alleging a crisis in the "fragile and tentative" masculinity of twelfth-century men, comments, "It requires strong social support to maintain fictions of superiority based solely on a measure of physical strength."[8] The requisite social support came in the form of the age's most important sports institution. The medieval tournament was a theater for the ostentatious demonstration of political dominance, a stage on which the powerful few flaunted the symbols of their authority in front of the more or less powerless many, and a showcase for vaunting proud masculinity. Tournament lists may seem far removed from the domain of eros, but the relationship between feats of arms and the code of courtly love was strikingly direct. Recent scholarship on the tournament is no longer hesitant to acknowledge an erotic component. This component must have been glaringly obvious when the victor's prize was a "nicely dressed young girl" (*puellam decoram valde*), which was the case at a tournament held at Merseburg in 1226.[9]

The medieval tournament began in the twelfth century as a deadly free-for-all combat among an undisciplined crowd of armored warriors who assaulted each other with a deadly passion. (Georges Bataille might have argued that their passion was erotic precisely *because* the combats, fought with appropriately phallic swords and lances, involved the risk of death.) As the sport evolved, over a period of some four hundred years, it underwent what the German sociologist Norbert Elias has referred to as a "civilizing process." In time, the frequently deadly mock battles became theatrical performances full of allegorical pageantry. The tournament appears in fictional form in the romances of Chrétien de Troyes and Sir Thomas Malory. The romance, in turn, influenced the subsequent development of the tournament.

Parallel to the political structures of feudalism there developed the conventions of what Max Weber called "erotic vassalage."[10]

More recently, Louise Olga Fradenburg has argued that the tournament had "crucial homosocial functions in the later Middle Ages." In order to ward off suspicions of effeminacy and to "constitute themselves as 'men,' " knights battled one another before the admiring eyes of women who were both spectators and prizes. "The lady dramatizes the masculinity of the warrior by being what he is not and by watching his effort. . . . The knight, in fighting over the female, proves that he is not a female."[11] Adhering faithfully to the folderol of courtly love, the customary practices of the late medieval tournament called for a love-smitten knight to knot his beloved's scarf around the tip of his blunted (but still presumably phallic) lance and then to display his courage and his military skills as a means to win her favor. Around the joust there exfoliated a fantastic make-believe world of giants, dwarfs, magicians, enchanted castles, and dutiful unicorns that laid their heads in ladies' laps (if the ladies were really the virgins they were supposed to be). At the *Pas de l'Arbre d'Or* held at Bruges in 1468 to celebrate the marriage of Charles of Burgundy to Margaret of York, "the tournament had become a vehicle for fantastic, even prodigal, artistic expression." Sydney Anglo's description is the best:

> There were two entrances to the lists, one painted with a golden tree from which was suspended a real golden hammer, the other built with two towers which were filled with trumpeters during the contests. Opposite the ladies' seats was planted a pine tree with gilded trunk—the Tree of Gold itself—and a so-called *perron* with three pillars which served as a stage for the Arbre d'Or Pursuivant, his dwarf, and the captive giant.[12]

When the late-medieval or Renaissance tournament took the popular form of the *Table Ronde*, the participants in the allegory masqueraded as Lancelot and Guinevere, as Tristan and Isolde, or as other romantically Arthurian figures. After the bold knight rescued the distressed damsel, the two of them retired to the Temple of Love, where he doffed his battered helmet and received his kiss of

gratitude. While the military and political functions of the tournament never wholly disappeared, the erotic function—suitably con-
ventionalized—became increasingly prominent as *la force* was
replaced by *la prestance*.[13]

One of the odder aspects of late medieval tournaments was the
appearance of jousters in drag. The museum-goer who comes upon
prints of a *Frauentournier*, as I once did in Dresden, can easily
arrive at the false conclusion that women fought in tournaments,
but the *Frauen* depicted are actually men involved in what has to be
recognized as transvestite play. *Frauendienst*, a comic epic written
by Ulrich von Liechtenstein, indulges in the same sort of quirky
fantasy. When the chivalric hero is rebuffed by his lady love, he
chops off a finger and sends it to her to signal his submission to her
whims. Symbolically castrated, he then disguises himself as a
woman. Whom does he choose for his female persona? Venus.
Masquerading as the goddess of love, he gallops and thrusts his
way through a number of jousts until he earns the right to
straighten skewed gender lines and to renew his courtship.[14]

Some medievalists, assuming nothing is too rum not to have
happened, accept Ulrich's poem as autobiography, but most scholars agree that it is a work of fiction. As such it is comparable to the
many illuminated manuscripts depicting medieval women engaged
in fabulous jousts. Robert de Borron's *Histoire du Graal* and the
anonymous *Lancelot de Lac* are ornamented with pictures of
mounted women wielding distaffs and spindles and charging at
obviously disconcerted knights and monks. A marginal illustration
to Pierart dou Tielt's *Saint Graal* shows a titillating contest
between two naked women armed with distaffs, one upon a goat,
the other on a ram. The early-fourteenth-century *Breviary for
Marguerite de Bar* repeats the goat-ram theme with a peasant
woman on a goat and a knight about to be unseated from his ram.[15]
These marginalia portrayed an imaginary topsy-turvy world—
eine verkehrte Welt—in which women astride notoriously lustful
mounts enacted forbidden roles. The point here is not the historic-

ity of such images but the association, in the minds of these clerical misogynists, of eros and sports.

While lords and ladies amalgamated the tournament within the
game of love, the relationship between sport and sexuality took a
crasser form at the other end of the social hierarchy. Peasants who
had never heard of Chrétien de Troyes or seen a *Table Ronde* played
folk-football, a rough sport that matched village against village
or, more anthropologically interesting, the married against the
unmarried. The rules varied from locale to locale, as they always do
for traditional games, but a typical contest was one in which the
men, women, and children of two neighboring villages struggled to
carry, kick, or throw a ball or some other portable object into the
portal of their opponents' parish church.

In twelfth-century England and France, these tests of strength,
swiftness, endurance, and the ability to survive rough treatment
were often played on Shrove Tuesday. In addition to the game's
Eastertide setting, some of its associated customs point to its origins
as a religious ritual. Folk-football may have begun as part a fertility
rite, a lively way to mark the vernal equinox and celebrate the
rebirth of vegetation after winter's death. Shrove Tuesday contests
that pitted the married against the unmarried visibly stressed the
difference between those who were sexually active and those who
were—at least officially—still celebate.[16] Helping us to imagine the
ribald shouts and obscene gestures of the spectators, folklorists point
to modern clues to medieval behaviors. In France, at Boulogne-la-
Grasse, the rituals that accompanied the game, played on *le jour de
mardi gras,* survived into the nineteenth century. The sexually suggestive paraphernalia of the day included a basket of eggs and a staff
from which a beribboned leather ball was suspended.[17]

The vital association of eros and sports can be also be detected in
accounts of the many seasonal fairs and saint's-day festivals that
brightened the medieval year. Men wrestled, fought with staves,
and performed prodigious feats of strength. Winners won plaudits
from their peers. "In the game of gander-pulling, the young man

demonstrated his vigor and skill and, if he won, he offered his prize to his intended amidst the cries, the appreciative remarks, and the applause of the crowd."[18] The women, meanwhile, ran races. Contests among prostitutes were a common attraction. In the south of France, for example, races for prostitutes were mentioned in conjunction with saint's-day fêtes at Pernes (in 1458).[19] German customs were similar. Typically, the "public women" competed after the men's archery contest and before the footraces for children. Sometimes the prostitutes competed against their untainted sisters, as they did in Nördlingen in 1442, and sometimes the fallen women had the field to themselves, as they did in Augsburg in 1452.[20] Just as in the tumult of folk-football, the women ran "with skirt tuckt very high."[21] Commenting on the carnival-time contests in Basel, one historian remarks that the lightly clad prostitutes were exemplars of *Liebesübungen* rather than *Leibesübungen* ("exercises in love" rather than "exercises of the body").[22]

During the Renaissance, fencing matches rivaled tournaments as occasions for the presentation of a manly self—although the conceptions of masculinity each sport implied were very different. In fencing, quickness and agility were prized above "brutish" strength. The difference between the vertical slash of the heavy, difficult-to-wield two-handed tournament sword and the horizontal thrust of Hamlet's light rapier signals a transformation in European culture. Like other cultural transformations, this one had its critics. George Silver, one of Shakespeare's traditionalist contemporaries, complained in 1599 about the decadent influence of "these Italianate weake, fantasticall and most divellish and imperfect fights."[23] (Was Silver aware that Venetian fencing schools had become nodal points of a homosexual subculture?[24])

The lower classes held longest to familiar customs. In 1705, Thomas Brown witnessed an exhibition of good old-fashioned swordplay at London's "Bear-garden": "Seats fill'd and crowded by Two: Drums beat, Dogs yelp, Butchers and Footsoldiers clatter their Sticks: At last the two Heroes in their fine borrow'd Holland shirts, mount the Stage about Three; Cut large Collops out of one another to divert the Mob, and make Work for the Surgeons."[25] Bloody occasions of this sort persisted through the "Age of the Enlightenment," as did bouts between lusty men armed with staves, but the historical current ran against them. In the apogee of the *ancien régime*, such entertainments seemed atavistic. As late as the nineteenth century, Frenchmen sniffed that the English were a nation of beefy shopkeepers whose regressive admiration for boxers compared unfavorably with the "dignity and delicacy" of the French, who appreciated the fine points of the fencer's art.[26]

"For the Renaissance fencer," writes Henning Eichberg, "the charm of his sport clearly lay in the exercise of every spatial and positional possibility."[27] Treatises on the "Italianate" sport emphasized the aesthetic appeal of the fencer's movements. Camillo Agrippa's *Trattato di Scientia d'Arme* (1533) and Girard Thibault's *L'Académie de l'espée* (1628) were illustrated by diagrams of the appropriate positions to take before, during, and after a match. For his copperplate print, *The Fencing Hall* (1608), Willem Swanenburgh arranged his fencers around a complicated geometrical pattern drawn in the middle of the tiled floor. The picture is an epitome of elegance.

The shift in emphasis from force to finesse can be seen in the advice offered by Baldasarre Castiglione in *Il Cortegiano* (1528). How should the courtier behave when at play?

> If he happens to engage in arms in some public show—such as jousts, tourneys, stick-throwing, or in any other bodily exercise— mindful of the place where he is and in whose presence, he will strive to be as elegant and handsome in the exercise of arms as he is adroit, and to feed his spectators' eyes with all those things that he thinks may give him added grace; and he will take care to have a horse gaily caparisoned, to wear a becoming attire, to have appropriate mottoes and ingenious devices that will attract the eyes of the spectators even as the lodestone attracts iron.

Contest makes way for spectacle and the primary focus is on the spectacle's effects. Castiglione's enthusiasm for elegance and grace was not, however, unbounded. Men who pampered themselves, men who plucked their eyebrows and curled their hair, were liable to become "soft and feminine." Castiglione had only scorn for men "so tender and languid that their limbs seem to be on the verge of falling apart." Despite the revolution in manners, "The principal and true profession of the Courtier must be that of arms." Wrestling was especially prized because it "frequently accompanies the use of weapons on foot."[28]

The ludic evolution from manly roughness to not-quite-effeminate refinement is observable in football as well as in fencing. In Italy, the peasant's bruising, brawling free-for-all became the aristocrat's minutely regulated recreation. In the elegant game described by Giovanni de' Bardi's *Discorso sopra il Giuoco del Calcio Fiorentino* (1580), there was no trace of the "beastly fury . . . and extreme violence" that Sir Thomas Elyot observed in English folk-football.[29] The contestants, wrote de' Bardi, should be "gentlemen, from eighteen years of age to forty-five, beautiful and vigorous, of gallant bearing and of good report." It was important that the players wear "goodly raiment and seemly, well fitting and handsome." Why did de' Bardi stress the participants' appearance? Because "the fairest ladies of the City, and the principal gentlemen are there, to look upon the game; and he who appeareth badly clad maketh but an ill show and acquireth evil report thereby."[30]

To compete in this and other sports favored by Renaissance men, the young patrician had no need for extraordinary strength and the cultural ideal for men's bodies was less obviously athletic than during Greek and Roman antiquity. Although art is never simply a mirror of social reality, and individual variations in artistic style make generalization especially risky, statues and paintings provide clues to Renaissance conceptions of the ideal body. There are many images of powerful physiques. Michelangelo's marble *David*, while not as exaggeratedly mesomorphic as the sculptor's wrestlers, is a beautifully proportioned, muscular, unashamedly naked young man. The beautiful body of his equally famed Sistine Adam looks more Olympian than Biblical. Antonio Polliauolo's bronze statue of Hercules hoisting and crushing Antaeus seems almost herculean. "Pollaiuolo clearly derived both scientific and erotic pleasure from the accurate delineation of the muscles as they bunch and tense beneath the skin."[31] Like Pollaiuolo, Marco Dente DaRavenna chose a classical subject—this one from the *Aeneid*—when he wanted to portray the physical combat of powerful men. In sharp contrast to these artists, there were others whose masculine ideal seems anything but manly. Donatello's *David* is a slender androgyne with "droopy buttocks and . . . soft stomach muscles."[32] Caravaggio's *David* seems hardly strong enough to hold the sword that has decapitated Goliath and his *Bacchus* has been described as "epicene."[33] Michelangelo was immensely excited by the discovery of the *Laokoön* in 1506, but most artists seem to have been repelled rather than attracted by the straining limbs and agonized expression of the powerfully built Trojan priest caught, together with his sons, in the coils of a serpent. Far more influential as a model and an inspiration for Raphael and other Renaissance artists was the smooth and slender body of the *Apollo Belvedere*, discovered in 1479.[34]

As Georges Bataille has shown in *Les Larmes d'éros*, Northern artists like Cornelius van Haarlem were more likely than the Italians to depict the erotic in the form of muscular male bodies.[35] Peter Paul Rubens and Michael Sweerts were bold exceptions. As an admirer of ancient athleticism, which he encountered in the *De Arte Gymnastica* (1569) of Hieronymus Mercurialis, Rubens lamented the "weak and puny" bodies of his contemporaries.[36] He painted a number of markedly robust male figures. The mesomorphic wrestlers and bathers painted by Michael Sweerts are another startling contrast to the more typical wrestlers portrayed by Hans Burgkmair the Elder, Albrecht Dürer, and Lucas Cranach the Elder. These athletes are fully clothed and awkwardly posed. It is difficult to imagine them as icons of masculinity. In fact, Cranach's

wrestlers seem positively spindle-shanked. The Renaissance emulation of pagan antiquity was still too much under the influence of
medieval Christianity to embrace fully the Greek celebration of
erotic athleticism.

From antiquity to the Renaissance, the range allowed the ideal
female body has usually varied beyond that allowed for the ideal
male body, but the Renaissance may have been an exception to the
rule. Except for the virtually peerless Michelangelo, artists were
mindful of their patrons' rather restricted tastes and rarely painted,
carved, or cast an athletic female body.

Aristocratic women were not encouraged to fence, to participate
in the game of *calcio*, or—how unlikely!—to wrestle, but they
were frequently indulged in their passion for field sports and
Renaissance artists sometimes painted them in the guise of Diana.
If we expect the huntress goddess to look even remotely like Paul
Manship's splendidly athletic bronze *Diana* (1925), we will be dis-
appointed. Diane de Poitiers, mistress of Henri II, posed as her
eponym in a portrait executed by Francesco Primaticcio. Standing
uncertainly on a pair of tiny feet, with her right leg awkwardly
positioned behind her left, dangling an arrow from her right hand
and holding a bow in her left, surrounded by six playful infants and
three friendly dogs, she looks no more athletic than the Virgin
Mary (whose color—blue—she wears). Similarly, the Diana carved
by Jean Goujon has the softly rounded body of more sedentary
goddesses. The versions of Diana painted by Titian and by Rubens
are both Rubensesque, with the goddess passively bathing rather
than actively hunting (as she did in Greek depictions). Guido Reni
drew on Ovid's *Metamorphoses* and portrayed a female athlete in
motion, but his Atalanta is too plump to win her mythic race even
if Hippomenes, in hot pursuit, were to pause and stoop for a whole
basket of golden apples. When François Girardon restored a replica
of a statue by Praxiteles, the *Venus d'Arles*, he followed instruc-
tions from Louis XIV and "smoothed . . . the whole body, since the
King was offended by the sight of ribs and muscles."[37] In the

Bargello in Florence, Bartolommeo Ammanati's bronze *Venus* shares space with Donatello's effeminate *David*. She has the body and the stance of a powerfully athletic woman. To a twentieth-century eye (mine), she is a forceful embodiment of eros, but she has never earned the admiration lavished upon Sandro Botticelli's famous image of newborn Venus as a smoothly rounded, sweetly smiling deity, an angelic creature who seems to float over rather than stand firmly upon her mythic seashell.

4

Modern Times

There is only one god. Muscle!
—Paul Gurk[1]

Give me muscles.
—Mae West[2]

In the seventeenth and eighteenth centuries, when Baroque and Rococo styles spread from France to the rest of Europe, erotic athleticism was not in fashion. Tournaments remained popular, but the knight in armor was replaced by the courtier in embroidered hosiery and the clang of sword against shield gave way to the tinkle of a spear as it passed through a brass ring. As can be seen in the work of Chrispyn DePasse, the symbolism was as sexual as ever, but it was hardly athletic. With the exception of Jean-Jacques Rousseau, who advocated physical education and a more "natural" use of the body, the *philosophes* who criticized the *ancien régime* tended to be as inattentive to sports as the courtiers whom they condemned for their lives of parasitic indolence. For the philosopher as for the courtier, the venue for the game of love was the *salon*, where reputations were made with the thrust and parry of *bons mots*. The lovely children painted by Chardin play shuttlecock, spin tops, build houses of cards, and blow bubbles, but their elders, portrayed by Watteau and Fragonard, seem seldom to have indulged in recreations more physically strenuous than playing featherball, ambling to a *fête champêtre* or swaying on a garden swing. (The latter activity allowed one of Fragonard's young gallants to peek beneath his beloved's skirts while she experienced a bit of vertigo.) The male nude of Rococo art was so feminized that François Boucher "hardly [saw] the male body at all, and even his more muscular males seem to be patterned and posed after his girls."[3] The athletes drawn by Christian Müller and the stalwart, muscular, heroically posed Roman warriors of Jacques-Louis David's neoclassical canvases represented a revolution in the social construction of the body as well as in the artistic composition of a picture.

Did lusty peasants and urban artisans, accustomed to heavy work, compete in rough sports as a way to vaunt their masculinity and mark their distance from the foppery of the court? Since medieval folk-football survived into the nineteenth century, when antiquarians and folklorists began to record its presence among the peasantry, it must have been played in the intervening sixteenth, seventeenth, and eighteenth centuries. Social historians have also begun to observe signs of other sports among the lower classes. A lively game of pelota appears in a picture by Francisco José de Goya and Goethe observed a similar scene on his Italian journey.[4] At Saint-Ovide and the other great urban fairs of eighteenth-century Paris, there were singers, dancers, pantomimists, acrobats, mountebanks, and strong men. In 1754 there was even an exhibition by *les femmes fortes*, who supported great weights on their stomachs while they stretched supine with their heads on one chair and their feet on another.[5] In the sports of continental Europe's peasantry and urban poor, eros probably played a greater role than it did among the aristocracy and the bourgeoisie, but the evidence is scanty.

In England, "the birthplace of modern sports" and the favored venue of the sports historian, the situation was very different. The Puritans, always suspicious of sensuality, were hostile to traditional sports and pastimes, which they condemned as pagan or—even worse—"papist." During Oliver Cromwell's Puritan Commonwealth, English sports were suppressed, but they reappeared in 1660 when Charles II, famous as a sportsman and notorious as a rake, returned from exile and made England merry once again. During the Restoration and throughout the eighteenth century, great lords and lesser gentry indulged themselves in field sports. In the colorful scenes painted by George Stubbs and the other masters of English sporting art, images of the hunt—the horses, the dogs, the guns, the downed bird and the dismembered vixen—became emblems of masterful virility. The hunt, like the increasingly popular game of cricket, was a distillation of what it meant to be authentically English. The urban middle class, strongly influenced by Methodism, tended to hold itself aloof from the sporting life, which often included an un-Christian enthusiasm for the horse track and the cock pit; but the top and the bottom of the social hierarchy allied informally in support of almost every kind of sport. Although historians have a tendency to exaggerate the frequency and intensity of English sports participation, which certainly did not reach the levels attained in the nineteenth and twentieth centuries, sports did once again begin to assume importance they had had in antiquity.

While sedentary members of the nobility wrote verses and aspired to the dignity and decorum of a Chesterfield, their more active peers gloried in their sponsorship of pugnacious butchers. The Duke of Cumberland was famous for his patronage of John Broughton, a bare-knuckles brawler who was formally celebrated as the boxing champion of England and informally admired as the finest embodiment of virile English manhood. When Broughton was about to lose his title, in 1750, against Jack Slack, the battered boxer was gibed by the Duke, "WHAT ARE YOU ABOUT BROUGHTON— YOU CAN'T FIGHT!—YOU'RE BEAT!" To these taunts Broughton replied, "I can't see my man, your highness—I am blind, but not BEAT." Broughton lost the fight and his noble patron lost several thousand pounds, which diminished but did not eliminate his enthusiasm for pugilism.[6]

When noblemen did not arrange the combat, they "honored" it with their presence. Referring to James Figg, who covered all bets by performing as a stickfighter, a fencer, and a boxer, a contemporary remarked in 1749 that "most of the young Nobility and Gentry made it Part of their Education to march [as spectators] under his warlike Banner."[7] For a bout at Brighton's racetrack in 1788, "the race-stand was crowded to excess with nobility and gentry; among whom was his Royal Highness the Prince of Wales."[8] The tradition of upper-class patronage and popular enthusiasm continued into the early nineteenth century. Lord Byron, for instance, admired John Jackson and decorated a firescreen with the boxer's pugilistic poses. At Jackson's rooms, wrote a contemporary journalist, "all the elite of the fashionable world were daily assembled."[9]

Young noblemen like Byron were, of course, a small minority of the "fancy" that flocked to see Henry Pearce, John Gully, Tom Cribb, and other pugilists of the Regency era. "The Johnny Raws in rural England and the millions who lived in the narrow rooms and dirty alleys of London and the new industrial towns, these were the men who made up the enormous crowds that thronged to every prizefight."[10] In *Tales of a Traveller* (1824), Washington Irving described the "fancy" as "a chain of easy comunication, extending down from the peer to the pick-pocket, through the medium of which a man of rank may find he has shaken hands at three removes, with the murderer on the gibbet."[11]

What brought the "fancy" to ringside? What did the sport mean to them? Pierce Egan, who witnessed many if not most of the bouts described in his five-volume history of the sport, boasted that the British were "a far more manly and courageous people than the Greeks or Romans ever were." The word "manly" became a journalistic talisman. It seemed only natural to those who wrote for the popular press that "freeborn Englishmen" exhibited "an unsophisticated admiration of courage or manly vigour." Boxers were real men, immune from the vices of "selfishness and effeminacy," while bourgeois opponents of the pugilism suffered from an "unmanly dread of generally transient pains."[12] That boxers were icons of beef-eating, ale-drinking, hard-living masculinity is undeniable. Exemplifying the manly ability to batter and be battered, they were praised for their "bottom."[13] Debating the virtues of their pugilistic idols at the local pub, fight fans probably used a less euphemistic term.

Whether or not women had "bottom" was an unanswered question, but a number of them squared off and fought bare-knuckles bouts. In his narrative of a visit to London in 1710, Zacharias Conrad von Uffenbach reported that he encountered a woman who "had fought another female in this place without stays and in nothing but a shift. They had both fought stoutly and drawn blood, which was apparently no new sight in England."[14] If it *was* a new sight, it soon became a familiar one. John Trenchard's *London Journal* for June 23, 1722, referred to a battle between "two of the Feminine Gender" who "maintained the Battle with great Valour for a long Time, to the no small Satisfaction of the Spectators." Martin Nogüe's *Voyages et Avantures* (1728) reported matches between girls and grown women "stripped to the waist."[15] James Pellor Malcolm's *Anecdotes of the Manners and Customs of London* (1810) collected numerous references to boxing women at Hockley in the Hole and at James Figg's "Amphitheatre," two of the most common venues for combat sports.[16]

A vivid account of impromptu female pugilism occurs in the memoirs of William Hickey, a late-eighteenth-century rake. At Wetherby's near Drury Lane, Hickey found two women

> engaged in a scratching and boxing match, their faces entirely covered with blood, bosoms bare, and the clothes nearly torn from their bodies. For several minutes not a creature interfered between them, or seemed to care a straw what mishap they might do to each other, and the contest went on with unabated fury.[17]

This fight, about which Hickey was quite ambivalent, may have been nothing more than a bar-room brawl, but the *London Times* continued to publish accounts of regular matches conducted under the same rules as men's fights.

It can hardly be denied that the mostly male spectators for these fights were attracted by the same voyeuristic motives that drew them to "smock-races," contests to which "the female competitors were often encouraged to come lightly clad."[18] Most of these races were contested by rural maidens, but London's Pall-Mall was the site of an October 1733 race that "attracted an amazing number of persons, who filled the streets, the windows, and balconies."[19] The *Penny London Morning Advertiser* for June 11, 1744, recorded a race run by "two jolly wenches, one known by the name of The Little Bit of Blue (the Handsome Broom Girl) at the fag end of Kent Street, and the other, Black Bess, of the Mint." The erotic element was obvious; the newspaper commented that the girls were "to run in drawers only, and there is excellent sport expected."[20] Thomas Rowlandson's print *Rural Sports: Smock Racing* (1811) underscores the rampant sexuality of these events. In this rustic scene, uninhibited male and female bumpkins cavort and brawl while bare-breasted girls run races. In eighteenth-century England as in ancient Sparta, such demonstrations of female physical prowess were often an enticement to courtship.[21] A correspondent to *The Spectator* for September 4, 1711, noted that "nothing is more usual than for a nimble-footed Wench to get a Husband at the same time she wins a Smock."

César de Saussure, Antoine de Prévost, J. B. LeBlanc, and other French visitors to England were shocked that "intrepid Amazons"[22] fought like men and they were puzzled that men's sports were perceived as a measure of manhood. That a nobleman rebuked an impudent butcher with his fists rather than with his sword seemed *indigne*. Their disapproval of the strange customs of *les anglais* was an indication of the relative unimportance of physical prowess in the life of the French aristocrat.

And yet, the English nobleman who patronized pugilists and scorned urbane French courtiers as unmanly, effeminate, and probably homosexual[23] looks, in retrospect, hardly more athletic than the despised gallic poppycocks of Versailles. "In the eighteenth century, both men and women of the aristocracy . . . were equally partial to ample displays of lace, rich velvets, fine silks, and embroideries, to highly ornamental footwear, to coiffures, wigs, and hats of rococo embellishment, and to lavish use of scented powders, rouges, and other cosmetics."[24] At English country houses as well as at Frederick the Great's Sans Souci and scores of smaller Continental courts, men and women adopted fashions that all but immobilized them. The imperious dictates of proper attire called for a sexual *rapprochement* of dress that seemed to deny the distinctions emphasized by the anatomy books.[25] A modicum of physical agility was necessary to bow or curtsey without the loss of one's *perruque*, but the sports participation of the English elite seems to have been limited to an occasional game of cricket, the seasonal pleasures of the chase, and frequent sponsorship of ruffians in the ring. Neither in England nor on the Continent did early modern sports play the leading role allotted to them in antiquity. For the sports of London (and Paris and Berlin) to become as culturally central as the sports of the ancient *polis*, it was necessary to move into the industrial age.

Investigating the complicated story of modern manhood, historians have found that patterns of behavior have varied as they usually do in accordance with the usual demographic factors. The American frontiersman who bragged of his virility and demonstrated it in a stomp-and-gouge bar-room brawl[26] lived—more or less—in the same world as the hopelessly ineffectual Bronson Alcott, whose Transcendental philosophizing was financially supported by his daughter's fiction. The most that historians of masculinity have been able to accomplish thus far is to describe some of the major social changes of the nineteenth and twentieth centuries and to relate them to a dominant (but hardly an exclusive) model of masculinity.[27]

Since masculinity is usually constructed in opposition to femininity, some very brief comments on nineteenth-century women are in order. Although revisionists have already called attention to exceptions to the "cult of domesticity," there is still a consensus among social historians that the economic changes wrought by nineteenth-century industrialization tended to restrict middle-class women to domestic roles.[28] These economic changes were associated with an ideology that explicitly separated men's lives from women's. While men dominated the public realm of politics and economics, women were expected to administer the household and to foster religion and the arts. The doctrine of "separate spheres" was, however, limited to the middle class (whose watchword, on the European continent as well as in the English-speaking world, was "respectability"[29]). While "ladies" were more or less confined to the home, as wives and mothers, working-class women found paid employment in factories or in domestic service.

There were, as always, class differences in sexual behavior and erotic ideals. Working-class women seem increasingly to have ignored the proscriptions against premarital and extramarital sex. Although the "respectable" poor emulated middle-class sexual morality, there was apparently enough disreputable behavior for demographers to record a steep rise in the rate of illegitimacy. There was also a gradual decline in the age of first marriage.[30] Part-time prostitution, which was not exactly a new phenomenon, became widespread. "Some [part-time prostitutes] were forced, some sought money, some gained direct physical pleasure or companionship and asked for no more, but most undoubtedly saw it as a way to achieve marriage."[31] In the middle class, however, moral reformers intensified their traditional emphasis on female chastity (and some, like Margaret Fuller and Henry David Thoreau, hoped to implant the same high-minded ideal in male hearts). There was a measure of indulgence for the middle-class man, especially in Europe, but Victorian woman "now symbolized purity. She alone was fit to rule the home, and Victorians considered the home the true center of life."[32] She was, in the saccharine phrase popularized by the English poet Coventry Patmore, "the angel in the house."

And she seemed to many medical experts, and to an unknown but probably considerable number of laymen, most angelic when least active, when bedridden by "consumption" or some other debilitating illness.[33]

Ethereal women were not, however, the only ones to stir the male imagination. American "dime novels" introduced young readers to Calamity Jane, Hurricane Nell, and other powerful women; a number of British poets sang the praises of Atalanta; and Walt Whitman, sounding almost like a modern feminist, was lyrically exuberant about athletic women who "know how to swim, row, ride, wrestle, shoot, run, strike, advance, resist, defend themselves."[34] The transvestite athletic heroine of Théophile Gautier's *Mademoiselle de Maupin* (1835) rides, fences, and attracts lovers of both sexes. She fulfills the fantasies of the hero, who feared that "Christ has enveloped the world in his shroud" and had driven away the handsome Athenian wrestlers and the "young Spartan girls who danced . . . and ran naked to the summit of Mount Taygetus."[35] The ethereal hero of *A Rebours* (1884), by Joris-Karl Huysmans, falls in love—briefly—with the hard body of a female acrobat; he is attracted by her "suppleness and strength," by her "muscles of steel."[36]

At least two of the nineteenth century's finest artists were inspired by memories of Spartan girls. Eugène Delacroix, always fascinated by exotic embodiments of physical energy, drew them as wrestlers, "their bodies round and solid, like the nudes in Michelangelo's *Deluge*."[37] Inspired by his reading of Euripides' *Andromache* or Plutarch's *Life of Lycurgus*, Edgar Degas, whose brush and pen were more commonly activated by the sight of dancing or bathing women, imagined the Spartan girls challenging the boys to a wrestling match. At least one art historian sees these boys and girls as not-very-erotic "bare-rumped teen-agers who could just as well be from the alleys of nineteenth-century Monmartre or the suburbs of Naples as from ancient Greece,"[38] but the slender, athletic bodies are in fact rather similar to those of the artist's familiar ballet dancers. Although Degas has often been accused of misogyny, he endowed these bold girls with an "aggressive and competitive spirit" and posed them in a way that suggests "equality between the sexes."[39] Diana the Huntress attracted a number of sculptors, as she always has, Augustus St. Gaudens and Jean-Alexandre-Joseph Falguière among them.[40] The game of croquet, widely played by mixed groups of men and women, hardly seems in retrospect like a venue for physical passion, but a poem published in 1869 likens a maiden's "little foot" placed upon the ball to the arrows shot by "Cupid's bow." Croquet appears in a number of Winslow Homer's pictures—with only a subdued undercurrent of eroticism.[41] In James Tissot's more blatantly sexual *Croquet*, a young woman uses the phallic mallet to pin back her crooked arms and thereby to thrust forward her breasts. The saucy *déhanchement* of her stance completes the picture. On the whole, however, images of athletic women were relatively infrequent compared to the proliferation of etiolated female cadavers—like those in Henry Fuseli's *The Nightmare* and John Everett Millais's *Ophelia*—that littered nineteenth-century art.[42] Since most artists and most patrons preferred to contemplate women who were neither athletic nor dead, the modal image appears, softly voluptuous, in canvases as different as those of Jean-Auguste-Dominique Ingres and Auguste Renoir. In the latter's work, the female body seems as roundly immobile as a bowl of fruit. Yet even Renoir told his son that he admired the bodies of the supple acrobats at the *Cirque d'Hiver*, "stocky girls solidly planted on wrestlers' legs."[43]

If Victorian culture scripted narrow, rigid, nonathletic roles for middle-class women, which is what most social historians seem to believe, how were men supposed to behave? Stearns, who begins his survey of men's lives in prehistorical times, argues that the nineteenth century was the era when "traditional male roles were fundamentally changed." Industrialization removed men from the fields, where they had often worked in the proximity of women, and placed them in mines and factories, where they labored at tasks increasingly unfamiliar to their female relatives. Strength and endurance were prized because industrial labor was then no easier than a peasant's or an artisan's had been. Iron mills powered by steam engines required strong workers and the "dark shaft of a coal mine was one of the real tests of nineteenth-century masculinity."[44] Construction work, which was often quite dangerous, also required significant muscular force and endowed those who possessed it with considerable masculine prestige. Among twentieth-century factory hands, this attitude persists. "It was eight hours full of filth and dirt and grease and grim and sweat," recalls one of them; it was "manual labor and a manly atmosphere."[45]

While working-class men experienced what may well have been an enhanced sense of manhood, at least until progress in mechanization threatened to devalue completely John Henry's legendary physical strength, middle-class men entered what many social historians have interpreted as a prolonged crisis of masculinity. "American men," lamented Michael Kimmel, "have been searching for their lost manhood since the middle of the nineteenth century."[46] Neither the practice of a profession nor the routines of an office provided many opportunities for the demonstration of courage or the display of brute strength. Middle-class men seem haunted by an unspoken question: "A man in any culture is supposed to be strong, tough, adept and courageous; clearly that was true of primitive hunters and warriors, but is it true of us?"[47]

Reinforcing the notion that middle-class occupations were somehow "effeminate" was the disturbing fact that the women who were admitted into them performed as well as men did. While men accepted, without much fuss, the notion of salesgirls and "typewriters," they resisted women's access to the more prestigious, traditionally male professions. Privilege was ingeniously defended with an array of arguments about innate physical and psychic differences between males and females, but men were gradually, reluctantly, forced to admit that "the weaker sex" was equal to the demands of doctoring and lawyering as well as those of teaching and nursing.

Economic changes undermined middle-class manhood in more subtle ways. Incomes rose in Europe and in North America but, paradoxically, paternal authority weakened as the agricultural sector declined and men were less likely to inherit, acquire, and bequeath land. While the sons of skilled manual workers were often able to follow their fathers' occupational footsteps, especially after the rise of exclusionary labor unions, middle-class sons were increasingly required to go their own way. As formal education supplanted workplace or domestic apprenticeship, opportunities diminished for the transmission of vocational skills from father to son. Conflicts intensified because "too many fathers were asserting authority that they no longer really possessed."[48]

While both sexes play different social roles in all societies, the Victorian middle class went to extremes in its effort to encourage the flowering of the "softer sentiments" in women while pruning them back in men. Romanticism in literature and visual arts abounds with expressions of male emotion that seem to contradict this generalization:[49] Alfred Lord Tennyson expressed his love of Arthur Hallam in *In Memoriam*, Walt Whitman wrote lyrically of "amativeness" between men, and Herman Melville drew on marital metaphors to describe the embraces of Ishmael and Queequeg, "a tender, loving pair." But—with the exception of the clergy—their more typical contemporaries looked askance at such signs of unmanly sentiment.[50]

"Manly debility" was not a slogan to stir the blood. In Boston's *Atlantic Monthly*, a periodical treated like an oracle in middle-class homes, Oliver Wendell Holmes, Sr., and Thomas Wentworth Higginson brushed aside the notion that meekness and weakness might be virtues. "I am satisfied," intoned the "Autocrat of the Breakfast Table," "that such a set of black-coated, stiff-jointed, soft-muscled, paste-complexioned youth as we can boast of in our Atlantic cities never before sprang from loins of Anglo-Saxon lineage."[51] John Bull's American progeny were a degenerate lot. It was high time for them to shape up.

For middle-class men who worried about a loss of virility, life on the frontier and on the battlefield offered substantial reassurance. Roughing it in the wilderness or moving bravely forward through a hail of bullets were two ways to eliminate the stigma of effeminacy. Francis Parkman's *Oregon Trail* (1849) demonstrates how hardships and danger encountered in the West gave at least one sickly Easterner a chance to prove himself a real man. The horrors of the Civil War granted countless others confirmation of their masculinity. Idealistic young Oliver Wendell Holmes, Jr. enlisted when only twenty and was badly wounded, four months later, in the Battle of Bull's Bluff. By the end of the war, he had had more than enough of bloodshed and boredom, but he admitted, in a letter to his parents, "I started in this thing a boy. I am now a man."[52] Higginson's memoir, *Army Life in a Black Regiment* (1870), is a proud account of the physical ordeals and the dangers of soldiering. Charles Francis Adams, Jr., had a similar reaction to military service. The war, he wrote, "gave me just that robust, virile stimulus to be derived only from a close contact with Nature and a roughing it among men and in the open air, which I especially needed."[53] Theodore Roosevelt drew on both these sources of masculine reinforcement, the frontier and the battlefield, in his celebration of "the strenuous life." As a rancher, he held his own against men who bragged that they had been born in the saddle. As a Rough Rider, he excelled in militarily unwise acts of masculine bravado.

The conflict with Spain was "a splendid little war," but, since wars threatened to become distressingly infrequent, Roosevelt availed himself of a third source of reassurance that is mentioned by many social historians and discussed by few. For most American men born between 1865 and 1900, sports were one place where men felt that they were really men.[54] There can hardly be a better example of compensatory athleticism than Roosevelt's metamorphosis from a pampered, squeaky-voiced, bespectacled patrician into a virile sportsman who traded punches with frontier toughs, hunted big game in Africa, and ventured upon unexplored South American rivers. In *The Strenuous Life* he echoed the sentiments of the elder Holmes:

> Forty or fifty years ago the writer on American morals was sure to deplore the effeminacy and luxury of young Americans who were born of rich parents. The boy who was well off then ... lived too luxuriously, took to billiards as his chief innocent recreation, and felt small shame in his inability to take part in rough pastimes and field-sports. Nowadays, whatever other faults the son of rich parents may tend to develop, he is at least forced ... to bear himself well in manly exercises and to develop his body—and therefore, to a certain extent, his character—in the rough sports which call for pluck, endurance, and physical address.[55]

Roosevelt urged manly young men to plunge into a game of football. Many did and some were killed. When educators, appalled by football's violence, contemplated banning the game from the campus, Roosevelt quickly intervened and persuaded them that reform, not abolition, was the solution. There was no need to turn undergraduates into mollycoddles.

Roosevelt reveled in excess, but he was a representative figure whose convictions were widely shared on both sides of the Atlantic. Although the emergence of modern sports and their worldwide diffusion in the nineteenth and twentieth centuries is a complicated phenomenon resistant to easy explanation,[56] one reason for sports' nearly universal popularity is that they offer a chance for "man-the-breadwinner" to become, for a brief but glorious moment, "man-the-hero."[57] In an era of increasingly sedentary and cerebral work, sports provide an opportunity for men simultaneously to prove their physical prowess and to recover the intimacy of a Damon-and-Pythias friendship. It is no accident that middle-class men—in every modern or modernizing society—are much more likely than the men of other social strata to participate actively in organized sports.[58]

This over-representation, which is often obscured by the fame of professional athletes of working-class origins, is the result of both economic and cultural factors. Middle-class men can afford the time and money required for participation and they are especially susceptible to the need to prove their masculinity. In other words, for men too committed to domesticity and urban life to join the army or to seek adventure on the American frontier or in the Australian outback, sports "offered the potential of an invigorated manhood in which power, efficiency, and fairness ideally blended together."[59] The American and the European middle classes took to baseball and the various "codes" of football at a time when gentlemen were expected, in most social situations, to be genteel. As Roberta J. Park has shown, it was in "the crucible of athletic competition that the male character was to be forged." In Great Britain and the United States, sports gave "concrete—and spectacular—attention to action through the medium of the male body, the ideal for which had changed from lean and lithe to mesomorphic by the 1890s."[60]

The athletic ideal was certainly not limited to the United States and Great Britain (although Americans and Britons liked to think they had a monopoly on it): "The emerging ideal German man was heroic and tall, regularly presented in postures of action, combat, or struggle with muscles tensed and visible, honed through gymnastic exercises and physical training."[61] Frenchmen, humiliated by their quick defeat in the Franco-Prussian War, took to gymnastic exercises, in imitation of their German conquerors, or to modern sports, in emulation of their British rivals.[62]

European and American art of the nineteenth and early twentieth centuries has numerous depictions of the athletic body. Although a myriad of equestrian pictures testified to humankind's perennial love affair with horses, internationally celebrated artists also portrayed an amazing number of wrestlers and boxers (along with a growing contingent of oarsmen, baseball players, golfers, and tennis players). Gustave Courbet exhibited his *Wrestlers* in 1853, revealing "as sensuous a feeling for the muscular male body as for female softness; the two heavy wrestlers are locked awkwardly together, as totally involved with each others' bodies as a pair of lovers."[63] In 1867–68, Honoré Daumier, who caricatured the grotesqueries of every social class, depicted a trio of ungainly grapplers whose relationship to the beautifully sculpted bodies of antiquity's wrestlers was "not unlike that between Venus and a modern Parisian courtesan."[64] The eight young men who appear in Frédéric Bazille's *Scène d'été* (1869) swim, wrestle, and observe one another with what looks unmistakably like erotic interest. Max Slevogt's *Wrestling School* (1908) depicted four naked men, one tightly gripping his motionlessly prone opponent, two looking on as if spellbound. Like Slevogt's pair, the wrestlers painted by Thomas Eakins and George Luks lie on the ground, where they strain to keep or break a hold. Eakins, who produced a number of canvases devoted to hunting, sailing, rowing, and playing baseball, was intensely interested in the male body, whose actions he captured with his camera as well as with his brushes and pencils. One sees this in his portraits of boxers: *Salutat* (1898), *Taking the Count* (1898), and *Between Rounds* (1899). (The first of these pictures alludes visually and through its title to Jean-Léon Gérôme's sensuous "paintings of Roman gladiators in the arena."[65])

Another depiction of the athletic male body bears the unexpected signature of John Singer Sargent, remembered today for his elegant portraits of the social elite. Far better known than Sargent's atypical *Man Wearing Laurels* (1880) are the many boxing scenes painted by George Bellows. *Stag at Sharkey's* (1908) and *Both Members of the Club* (1909) confront the viewer with men who have been reduced to their bodies, bodies whose atavistic combat excites the spectators to a frenzy.

We shall never hear the cat-calls and shouted encouragements of those spectators, but there are indications of what they felt. Nineteenth-century journalists, who never had to tremble at accusations of "latent homosexuality," were free to express their emotional response to the bodies of other men. Of two boxers who stripped for their weigh-in, *The Spirit of the Times* reported, "If [Chris] Lilly's appearance was fine, [Tom] McCoy's was beautiful. His skin had a warmer glow than the former's; his form was more elegantly proportioned, and his air and style were more graceful and manlike. His swelling breast curved out like a cuirass: his shoulders were deep, with a bold curved blade, and the muscular development of the arm large and finely brought out."[66]

Fiction, as always, is another indicator of attitudes. George Bernard Shaw wrote, in an early novel, of a boxer whose "broad pectoral muscles . . . were like slabs of marble." In the eyes of the heroine, he seemed like "an antique god in his sylvan haunt." Louis Hémon, one of Shaw's French contemporaries, wrote ecstatically about a "pale adolescent [boxer] whose eyes flamed, who struck with both hands like a young hero whom Zeus protected."[67] In those days, if not in ours, it was manly to admire the bodies as well as the prowess of male athletes.

Meanwhile, the influential turn-of-the-century psychologist G. Stanley Hall articulated an atavistic theory of male adolescence in which boxing and other rough sports figured as the teenage boy's most appropriate activity. Since young males are naturally aggressive, their "inborn and more or less savage instincts can and should be allowed some scope." Like Theodore Roosevelt, Hall believed that "to be weak is to be miserable, to feel strong is a joy and glory." It was also to shine in the eyes of the opposite sex. "A subtle but potent intersexual influence is among the strongest factors in adolescent sport. . . . The presence of the fair sex gives tonicity to a youth's muscles and tension to his arteries to a degree of which he is rarely conscious." What, according to Hall, was the response of the "fair sex" to all that youthful masculine muscular tonicity? "Physical force and skill, and above all, victory and glory, make a hero and invest him with a romantic glamour, which . . . is profoundly felt and makes the winner more or less irresistible."[68] Hall was clearly not among those timid souls who envisioned sports as a means to fortify the will against the dread forces of adolescent sexuality.

For most adolescent boys, today as in Roosevelt's time, unusual athletic ability continues to guarantee heroic status while failure to perform well is tantamount to social ostracism, a truth amply documented by James Coleman and a number of other sociologists of adolescence.[69] This truth was movingly dramatized in Peter Bogdanovich's film *The Last Picture Show* (1971), in which failure to win a high-school football game instantly reclassifies the young protagonist from hero to pariah.[70] Since the "rites of fall"[71] take place before thousands or even tens of thousands of spectators, the shame and humiliation of athletic failure is intense. The phenomenon is certainly not limited to the United States. When a young man drops the ball or fails to block the kick, the psychic costs are as severe in Finland as in Texas: "I was in [the] goal in my first junior game against the other team of the town," writes Arto Tiihonen in an essay on masculinity. "I let in three goals in the first half and was replaced. It was enough for me. I was humiliated."[72] For the athletically inept male, sports—whether they are part of a physical-education requirement or a company picnic—are a "degradation ceremony."[73]

Adolescent male physicality has been expressed by romantic wandering through the German forest as well as by blocking and tackling in small-town football stadia. As young Germans experienced the pleasures of the *Wandervogel* movement of the early twentieth century, their worried elders felt impelled to distinguish between sexuality, associated with earthy nature, and eros, associated with the realm of spirit. In books entitled *Die deutsche Wandervogelbewegung als erotisches Phänomen* (1912) and *Die Rolle der Erotik in der männlichen Gesellschaft* (1917), Hans Blüher praised homoerotic and condemned homosexual relationships. Gustav Wyneken, seeking to propagate "a new sense of the body," wrote a book entitled *Eros* (1921) and defended the affectionate camaraderie that developed among young people who hiked through the woods, slept beneath the stars, and sang sentimental ballads around the campfire. This high-minded distinction between eros and sexuality was too fine for Wyneken's colleagues at the Freie Schulgemeinde Wickersdorf, the progressive school he had founded in 1906. He was expelled.[74] To most Germans, the pedagogical effort to distinguish between the homoerotic and the homosexual was unpersuasive.

As German youth began in the postwar years to abandon the *Wandervogel* movement for the more strenuous competitive physicality of sports, fears of male homosexuality diminished. In Europe as in America, sports participation seemed to certify that a young man's sexual proclivities, if ever he acted on them, were safely heterosexual. Even today, the association between sports and heterosexual masculinity remains so strong that psychological tests like the Minnesota Multiphasic Personality Inventory score a male's dislike of sports as an indication of homosexual tendencies, especially when coupled with a preference for the arts. In European and American popular culture, a young man's athletic inadequacy is commonly ridiculed with sexual taunts. Irate football coaches scream that the faltering defense is a bunch of "faggots" and urge the ineffective offense to act as if they had "balls."[75]

England's "football hooligans" shout that opposing players and rival fans are "cunts" or effeminate "wankers" who ought to be "matched with an Englishman's arse."[76] French and Italian soccer fans are equally obscene in boasting of their own virility and sneering at their rivals' lack of it. In one of the most horribly memorable boxing matches of the century, middleweight contender Emile Griffith battered Benny Paret to death because Paret, before the fight, had insinuated that Griffith was a homosexual. On the other hand, homosexuality seems to be quite acceptable if the "real man" is the active partner and if he acts sadistically. Argentine soccer enthusiasts chant that the only *authentic* fans are those who "fuck and tear open the anuses of all other fans."[77]

Although the idea may be anathema to the Argentine soccer fan, modern sports have also been a means to construct a positive, self-aware homosexual identity. This was true even in the nineteenth century, when a coterie of scholars defended the cult of athleticism by associating it with a passionate evocation of classical antiquity. "Greek athletes and athletic prowess, the *gymnasia*, the lithe bodies stripped for action," writes Jeffrey Richards, "were . . . regularly extolled by Hellenists. . . . Edward Cracroft Lefroy [reveled] in the sight of latter-day Antinous' and Praxitelean Hermes' on the football field."[78] No one exemplifies this homoerotic disposition better than Walter Pater, whose *Plato and Platonism* is certainly a *locus classicus*. The beauty "of these most beautiful of all people was a male beauty," wrote Pater. It had "the expression of a certain *ascêsis* in it; it was like unsweetened wine."[79] In *The Renaissance*, Pater meditated on "the beauty of the *palaestra*,"[80] where naked men wrestled under the protective gaze of images of Eros. Pater's last published story, "Apollo in Picardy," was a version of the Greek myth in which the god of the sun falls in love with a youth named Hyacinth. In Pater's redaction, the pagan deity enters a medieval monastery in order to court his beloved, whom he teaches to wrestle and to bend the bow with erotic grace.[81]

In Springfield, Massachusetts, as well as in Picardy, eros appeared in the guise of homage to antiquity. At the very YMCA where the game of basketball was invented in 1891 athletic young men participated in *tableaux vivants* in which they posed, nearly naked, as Greek statues. Tensed muscles were coated with a patina of bronze powder and wallpaper paste, which reassured the young men and their admirers that the excitement they felt was high-minded philhellenic awe.[82]

Although British games masters and American physical educators praised sports as a healthy alternative to fornication and "self-abuse," the combination of Hellenism and athleticism actually contributed to the sexual activity that was rife in schools like Eton and Groton. The experience of John Addington Symonds, for instance, was more like that of the ancient Greeks than his Harrovian teachers imagined: "Every boy of good looks had a female name, and was recognized either as a public prostitute or as some bigger fellow's "bitch." Bitch was the word in common usage to indicate a boy who yielded his person to a lover. . . . Here and there one could not avoid seeing acts of onanism, mutual masturbation, the sports of naked boys in bed together."[83]

Twentieth-century memoirs of English "public-school" life attest to the continued prevalence of homosexuality among healthy adolescents tutored by naively moralistic mentors. In *Enemies of Promise* (1938), Cyril Connolly recalled his schooldays at sports-mad Eton and added that homosexuality was "the Forbidden Tree around which our Eden dizzily revolved."[84] (Like a typical first-year student, Connolly fell in love with a boy who was "good at games and older than I."[85]) Headmasters like Edmund Warre engaged in "a futile attempt to stop Etonians from sinning by running them off their feet,"[86] but rowing and cricket probably did more to inflame than to dampen animal ardor.[87] The same kinds of socially deviant behavior were rampant in German military schools. Of his *Kadettenanstalt*, one officer remembered, "In addition to these friendships, love affairs developed between younger and older boys. . . . There were stormy embraces, hot kisses, and even acts of sexual intercourse."[88]

At late-nineteenth-century German military schools, rigid drill was preferred to sports (which were perceived as an unwelcome import from the weakly unwarlike English). At British public schools, rugby was the preferred manly activity and its derivative, American football, became so important a part of collegiate life in the United States that critics began to wonder, as early as the turn of the century, if students retained any interest at all in studying. Physical strength is an important part of every "manly" sport, but better still is the ability to mete out and to absorb pain, which suggests that sadism, masochism, and the risk of death are all aspects of the sports most strongly associated with masculinity. Rugby and American football fill the bill, but they are certainly not the only sports for "real men." Americans are not likely to think of soccer football as an epitome of masculinity, but that is exactly how the

sport is perceived by most of the world, for whom Franz Beckenbauer and Diego Maradona were more potent symbols than O.J.
Simpson or Michael Jordan. "The potency of the great player,"
writes a specialist on Latin American soccer, "is akin to sexual
power." The great player "is expected also . . . to be a prolific
lover."[89] And the object of countless male and female fantasies.

Consider also the Spanish *corrida*. Its human protagonist is the
matador, whom Alfonso Lingis has described as eros incarnate:

> No woman spread-eagled in a stripshow is as brazenly exhibited as
> the matador in the corrida. His body and his blood are exalted in a
> monstrance of scarlet velvets, spun-silver lace, and jewels over
> against the black fury of the bull. Insolence flaunts his torso, con-
> tempt splays his thighs, flash-fires of foolhardy intelligence crackle
> across his tensed and cynical posturing, his testicles and penis jeweled
> in the codpiece and provocatively exposed to the lusts of the crowds.[90]

The rhetoric of this comment is hyperactive, but the allusion to the
"lusts of the crowds" seems appropriate for this intensely sexual
sport. A quiver of hesitation in the face of the awesome taurine
adversary can bring forth taunts about a lack of *cojones*. A moment
of thoughtless bravado can mean emasculation or death.

Toreros perform in Iberia and Latin America. Pugilism, considered in the eighteenth century as an appropriate symbol of British
pugnacity (Latin: *pugnus*, the fist), is now widely condemned
because it is a brutal atavism. It is widely admired for the same reason. The sport, writes Joyce Carol Oates, "celebrates the physicality of men even as it dramatizes the limitations, sometimes tragic,
more often poignant, of the physical." (She deems the sport "powerfully homoerotic," but her own fascination seems conventionally
heterosexual.)[91]

No sport has produced more heroes. In the early years of the
nineteenth century, Tom Cribb, feet squarely planted and arms
cocked, appeared in lithographs hung from the walls of a thousand
British pubs. His two victories over an American black, Tom

Molyneaux, were taken (in Britain) as proof positive of British manhood. Fifty years later, in 1860, the fight between Thomas Sayers and John C. Heenan was another international event that pitted an English hero against an American challenger (who was also the paramour of Broadway's famously erotic Adah Isaacs Menken). Sayers won. "Throughout the land—in respectable Victorian homes, as in respectable Victorian newspapers—millions who normally ranked pugilists with common criminals hailed an illiterate bruiser as a national hero."[92] At the end of the century, John L. Sullivan defeated Jake Kilrain in the last of the bare-knuckles championships and then bragged his way through the nation's bar-rooms: "I can lick any man in the house!"[93] Men cringed and women moaned. Although the "Boston Strong Boy" eventually lost the struggle against obesity as well as the famous 1892 bout against James Corbett, Sullivan continued to represent a popular incarnation of masculinity.

When Jack Johnson became the first African-American heavy-weight champion, in 1908, racist hysteria required a "great white hope" to reclaim the title and banish what was obviously felt to be a threat to white womanhood. This fear of Johnson's irresistible erotic appeal was not wholly irrational. Women did, in fact, badger the "hypermasculine" black boxer for sexual favors; like many African-American athletes, he was "sexualized and eroticized by women and men of all races."[94] There is no need to recite the litany of other twentieth-century fighters who have served as icons of masculinity, but I must note that Norman Mailer, a virtuoso writer who has composed literary fugues on the theme of virility, wrote a book to express his admiration of Mohammad Ali. "If Ali never opened his mouth to quiver the jellies of public opinion, he would still inspire love and hate. For he is the Prince of Heaven—so says the silence around his body when he is luminous."[95]

The boxer's body, like the wrestler's, is on display. In other sports strongly associated with masculinity, uniforms and equipment are used to enhance the erotic effect (as clothes and cosmetics have been used, conventionally, to heighten a woman's sexual allure). In American football, for instance, the visual emphasis on masculinity approaches parody. Although the players, stripped naked, dwarf the average American male, the promoters of the game are dissatisfied with the merely superhuman. Pads extend the shoulders to megatheric broadness and exaggerate the bulk of thighs that are already massive. The waist is not exactly girlish, but bellies of substantial size seem small in relation to the rest of the outsize body. The uniforms are usually cut so that muscular arms are visible. Heads are helmeted and faces, the most individualized part of the body, disappear behind masks. The result is the generic *homo potens*.

An even more obvious example of outfits and equipment designed to intensify the association of eros and sports can be observed during Fox Television's weekly show, *American Gladiators*. Extremely muscular men and women, who have obviously spent innumerable hours "pumping iron," compete in a series of unique physical contests. Dressed in a variety of skimpy science-fiction outfits that accentuate different parts of their anatomy (e.g., women's thighs, men's pectoral muscles), the contestants wrestle, batter one another with padded poles, swing from rings, climb a cushioned pyramid from which other contestants try to hurl them to the floor, scale a wall under the same adverse condition, race up inclined treadmills that roll them backwards if they weaken, endeavor to knock or to pull each other from elevated platforms, and compete in a number of other newly invented sports, most of which allow for the ample demonstration of physical prowess and the generous display of secondary sex characteristics. The women, who seem invariably to be blonde if they are not African Americans, compete in exactly the same sports as the men. When not competing, the male and female contestants smile, gyrate seductively, flex and swagger. It is difficult to imagine a more egregious assertion of the erotic element in sports.

two
·

THE GUISES
OF EROS

Johnny Weissmuller as Tarzan.

Movie Stills Archive.

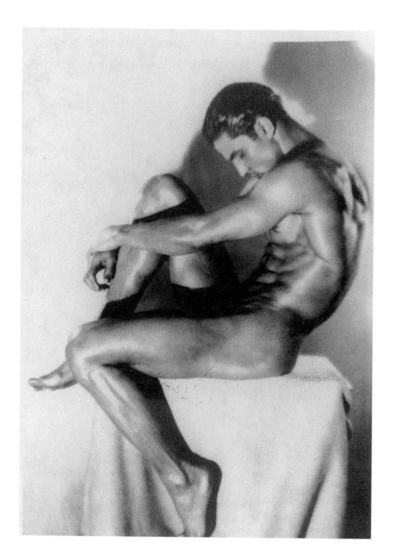

Tony Sansone

Todd-McLean Collection, Austin.

Gisele Mauermeyer at the 1936 Olympics, Berlin.
Collection of Gertrud Pfister, Berlin.

Jesse Owens at the 1936 Olympics, Berlin.
Author's Collection.

Diving sequence from Leni Riefenstahl's *Olympia* (1938).
Courtesy, Library of Congress.

Billie Jean King (ca. 1960).
Patrick DeLuca.

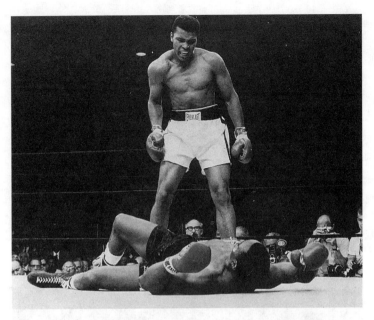

ABOVE: Muhammad Ali (then known as Cassius Clay) versus Sonny Liston (May 25, 1965).
Bettmann Archive.

BELOW: Jean-Claude Killy at the 1968 Olympics, Grenoble.
International Olympic Committee.

ABOVE: Mark Spitz at the 1972 Olympics, Munich.
AP/Wide World Photos.

BELOW: Ludmilla Tourischeva at the 1972 Olympics, Munich.
Author's Collection

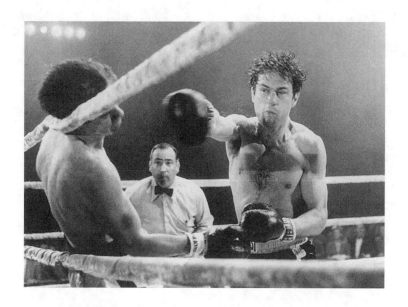

Robert DiNiro in *Raging Bull* (1980).
Movie Stills Archive.

Mariel Hemingway in *Personal Best* (1980)
Movie Stills Archive.

Katarina Witt at the 1968
Olympics, Calgary.
*Nationales Olympisches
Komitee der DDR*

Florence Griffith-Joyner at
the 1988 Olympics, Seoul.
Bettmann Archive.

Denise Gader—the diver's body.

Todd-McLean Collection, Austin.

Cory Everson—the body-builder's body.

Todd-McLean Collection, Austin.

Silken Lauman at the 1992 Olympics, Barcelona.
AP/Wide World Photos.

ABOVE: Franz Beckenbauer at the Parc des Princes, Paris. *AP/Wide World Photos.*

BELOW: Kristi Yamaguchi at the 1992 Olympics, Albertville. *Bettmann Archive.*

Greg Louganis.
Neil Leifer.

Michael Jordan.

Bettmann Archive.

5

Erotic Athleticism and Popular Culture

Although it is less conventional than the other shows that jostle it for a share of the Saturday afternoon television market, *American Gladiators* does at least present the spectator with athletes who engage in authentic competitions. Theatrical entrepreneurs, well aware of the profitable combination of sports prowess and erotic appeal, have also marketed spectacles that have little or no resemblance to sports performances. There is, indeed, a long tradition for this sort of commercial exploitation. A century ago, Australian playwrights inserted boxing matches into plays whose plots had nothing whatsoever to do with pugilism.[1] In this country, John L. Sullivan's lack of dramatic talent did not prevent him from earning more on the theatrical stage than he did in the ring. He flexed his biceps, chopped wood, rescued fair maidens from improbable dangers, and stammered his way from coast to coast.

Sullivan's path must have crossed a number of times with that of Eugen Sandow, the German-born weightlifter and body-builder who was perhaps the first claimant of the title, "the World's Most

Perfectly Developed Man." Although his Institute of Physical Culture was located in London (1897), Sandow also lifted and posed in the United States, on the European continent, and in the Far East. In the theaters of New York, Chicago, San Francisco, and many other cities, female members of the audience "responded enthusiastically to the strongman." For the privilege of a private backstage performance, women were asked to donate $300 to charity.

> At one of these highly charged shows, Sandow took a woman's gloved hand in his own and ran it slowly across the muscle in question. Apparently, this was too much excitement for the delicate creature, for she suddenly paled and staggered back. She was only able to gasp, "It's unbelievable!" before emotion got the better of her.[2]

She swooned. Anonymous admirers sent Sandow flowers and famous courtesans like Caroline Otéro, who included the Prince of Wales among her many royal conquests, attempted to seduce him. In the bedrooms of their Newport mansions, dazzled maidens kept photographs of Sandow, nude except for the traditional figleaf. (Photographs were, in fact, the basis of the modern cult of bodybuilding.[3]) What Anthony Comstock and other vigilant defenders of Christian morals thought of Sandow's public display of sexy musculature, enhanced by an ithyphallic sword, is not on record. Comstock did, however, do his best to thwart physical culturist Bernarr Macfadden's highly publicized quest for America's most perfectly developed woman.[4]

A generation later, female hearts fluttered at the sight of the legendary Bronko Nagurski, a Bunyanesque hero who laid down his axe in order to achieve greatness as a football player at the University of Minnesota and then with George Halas and the Chicago Bears. To supplement his income, Nagurski became a professional wrestler. "Hollywood," reported the *Minneapolis Journal*, "went gaga" at the sight of his physique.[5] The producers offered him a chance to move from the ring to the screen, but he spurned their proposals. When Rudolph Valentino died, Tony Sansone, the epitome of erotically charged athleticism, "a seductive and swarthy Pan," was asked to replace the deceased film idol, but he too refused the chance.[6] The moguls eventually discovered an athlete eager to exploit the opportunities Nagurski and Sansone rejected. Johnny Weissmuller, an Olympic swimming champion, was chosen to play the role of Tarzan to Maureen O'Sullivan's Jane because the producers at Metro-Goldwyn-Mayer believed correctly that he had enough sex appeal to entice millions of women to the box office. The producers stripped him of his Olympic swimsuit, wrapped him in a loincloth, and filmed his African adventures. Between 1932 and 1948, MGM and RKO cast Weissmuller in twelve Tarzan films. The dream-merchants knew exactly what they were doing. Swinging from vine to vine (accompanied by a friendly chimpanzee), Weismuller thwarted savage plots and captivated civilized hearts. Katherine Albert, reviewing *Tarzan the Ape Man* in *Photoplay*, marveled that "a lad who had never been in a picture before, who had been interested in nothing but swimming all his life, and who frankly admits he can't act, is the top-notch heart flutterer of the year."[7]

Producers and directors who transmuted athletes into movie stars were also adept at reversing the process. They touted the athleticism of their actors. Douglas Fairbanks, for instance, "was marketed as a virility symbol and fitness fanatic." His daily schedule, which included boxing, wrestling, running, and swimming, was "as strenuously publicized as his screen career."[8]

Theatrical promoters also recruited female athletes for popular entertainments, some of which were as tacky as burlesque shows. The *Police Gazette* sponsored boxing and wrestling matches for lightly clad young women and French cabarets lived up to their lurid reputation by providing even more exaggeratedly sexual contests. Max Viterbo, for instance, recalled a 1903 visit to a *boui-boui* on Rue Monmartre. Although there was music to mollify the waiting crowd,

> the room was wild with impatience. The stale smell of sweat and foul air assaulted your nostrils. In this overheated room the spectators

were flushed. Smoke seized us by the throat and quarrels broke out.
. . . [A] lubricious gleam came to the eyes of old gentlemen when two
furious women flung themselves at each other like modern baccha-
ntes—hair flying, breasts bared, indecent, foaming at the mouth.
Everyone screamed, applauded, stamped his feet.[9]

Sandow's feats of strength were imitated by a number of women,
the most famous of whom may have been Kate Roberts, an Irish
girl who performed as "Vulcana." Among her achievements was
hoisting a 120-pound barbell to her shoulders and then lifting it
overhead with one hand. She appeared, flexing and observing a
very impressive right arm, on the cover of *La Santé par les Sports*.

Turn-of-the-century boxers, wrestlers, and strongwomen performed primarily for working-class spectators whose preference in
women was for the oaken rather than the willowy. By the twenties,
a number of entrepreneurs sought to profit from the erotic appeal
of female athletes more respectable than "Vulcana" or "Sandwina."
Sports clothes became an important part of the apparel industry.
Whether or not one accepts Valerie Steele's dictum that "the concept of beauty is sexual in origin" and "the meaning of clothing in
general and fashion in particular is also erotic,"[10] there is no reason
to doubt Anne Hollander's somewhat less sweeping claims about
twentieth-century fashions. In *Sex and Suits,* she asserts that "the
erotic force of female bodily movement and bodily surface, and of
clothes that not only showed them but emphasized them, were at
last publicly acknowledged by fashion."[11] No one better illustrated
this than France's Suzanne Lenglen and America's Helen Wills, two
champion tennis players who were "clearly perceived . . . as attractive, erotic women." They, like Amelia Earhart, were promoted
with "an undertone of explicit . . . sexuality." Lenglen, wearing
sleeveless outfits, colorful sashes, and a kind of turban, set fashions.
Her appeal "lay precisely in the way she fused athletic ability with
heterosexual allure. With her unusual dress and dancelike movement, she pioneered an ideal of the female body as physical and

actively erotic."[12] Lenglen's matches drew an unprecedented number of spectators. Her match against Helen Wills is remembered as an encounter between "the goddess and the American girl."[13]

The Amateur Athletic Union of the United States, which did much more in the twenties than the colleges did to sponsor serious sports competition for young women, borrowed a gimmick from commercial promoters and staged beauty contests at national championships in women's basketball. The players were the contestants. "The depiction of athletes as beauty queens sent physical educators into a rage."[14] The female physical educators who controlled women's sports at the high-school and collegiate levels were equally horrified by the shorts and jerseys worn by basketball players like the Golden Cyclones, whose team, on which Mildred "Babe" Didrikson played, was sponsored by Employers Casualty insurance company. (The uniforms boosted attendance from under 200 to some 5,000 a night.)[15] The properly middle-class leaders of the Women's Division of the National Amateur Athletic Federation, which effectively controlled scholastic and collegiate sports, routinely denounced "abbreviated costumes," especially when worn in the presence of male spectators.[16] They condescended to working-class women, like "Ida the Industrial Girl," who snapped the bonds of middle-class decorum. "She wants strenuous athletics, jazzy music, snappy dramatics or musical comedies, thrilling parties, not for the benefit she will receive, but because she will show off to good advantage before an audience of the opposite sex."[17] In the eyes of the Women's Division, the sports spectacles staged by the Amateur Athletic Union and by industrial leagues were little better than peep shows.

In the twenties, the German film-maker Arnold Fanck produced several "mountain films" starring the very athletic Leni Riefenstahl (about whom more later). Although they too were tempted by the box-office potential of athletic women, Hollywood producers were at first surprisingly hesitant to recruit them. The Australian swimmer Annette Kellermann, the "Diving Venus" who was said to have had the world's most perfect body, starred in *The Daughter of the Gods* (1916) and "staggered" the United States, but producers seldom asked other female athletes to perform before their cameras.[18] Tennis star Helen Wills, whose classical facial features seemed perfect for the cinema, was "the object of romantic infatuation for tens of thousands of young men," but not for the scrutinizers of her screen test. They concluded that "her limbs were too developed and her body lacked the petiteness so necessary for film success."[19] The United States, it seems, was not quite ready for a cinema goddess whose arms had been described, in *Collier's*, as "pistoning-columns of white muscle."[20]

That was 1927. A decade later, producers were emboldened enough to experiment with another beautiful athlete, Eleanor Holm, a champion swimmer from the Olympic Games of 1932 who became a *cause célèbre* in 1936 when her shipboard carousing caused her sudden expulsion from the Berlin-bound Olympic team. Playing Jane in *Tarzan's Revenge* (1938), Holm splashed about seductively while another Olympian, decathlete Glenn Morris, beat his muscular chest and gave voice to what has to be heard as a mating call. A third Olympian, Sonja Henie, combined athletic talent with a conventionally pretty face and skated her way from Chamonix to Hollywood. Reviewing her performance in a musical, *Thin Ice* (1937), *Variety* raved about "a flash of winter lightning, a great combination of muscle and music."[21] After Henie came a series of figure skaters whose figures (pun intended) allowed them, like her, to glide gracefully into show business. Indeed, Henie was followed by so many champion skaters that Tenley Albright's religiously motivated decision *not* to join the Icecapades seemed quirky.

The erotic appeal of figure skating can hardly be overlooked. The costumes are designed to accelerate the spectator's pulse and the choreography is accompanied by music that runs the gamut from nineteenth-century romanticism to the latest hit on MTV. By the Eighties, when Katarina Witt performed to the music from *Carmen*, it was impossible to pretend that the skater's athleticism is purely athletic or that aesthetic responses can be neatly separated from erotic ones. Nor was Witt the only skater to emphasize her sexual attractiveness. "No skaters ever danced like Britain's [Jane] Torvill and [Christopher] Dean on Valentine's Day in Sarajevo. . . . In their 'Bolero' routine, they took ice dancing out of the ballroom and skated it deliciously close to the back seat of a parked car."[22] In the journalistic melodrama of Nancy Kerrigan versus Tonya Harding, the former was type cast as the virginal beauty while the latter, who had appeared in *Playboy*, was characterized as little better than a slut. That was not the sort of contest that Pierre de Coubertin had in mind when he revived the Olympic Games in 1896, but it was unquestionably popular. The skaters at Lillehammer attracted the largest television audience of the 1994 games.

By the seventies, censorship of the arts had diminished to a trace element in the chemistry of European and North American cultures. Film-makers were free to indulge the public's appetite for the exciting combination of eros and sports. In the terminable (I hope) series of *Rocky I* (1976) through *Rocky V* (1990), an extremely muscular Sylvester Stallone poses and punches his way through a succession of increasingly implausible boxing matches. Referring to Stallone, among others, Yvonne Tasker comments in *Spectacular Bodies* (1993) that the world-wide "box-office success of the white male bodybuilder as star has been one of the most visible aspects of recent American action cinema."[23] Tasker argues that the cumulative effect of films like Martin Scorsese's *Raging Bull* (1980) has wrought a gradual redefinition of the image of masculine identity. In fact, gradual redefinition seems now to have accelerated into "a seismic shift in male body image." In "The Beefcaking of America," Jill Neimark meditates on the results of a survey conducted by *Psychology Today*: "In movies, heartthrobs from Alec Baldwin to Keanu Reeves are seen shirtless, with rippling pecs and lats; on fashion runways male models in skin-tight tanks and jackets unbuttoned to flaunt washboard bellies pace before cheering crowds." Neimark concludes that we are witnessing the emergence of a single standard for male beauty: "a hypermasculine, muscled, powerfully shaped body—the Soloflex man."[24] Samuel Fussell agrees: "Muscles are the latest props of the dandy."[25]

Feature films starring female athletes have been less successful at the box-office, but the list of Hollywood's athletic heroines includes Susan Anton in *Goldengirl* (1980), Mariel Hemingway in *Personal Best* (1982), Jamie Lee Curtis in *Perfect* (1985), Geena Davis in *A League of Their Own* (1992), and Meryl Streep in *The River Wild* (1994). Linda Hamilton, played alongside Arnold Schwarzenegger in the two *Terminator* films (1984, 1991). She trained for a year in order to create the body required for this role. "A central focus of the film is on actress Linda Hamilton's strong physique. In fact, the first image of [her] is of her developed biceps, the shot backing to show [her] working out."[26] She uses her physical strength to escape from unjust imprisonment and, eventually, save the world. On the basis of this role, Hamilton "quickly acquired a cult following" among lesbians.[27] "Unmuscled heft is no longer as acceptable as it once was," writes Susan Bordo. "Even Miss Soviet Union has become lean and tight."[28]

John Fiske's observations about televised sports also apply to feature films. The mediated spectacle differs from the spectators' *in situ* experience. In sports as in other filmed "masculine narratives," the temporal pace is routinely slowed during moments of intense action. "Slow motion is used . . . to celebrate and display the male body in action, to produce a sense of awe by making the physical performance appear beautiful. The male body in televised sport does not consist merely of brutish muscularity, but is aestheticized." Fiske is wrong to limit the effects to the male body, but he is right about slow motion. In televised sports coverage as in action drama, slow motion functions "to eroticize power, to extend the moment of climax."[29] Like slow motion, television's close-ups intensify "the erotic theatricalization of the athletic body."[30] Margaret Morse notes perceptively in "Sport on Television" that this is one context where "the male body . . . is a legitimate object of the male gaze."[31]

And the female gaze as well? An Australian media specialist, Beverley Poynton, is unabashed about her voyeurism: "What attracted my interest [to Australian Rules football] were the [televised] images of male bodies. Here were barely clad, eyeable Aussie male bodies in top anatomical nick. The cameras follow their rough and tumble disport with a relentless precision, in wide-angle, close-up and slow-motion replay." For this female sports fan, the choreographed spectacle is "lyrical, flagrantly masculine and erotic." One can safely infer that the producers of ABC's "Monday Night Football" agree. They screened a music video in which two members of the female rap group Salt N' Pepa performed a variation of their hit song, "Whatta Man," while the camera focussed on a pair of football players working out. The video was clearly an instance of "the sexual objectification of the male athletic body."[32]

While Hollywood and the world's television networks were enthusiastically relearning the profitable lesson of the Tarzan films, magazines devoted to fitness and sports proliferated. Since Bernarr Macfadden began to publicize the gospel of muscular hedonism in *Physical Culture* in 1899, periodicals like *Shape* and *Flex* are hardly a novelty, nor was it unprecedented that many of them were targeted for both male and female readers. (In 1932, ten of the twelve covers of Macfadden's *Physical Culture* pictured shapely women actively engaged in sports; Macfadden "frankly admitted the sexual energy implicit in body work."[33]). Japan has its own version of *Strength and Health*, in which the Japanese text is accompanied by photographs of European and North American body-builders. (This is very much in line with the Japanese penchant for using blue-eyed blondes in cosmetics advertisements.) Similar journals appeared at European kiosks. Two German publications—*Sport und Fitness* and *Sportrevue* —quickly achieved a combined monthly circulation of 250,000.[34]

In the Eighties, editors of general-circulation periodicals quickly hopped aboard the fitness express. Consumer culture seemed suddenly to have lost its last inhibitions and to have become obsessed "with the notion that the body is a vehicle of pleasure and self-expression." Everywhere one looked, there were "images of the body beautiful, openly sexual and associated with hedonism, leisure, and display."[35] *People* and the *New York Times Magazine* both investigated body-building in the spring of 1980. *Psychology Today* weighed in with "Iron Sisters" (in which Lisa Lyon asked, "Why should muscles be considered masculine?").[36] Mainstream women's magazines became daringly explicit about sports and bodies. In the April 1980 issue of *Vogue*, Mariel Hemingway posed with weights and urged other women to follow her example. *Glamour's* article on women's body-building (October 1981) included photographs of muscular women "pumped" and flexed. In April of 1983, *Cosmopolitan* crowed that female body-builders are "shapelier, firmer, *sexier!*" Meanwhile, in France, *Marie-Claire* and *Elle* were almost as quick to present images of trimmed and toned female bodies that conformed to the new "canons de beauté."[37] Writing in *Magazine Littéraire* for January 1986, the French man-of-letters Michel Tournier asserted, "Muscular women are by no means masculinized—not at all. The athletic woman who develops her body and its muscles has a totally feminine beauty. . . . There's nothing more beautiful than the female athlete."[38]

Surveying the British scene, Jennifer Hargreaves—another unusually acute observer—concluded that, although "muscularity has been associated with masculinity, it has now become a [generally] glamorized and sexualized condition."[39] John Updike has written as good a one-line summary of the transformation as we are likely to find: "Diana the huntress is a more trendy body-type nowadays than languid, overweight Venus."[40].

In recent decades, exercise manuals have flooded the market. Jane Fonda, who first attracted attention as the leggy astronautic heroine of *Barbarella* (1967), took to barbells and became better known as an icon of forty-year-old fitness than she had been as teenaged temptress. Videocassettes followed the manuals in such numbers, and with such physically attractive demonstrators, that uncritical viewers were tempted simply to sit before the TV and gawk at Sugar Ray Leonard, Martina Navratilova, O. J. Simpson, and company. "The body," writes an observer of contemporary German life, "is now the jewel; clothes are merely the setting."[41]

Comic books, which are a staple of popular culture, have always encouraged ninety-seven-pound victims of bullies on the beach to imagine physical transformation. ("Charles Atlas did it; you can do it too.") In the first comic books, Clark Kent became Superman. His muscles, developed for the environment of the lost planet Krypton, made him invulnerable, invincible, and—in the dazzled eyes of Lois Lane—irresistible. Today's children are beguiled by similar images of herculean men—and superhuman women. Wonder Woman, once an athletic anomaly in a comicstrip world where Blondie and Tillie the Typist were the norm, now has company. Germaine Greer has expressed amazement at the women who "prowl through thriller comics." Clouds of hair swirl about their heads, "the musculature of their shoulders and thighs is incredible, their breasts [are] like grenades, their waists [are] encircled with steel belts."[42]

The first images of Wonder Woman were inspired by tennis champion Alice Marble; she advised the cartoonists that Wonder Woman's star-spangled tennis dress be replaced by shorts—the better to reveal her muscular legs.[43] The televised Wonder Woman, played by Lynda Carter, was never as popular a heroine as Krystle (Linda Evans) and Alexis (Joan Collins) Carrington, but she has had her devoted followers. In a list of favorite entertainers named by a group of one-hundred twenty-eight schoolchildren (grades 3, 6, 9, and 12), Wonder Woman received more votes than Elvis Presley and almost as many as Bugs Bunny.[44] Perhaps it was her ability to perform extraordinary feats of strength while her breasts "seemed constantly poised to burst forth from their *Playboy* bunny-type container."[45]

Advertisers have rushed to sponsor televised displays of the athletic body and to have their products endorsed by prominent athletes. Coca-Cola led the way in the thirties and forties with advertisements picturing Johnny Weissmuller, Jesse Owens, Helen Madison, and Alice Coachman (all Olympic champions).[46] More recently, sponsors have been eager to pay huge sums of money for the right to picture Jim Palmer in his underwear, Bruce Jenner on a Wheaties box, Michael Jordan lofted by a pair of Nikes, Dorothy Hamill as a Breck girl, and Kristi Yamaguchi with a milk moustache. (Some kind of ultimate was reached when Fabergé advertised its perfume with pictures of Margaux Hemingway executing a karate kick.) Bernard S. Owett, senior vice-president of the J. Walter Thompson agency, announced that Madison Avenue wanted models with muscles because "athletic women are beautiful and sexy."[47] The issue of the marketers' trade journal in which Owett was quoted appeared with a flexed Lisa-Lyon-look-alike on its cover.

The manufacturers of exercise equipment are too clever to promise their readers a shot at Wimbledon or to guarantee a place on the Olympic team, but they do insinuate that the purchase of a Nautilis machine, a Nordic track, or a set of chromium-plated dumbbells will—if used according to the printed or videotaped directions—produce "buns of steel" and all the other attributes of the ideal physique. The message is clear and it is beamed at both men and women. You cannot realistically hope to become a champion athlete, but you *can* at least look—and love—like one. Medical experts assure us all that moderate exercise improves one's circulatory system and reduces our vulnerability to cardiac arrest, but five minutes in the supermarket checkout line ("Firmer Thighs Will Attract His Eyes!") are enough to persuade anyone that a desire for longevity is not the only thing that motivates to diet and exercise.

The assumption behind the advertisements for commodities as different as barbells and perfumes is that images of taut muscles and tight bodies will weaken a consumer's resistance and loosen his

or her purse-strings. Unfortunately, if a twenty-six-year-old feminist is at all representative, the advertisers' marketing strategy is
sometimes misconceived:

> I like slim men with tight asses and fairly broad shoulders, taller
> than I am, and [with] fairly good muscle tone. . . . Suits turn me off.
> Most men I look at are wearing earrings and radical pants. But have
> you seen that guy on the Calvin Klein billboards? I think he's deli-
> cious. I just wish he wouldn't wear those awful clothes.[48]

The right body, the wrong outfit.

The athletes whom the Broadway entrepreneurs and the
Hollywood moguls and the Madison Avenue hucksters showcase
are not unaware of their physical attractiveness. "Broadway Joe"
Namath marketed his sex appeal almost as successfully as he sold
his skills as a quarterback for the New York Jets. Wilt Chamber-
lain's notorious claim that he had slept with 20,000 different
women produced a spate of journalism in which other athletes
boasted that they too had had their pick of young women eager for
vicarious involvement in baseball, basketball, football, and ice
hockey. Rugby players are no exception. "Unlike beer," writes
Chris Laidlaw, "women on a Rugby tour are not compulsory.
Sometimes taken sometimes left, they are a commodity to be uti-
lized only if instantly available and free, which they usually are, in
considerable plentitude. The sex scene on Rugby tours is a woman
liberationist's nightmare."[49] Media specialist John Fiske believes
that many female sports spectators perceive the "display of male
bodies" as an opportunity "to mock masculinity." This may be the
case for some women, but the male athletes' sexual adventures
indicate otherwise. Fiske concedes as much when he adds that close-
ups and slow-motion replays "aestheticize the male body and turn
it into an object of feminine visual pleasure."[50]

When it comes to acknowledging one's own physical attractiveness, there has *not* been a contrast between manly boastfulness and
maidenly modesty. "Men," remarked female pentathlete Jane

Frederick, "go cuckoo for me." She was not offended by their delirium; she rather expected it. "As long as I love my body, everyone else does, too."[51] Another pentathlete, Cory Everson, became a highly successful competitive body-builder. She admits that she loves to admire herself in the mirror when "pumped up."[52]. "Athletes love physical expression," Lynda Huey proclaimed, "and sex is one of the best forms of it. . . . Physical strength [adds] to the whole sexual experience. How can anyone want anyone but an athlete?"[53] Florence "Flo-Jo" Griffith-Joyner is yet another example of a stellar athlete consciously presenting herself, with sharply defined quadriceps muscles and iridescent fingernail polish, as a source of exotic erotic delight. Olympic champion Jackie Joyner was no more willing than her sister-in-law to simper inanities and evade questions: "I love my body."[54]

Less celebrated believers in muscular hedonism are increasingly eager to testify (even if most physical educators are still too embarrassed to listen). Ordinary men and women agree with the Olympians and the Superstars that a devotion to sports has done more than improve their cardiovascular fitness. Stockbrokers in their forties take up afternoon squash and discover, after swatting the ball and working up a sweat, that they are no longer too fatigued for nocturnal sex. When a pair of feminist scholars interviewed eight female body-builders, they found that all of them "reported feeling sexier and more feminine as a result of their body-building."[55] Sports," comments a thirty-seven-year-old female softball player, make "me feel more attractive. . . . I feel sleeker, more fit, more feminine. And that carries over to my marriage."[56]

Awareness of the erotic potential of the athletic *body*, one's own or someone else's, is not, however, the same as awareness of an erotic element in the sports *performance*. Nonetheless, there is now a whole literature of ecstatic commentary on "the runner's high" and other forms of "peak experience." Athletes are increasingly vocal about what it is they feel. Skateboarders, wind-surfers, and hang-glider enthusiasts attest to ecstatic states comparable to "the pleasure that is derived from orgasm or drugs."[57] Mariah Burton Nelson has scathingly condemned sexism in sports, but she writes poetically of "pleasurable perceptions—two skis caressing a mountain; a hand rolling a heavy ball toward ten pins; the welcome ache of powerful thighs kicking through ocean waves."[58] Nelson's reference to "pleasurable perceptions" seems almost Victorian compared to Arnold Schwarzenegger's ecstatic claim that the athlete's "pump" is better than mere orgasm.[59] Athletes who once seemed devoted to secular asceticism are now eager to testify to the bliss experienced in moments of "flow" or the exhausted out-of-body sensation that follows one's utmost effort.

> I sometimes run up and down the stairs of a . . . skyscraper. After 144 flights, all I see are yellow walls, gray stairs, and red fire alarm boxes, one on every story. I take two stairs at a time, and my pulse races. When I reach the top, I just [lie] there. By then I'm beyond the physical, I'm somewhere else. I've used up all my stored energy and I'm totally dying, flying, and my legs are trembling. It's such a high and it's for my own satisfaction.[60]

The passionate language resembles the poetic discourse of mysticism (which Georges Bataille classified as a form of erotic experience).

Silken Laumann, a statuesque Canadian oarswoman who returned from Barcelona in 1992 with a bronze medal, seems to deny the erotic possibilities of her sport: "Rowing is a sport where you're really powerful, muscular and tall, and you sweat like crazy. . . . There's nothing glamorous at all."[61] Laumann's teammate Heather Clarke agrees about the muscularity but not about the lack of glamour. She refers to the tall, blonde, modest Laumann as "a youthful Valkyrie, a Nordic warrior goddess" and quotes her confidential desire "to be strong, lean and beautiful all at once"— which, in Clarke's eyes, she certainly was. Although Clarke has more to say about the athletes' *appearance*, she refers as well to the sensual pleasure experienced during the athletic *performance*: "Rowers," she writes, "love to glide through the mist with no sound but the catch-push of the oars hooking into the water. They love the physical feeling of the oar, their muscles, the water bubbling under the hull." Pushed by her coach to the point of exhaustion and beyond, she experienced "the physical ecstasy of being in top shape and celebrating the body's ability."[62]

To go beyond these attempts to communicate the ineffable sensuality that permeates at least some sports performances, it is not enough that one be an athlete. One has to be a verbal or a visual artist. It is time to look more closely at some literary and cinematographic manifestations of eros and sports.

6

Eros Imagined

NOVELS

Although twentieth-century American writers, from Ernest Hemingway to Joyce Carol Oates, have seemed almost to tumble over one another in their efforts to exploit the thematic possibilities of sports, it was European writers, especially the French and the Germans, who led the way.[1] Of the hundreds of modern writers, major and minor, who have produced novels, stories, poems, and plays with athletes as characters, four seem to have been especially fascinated by the theme of eros and sports: Henry de Montherlant, Ernest Hemingway, Kasimir Edschmid, and Jenifer Levin. Their dramatizations of the theme, like Georges Bataille's in *L'Érotisme*, may not be representative of Everyman's and Everywoman's experiences, but they widen the range of our speculations.

Reacting against the French intellectual tradition that had for centuries elevated mind above body, Marcel Berger, Dominique Braga, Maurice Genevoix, Jean Giraudoux, Louis Hémon, Paul Morand, and André Obey penned ecstatic descriptions of the "splendidly sculpted allure of . . . young bodies."[2] Even Marcel Proust managed to put Albertine on a bicycle. Although there were writers who sounded a note of asceticism, the majority agreed with Jean Prévost's assertion that the athlete's body should arouse "admiration with desire."[3]

Among the *auteurs sportifs* publishing novels and poems in the years before and after the 1924 Olympics (which took place in Paris), Henry de Montherlant was perhaps the most important. In a number of impressive novels and poems he celebrated "the sensuality and eroticism" of sports.[4] His experimental novel *Le Paradis à l'ombre des épées* (*The Paradise in the Shade of the Swords*) (1920) is a lyrical account of "the glory of the stadium."[5] The central characters, both athletes, are an anonymous narrator (whose surname the book's sequel gives as Riry) and his friend Jacques Peyrony, a youth whose physical beauty is described immediately after a reference to Plato's *Symposium* (which focuses on the theme of eros):

> When the water from the shower runs down his body, its reflecting surface, catching the light and creating shadows here and there, outlines the fine musculature as the varnish of a picture brings out its details. I dream of other illusions: of the plaster statues whose radiant whiteness makes them appear larger than they are, of statues of bronze whose clean contours give the impression of lengthened forms. Then the body is dry and its salients seem to be reabsorbed. A soft unity resolves them into one another as the light swells of a peaceful river resolve into one another.

Although Peyrony's young body is imperfect, it brings to mind the ideal of the human form expressed in "Greek athletic statuary." And the body seems, as it did to Plato, "like an image of the soul."[6]

Riry responds to the erotic appeals of girls as well as boys. While running a race, he becomes exhausted, stumbles, and cuts his hand on the frozen ground. When he seeks first aid, he notices "Mademoiselle V," a member of another athletic club, who has a bandage on her knee. He learns later that the bandage, reddened by her blood, was originally the white band with which she had tied back her hair. In the course of her cross-country run she too had fallen and cut herself badly on the shards of a broken bottle. Observing her, the narrator experiences a sense of erotic communion. "Ah! what a blow to the heart! Her blood! My blood!" Their blood is associated both with nuptial blood and with that shed by wounded soldiers. Riry feels "as if suffused from top to bottom by a flame, shaken by a trance." He experiences an "epiphany" and a rush of sexual desire for this body "because it bleeds." When her wounds are treated, she looks on gravely "and says not a word." Enamoured of her courage, he falls in love and realizes why he had not, before this epiphany, found women particularly attractive. "Diotima says [in Plato's *Symposium*] that it is impossible for our nature to love what is ugly. I realized that it was impossible for mine to love what is weak."[7]

After this scene, "Mademoiselle V" disappears from the story, but the arrival of "Mademoiselle de Plémeur," a champion runner, occasions a further meditation on the aesthetics and erotics of athleticism. While admitting that male athletes have often mocked their female counterparts, Riry insists that "feminine athleticism— running, jumping, throwing—provide intense pleasure, athletic as well as aesthetic." He realizes that "musculature is always beautiful, a woman's as well as a man's, if it is not excessive." This realization forces him to rethink his previous failure to respond positively to the appeals of the opposite sex:

> The bodies of women represented by contemporary painters and sculptors, those of the nude women whom I had seen, even the professional models considered to be "jolies femmes," were horrible. No matter that a unanimous opinion proclaimed that their pads of fat . . . were the most sublime expression, the sole expression, of Beauty with a capital "B."

Never having encountered young women with "the bodies of the women of Greek statuary," he had concluded that such were "the inventions of idealism." And then, visiting the stadia, he observed "athletically trained young girls. . . . What a revelation! Like that of a new sex. I realized then that a woman's body can be beautiful—if it is trained."[8]

Fascinated now by Mlle. de Plémeur, Riry narrates her story, telling how she, the best runner in the club, lost a race, became discouraged, abandoned her regimen, grew fat and flabby, but then returned to the track, and trained to set a record for 300 meters. He times her heroic effort, which fails by eight seconds. He comforts her, after which she disappears from his life.

In a sequel to this novel, *Les Onze devant la porte dorée* (*The Eleven Before the Golden Door*) (1924), Montherlant returned to the stadium, this time, as the "eleven" of the title indicates, with an emphasis on soccer. The narration is, however, interrupted by a number of poems that sing of the beauty and the erotic potential of other sports. "Les Coureurs de Relais," for instance, goes beyond the concept of a team in order to affirm the metaphorical identity of the relay's four runners:

> *Four and yet we are one. A perfect solidarity.*
> *A grand human accord, so just that one wants to sing.*
> *Each of us exercises the right to control the bodies of the other three.*
> *To my calves, because they are yours, I acknowledge your right.*
> *And your muscles, your nerves, your head—they matter to me*
> *because they are mine.*[9]

Other interpelated poems, "Soleil de Nuit" and "A une Jeune Fille Victorieuse dans la Course de mille Mètres," are evocations of the theme of female athleticism, but the climax of the book is yet another male communion. This one brings together the soccer players, one of whom asks if the somber force of the body's play is not "akin to love?"[10]

The final chapter takes the form of a one-act play whose main characters are the captain of a soccer team and Jacques Peyrony, who has decided to leave the team for a more prominent one. At first, Peyrony brusquely repels the captain's plea that he stay with his old comrades: "There's not a single person in the club that I'll miss." Eventually, however, he relents. Ritual seals the renewed pact. Just as "Romulus and his companions leaped above the flame, to purify themselves, when they founded the City,"[11] the two young men spring across the a pile of burning leaves. The bonds of male friendship mean more than mere ambition. With this strange symbolic act, the book ends.

Le Songe (1922) is Montherlant's somewhat less rhapsodic story of Alban de Bricoule, the devoutly Catholic scion of generations of French aristocrats. A professional classicist and an amateur athlete, he finds himself attracted by two women. The first of them, Douce (i.e., "Sweetie"), is quite conventional; the second, Dominique, whose name in this context suggests domination, is probably the most lovingly created female athlete in French (perhaps in any) fiction. Dominique is certainly Montherlant's most detailed portrait of the type. Driven by "the ideal of the Amazon," she is "a strong girl, with broad shoulders, a helmet of hair, and heroic hands that hurled the javelin across the field." The imagery is intentionally martial (the "helmet" of hair) and the sports that attract Dominique are those originally associated with warfare, an association that seems especially appropriate in a novel set during World War I, when images of "Marianne" became markedly more bellicose.[12]

Even more remarkable than this description is a long narcissistic scene in which Dominique poses before her mirror, stretching, turning, twisting, flexing, admiring. Defying the Romantic convention that shuns a kind of textbook anatomical exactness (what poet sings of deltoids and adductors?), Montherlant allows Dominique to name each muscle and to revel in her physical perfection:

> Without changing her pose, she contracted her muscles across the length of her body. . . . Her entire body was like a thing of delicately hammered metal. . . . The lateral ridges of her abdomen flexed, mounted, slid smoothly one above the other beneath her breasts.

Despite the poses, Dominique is not a body-builder whose physical development has become an end in itself. She runs. The exhilaration she experiences is closely detailed. When she races a friend, she feels an inexpressible ecstasy: "Intoxicating, intoxicating, intoxicating sensation of calling upon oneself and feeling oneself respond!" This sensation culminates in a mystic moment of exhausted plenitude when Dominique flings herself upon the earth and achieves a momentary unity with nature. Her bliss seems almost postcoital.[13]

Like many French writers familiar with Greek and Latin literature, Montherlant alludes often to pagan antiquity. The neoclassicism of the novel appears in many ways, but the most evocative passage comes early when Dominique and Alban study photographs of the Parthenon, the temple of Athena worshipped as the virgin goddess (*parthenos*). The two of them, comrades rather than lovers, marvel at the beauty of the equestrian statues and are entranced by the look of one of the youths as he seems to turn outward from the procession in order to stare at them across the centuries. Still, despite his love of pagan antiquity, Alban remains passionately Roman Catholic. He keeps a crucifix in his study and imagines Christ's expression to be as contorted as that of an athlete at the end of his race. In fact, when Dominique's face contorts and stiffens in the exertion of a race, her expression takes on a "splendid unattractiveness" not unlike that of the crucified Christ.[14] Her physicality simultaneously attracts and repels Montherlant's conflicted hero. Paradoxically, Dominique represents both temptation—the embodiment of eros—and a bodily perfection too pure to be sullied by the physical act of love. The two of them have a relationship that can accurately be called Platonic.

When Alban decides to volunteer for active military duty, Dominique becomes a nurse. She is sexually awakened by the wounded youths in the hospital where she works. He discovers that he *likes* to kill. When a German soldier tries to surrender to him, Alban calmly shoots him. He feels an erotic thrill (as does Norman

Mailer's Stephen Rojack in a similar scene in *An American Dream*). The war provides him not only with the chance to kill but also with the opportunity to love. Although the theme of homosexuality is covert, it is unmistakably clear that Alban is in love with a comrade, Stanislas Prinet, a prewar friend, with whom he endures a terrifying nocturnal bombardment. When Stanislas fears that he has been wounded, Alban holds him in his arms and brings him through the ordeal. The next day, however, Alban quarrels with Stanislas, then feels guilty about his un-Christian behavior, and subsequently begs absolution from a priest (who asks him to compose a triad of Latin hymns as his penance!). Risking his own life, Alban searches the battlefield for Stanislas, only to learn that he has been killed. In panic, Alban flees from the front (a minor wound is his official excuse).

At a hospital in the rear, he meets Dominique once again. Insistently, she declares her passionate love for him; just as insistently, he announces that she represents for him the *idea* of physical perfection. Mere physical desire repels him. "All progress," he declares, "comes not from following nature but from opposing nature." Bitterly, she accuses him of having manipulated her into sterility, "forcing me into this coldness from which you drew your icy pleasure!" His immediate response to her passion is to fall silent, but he subsequently agrees to sleep with her, only to draw back at the last minute, when the sight of her body fills him with conflicting emotions. He cannot bear "the transformation of the image of purity into the image of impurity." And he imagines the voices of Stanislas and other dead comrades reminding him of his patriotic duty. To Dominique, who is mad with desire, he declares his (still Platonic) love, and he departs into the purifying waters of a thunderstorm. As he returns to the front, he likens Dominique to Agamemnon's daughter Iphegenia, sacrificed by her father to the gods of battle. It is a strange and wonderful novel.[15]

In the course of writing *Le Songe*, Montherlant seems to have become so fascinated with the figure of Alban de Bricoule that he

subsequently wrote another novel, *Les Bestiaires* (1926), devoted
to Alban's athletic and religious adventures four or five years
before the time of his relationship with Dominique. In this novel,
which is even stranger than *Le Songe*, Alban is sent by his mother
to vacation in Spain because she senses that a planned visit to the
Catholic shrine of Lourdes might overexcite his religious sensibil-
ities. Her scheme goes awry when Alban falls in love—not with
Soledad, the beautiful young daughter of an aristocratic Spanish
family—but with the *corrida de toros*. He becomes a bullfighter.

In this novel, Alban succumbs, at least for a time, to the attractions of paganism. Like many who have written on the *corrida*,
Montherlant believes that it derives from the cult of Mithra. To
slay the bull is to re-enact the sun god's ritual sacrifice. Alban's
sense of kinship with the Persian deity is intensified by the fact that
the sun enters the constellation Taurus on Alban's birthday. The
god's ritual sacrifice, replicated in the *corrida*, is described as a sexual act. "The combat and sensuality [*volupté*] are brother and sister." The erotic occasion is one from which women are barred:
"Women are excluded from participation in his [Mithra's] mysteries." Although taming a wild horse gives Alban "a sensation of
virility . . . unlike any he had ever experienced," the thrill that
accompanies the thrust of his sword into the heart of the bull is
even more intense. The combat between the man and the animal,
likened to the communion of "the god and his priest," is "more
than a combat; it [is] a religious incantation elevated by pure gestures more beautiful than those of love." Alban slays the bull,
whose testicles are then removed by a boy named Jesus. As Alban
dedicates the slain bull to "the unvanquished Sun," he asserts that
there is no conflict between Mithraism and Christianity. The poly-
semic novel ends with the celebration of a Catholic mass.[16]

Ernest Hemingway's *The Sun Also Rises*, another novel in
which bullfighting is a basic metaphor, coincidentally appeared the
same year as *Les Bestiaires*. (Although Hemingway wrote the book
while living in Paris, there is no evidence that he knew

Montherlant or read his work.) Every *aficionado* of modern literature is aware that Hemingway was obsessed by sports. Among his
most memorable characters are not only the bullfighters of *The
Sun Also Rises, Death in the Afternoon,* and "The Undefeated" but
also hunters (*The Green Hills of Africa,* "The Short Happy Life of
Francis Macomber"), fishermen (the Nick Adams stories, *The Old
Man and the Sea*), boxers ("The Battler," "Fifty Grand"), and jock-
eys ("My Old Man")—and this list is far from exhaustive.
Although Hemingway, like Montherlant, was in love with sports,
his fiction differs from the French author's because Montherlant
tells us what he thinks we need to know while Hemingway leaves
it to his readers to infer the presence of eros from the nuances of
his prose.

The *Sun Also Rises,* Hemingway's most profound exploration of
the erotic element in sports, is probably his best book. It is certainly
his most complex. The two epigraphs—from Gertrude Stein's
chauffeur's comment on the "lost generation" and from the Book of
Ecclesiastes—contrast the linearity of History, where the loss of a
generation in World War I is irreparable, with the eternal return of
Myth, where "one generation passeth away, and another generation
cometh; but the earth abideth forever." History and Myth are local-
ized in modern Paris, where Jake Barnes leads a meaningless life, and
in primitive Spain, where Pedro Romero, defying the horns of the
bull, whirling the *matador's* cape, thrusting with his *spada,* symbolizes the masculine values Hemingway most prized. For many
details of the symbolic contrast between Paris, where the action
begins, and Pamplona, where it reaches its climax, Hemingway drew
upon T. S. Eliot's *The Waste Land,* published just four years earlier.
Subtle allusions to Eliot's elitist poem are the last thing one expects
of an author who prided himself on his "tough guy" image, but
there they are. Jake Barnes, for instance, rendered sexually impotent
by a wound suffered in the war, is the analogue to Eliot's emblem-
atic "fisher king," the waste land's impotent sovereign. What better
metaphor was there to symbolize what Hemingway, like Eliot, felt

to be the sterility of the modern world? And how ironic it is that Hemingway grants to his wounded narrator some moments of pastoral communion with other men—as a fisherman in Spain.

When the story begins, Jake Barnes is hopelessly in love with the bewitching Lady Brett, Hemingway's version of Eliot's version of Homer's Circe. She reciprocates—in her way—but both of them realize that there can never be a physical consummation to their love. She turns, instead, to Pedro Romero, the courageous incarnation of what has become, sadly, a cliché: grace under pressure. In this context, the overworked concept of "grace," which has become almost wholly secularized, retains much of its original theological force because Hemingway, whose modern urbanites have lost their faith in God, underscores the fact that the bullfight, which occurs within the larger context of Pamplona's annual fiesta, is a religious ritual.

In Jake's description of the *corrida*, it seems almost as if the bullfighter and the bull were a pair of lovers. Romero entices the bull to come toward him

> and then stopped and, standing squarely in front of the bull, offered him the cape. The bull's tail went up and he charged, and Romero moved his arms ahead of the bull, wheeling, his feet firmed. The dampened, mud-weighted cape swung open and full as a sail fills, and Romero pivoted with it just ahead of the bull. At the end of the pass they were facing each other again. Romero smiled. The bull wanted it again, and Romero's cape filled again, this time on the other side. Each time he let the bull pass so close that the man and the bull and the cape that filled and pivoted ahead of the bull were all one sharply etched mass. It was all so slow and controlled. It was as though he were rocking the bull to sleep.

When he is done with this deadly foreplay, he leans forward between the horns of the bull and thrusts his sword into the animal's shoulder "and just for an instant he and the bull were one."[17]

Jake Barnes, transfixed by admiration and by envy, realizes that Romero's performance is more than a religious ritual. It is also a

form of courtship. "I think he loved the bulls, and I think he loved
Brett. Everything of which he could control the locality he did in
front of her that afternoon. Never once did he look up. He made it
stronger that way, and did it for himself too, as well as for her.
Because he did not look up to ask if it pleased he did it all for himself inside, and it strengthened him, and yet he did it for her, too."

Peter Schwenger, discussing the symbolism of the bullfight in
the work of several twentieth-century writers, takes the sexual
associations a step further: "In the end, the *torero* enters the bull's
body in an act analogous to sexual penetration."[18]

That Brett, watching Romero twist and turn and thrust his
sword, finds him sexually irresistible, is obvious. She abandons
Robert Cohn, who "was once middleweight boxing champion of
Princeton," with whom she had had a brief love affair, and runs off
with Romero.[19] Why does she prefer the bullfighter to the boxer?
Jake Barnes provides the answer on the first page of the novel.
Cohn fought not because he loved the primitive thrill of man-to-
man physical combat, which is what attracted Hemingway to the
sport, but only "to counteract the feeling of inferiority and shyness
he had felt . . . as a Jew at Princeton."[20] He has the utilitarian
pugilistic skill to batter Romero in a fistfight, which he does, but he
cannot subdue the bullfighter's spirit. His farcical victory in an
unfair fight merely demonstrates to Brett and to all the others in
their party that Cohn is morally inferior to Romero.

Hemingway's disgusted response to "inauthentic" boxers also
appears in a tale told by one of Jake's friends. Bill Gorton returns
from Vienna with an account of a fixed fight between a bribed
African American and a local boxer too unskilled to hit an opponent
who wanted only to collapse into a plausible heap. When the hap-
less black fighter became the reluctant winner, he had to flee to
escape the enraged crowd.

There is still another sport that Hemingway uses as a foil to the
bullfight. Toward the end of the novel, just before Jake learns that
Brett has decided to leave Romero in order not to ruin him with her

wicked love, Jake encounters a team of professional cyclists. They represent, for Hemingway, the debased moral tone of modern—as opposed to traditional—sports:

> They were all French and Belgians, and paid close attention to their meal, but they were having a good time. At the head of the table were two good-looking French girls, with much Rue du Faubourg Montmartre chic. I could not make out whom they belonged to. They all spoke slang at the long table and there were many private jokes and some jokes at the far end that were not repeated when the girls asked to hear them. The next morning at five o'clock the race resumed with the last lap, San Sebastian-Bilbao. The bicycle-riders drank much wine, and were burned and browned by the sun. They did not take the race seriously except among themselves. They had raced among themselves so often that it did not make much difference who won. Especially in a foreign country. The money could be arranged.

It is all there: the estrangement from nature symbolized by the bicycles, the meaningless sexuality, the obscene jokes, the failure to take sports seriously, the dishonesty. The team's manager assures Jake that France is "the most *sportif* country in the world. It was bicycle road-racing that did it. That and football." Jake knows better. When the cyclists are gone, he swims out to sea in order to cleanse himself of their taint. The novel ends with Jake and Brett in a taxi on Madrid's Gran Via, wishing that the world were other than what it is. "Oh, Jake," she says, "we could have had such a damned good time together," to which he replies, "Yes. . . . Isn't it pretty to think so?"[21]

Of the German writers fascinated by sports, and they have been many,[22] Kasimir Edschmid was the one most clearly obsessed with sports' erotic component. Like Montherlant and Hemingway, he published his most important work in the twenties: *Sport um Gagaly* (1928). In an essay entitled "Sports and Literature in the Twenties," Wolfgang Rothe has maintained that Edschmid's novel is the only important sports fiction to appear between World War I and World War II.[23] Nonetheless, the book remains little known even among specialists of German literature.

The male protagonist is an Italian prodigy, Cesare Passari, a wealthy industrialist with a passion for sports, a man who considers the human body a work of art. Not only is he a runner and a tennis player; he is also an airplane pilot and an ardent *automobilista* who represents the Fiat motor company in deadly contests against rivals driving Peugeots. Bored by a career in diplomacy, he nonetheless wrote a study of Machiavelli's treaties before he abandoned the word for the deed. The name "Cesare" is appropriate.

Rothe refers to the book as "snobbish" and remarks disapprovingly that the reader "discovers not even a trace of social criticism in *Der Sport um Gagaly*."[24] In fact, there is plenty to be found, but it is not the kind Rothe was looking for. Cesare's allusions to Gabriele D'Annunzio and Benito Mussolini indicate that Edschmid may have shared Fascism's glorification of physical strength and its infatuation with the wonders of modern technology. Vigorous men (and women) in automobiles symbolize the mastery once associated with men on horseback. "Passari's conception of sports," writes Edschmid, "resembled Mussolini's State."[25] Although the fascination with Fascism, even in its somewhat milder Italian version, is repugnant, it is but one strand in a complexly woven work.

The novel's milieu is decidedly cosmopolitan and elitist. The first scenes are set at a Hungarian castle where an international cast of characters talk politics, ride, hunt, run, play tennis, and fall in love. Among them is Baron Tibor Banffy, crusty defender of premodern sports. He is proud that his trotter once set a record, and he refuses to loan the horse to a youthful countess: "he would rather put a bullet in the stallion's head than entrust it to an adolescent." Modern sports, however, baffle him. Observing Cesare's enthusiasm for odd forms of physical exertion, the Baron is puzzled: "He failed to comprehend why a man able to afford a horse ran around the race track in women's underwear."[26] Initially annoyed by Cesare's unconventional behavior, the Baron is mollified when he in his horse-drawn sulky seems to win a race against the Italian runner (who purposely slows down to appease the older man— *noblesse oblige*).

The plot centers not on different conceptions of sports, important as that theme is in Edschmid's novel (as in Hemingway's), but on the erotic triangle formed by Cesare and two sporty females. Cesare is attracted both to Gagaly Madosdy, a mature but still youthful woman, and to Contessa Pista Tossuth, an unmarried adolescent. The first is already and the second soon becomes a remarkable athlete. In one of the many classical allusions that pervade the book, Gagaly is "an Athena in tennis shoes." She is Cesare's "athletic and feminine ideal."[27]

Pista, on the other hand, is still unformed. Concluding that the "laws which can perfect this child are the laws of sports," Cesare undertakes—Pygmalion-like—to shape her to his ideal of feminine beauty. He teaches her to run properly and he trains her to defeat Gagaly, the national champion, at tennis. Because Cesare is sleeping with Gagaly while training Pista, his motives are not entirely clear. Apparently he wants to humble Gagaly because her aloofness in public seems incompatible with the clandestine passion of their affair. He officiates at the tennis match at which Pista challenges Gagaly, and he feels emotionally knocked about by the fact that he loves both of the contestants.

When not running or playing tennis, the three young people spend a great deal of time in automobiles. What the boudoir is to the vamp, the driver's seat is to Edschmid's modern lovers. As Cesare says to Pista, "You have to fall in love with the motor." She does. She learns to shift gears without the clutch. It is, in this highly erotic context, a very sexy accomplishment. The episode is reminiscent of Filippo Marinetti's Futurist essay on the love of the mechanic for his machines: "His is the minute, knowing tenderness of a lover caressing his adored woman."[28]

Cesare, Gagaly, and Pista admire each others' bodies as well as their aptitude with automobiles. Gagaly's legs are "perfectly beautiful, muscular, curved and firm, but nonetheless graceful." As for Pista, her "steel-slim body" assumes a "wonderfully elastic form" as she raises her head and tosses her mane of hair. Cesare admires this body, which seems to be made "of thin bronze." He is especially impressed by her flat belly, but, on the other hand, he notes that her "thighs were not entirely mature. Clearly she lacked the full proportions which gave [Gagaly] Madosdy her marmoreal gleam." Since the women eye him as closely as he inspects them, accusations of "sexism" are not really in order. Nonetheless, the references to bodies made of steel, bronze, and marble do indicate a rhetoric of hard physicality unmistakably reminiscent of Italian Fascism.[29]

The climax of the novel comes in Italy, where Cesare goes for an automobile race. The two women, too modern and emancipated simply to mope about, set off on their own Italian journey. In Venice, where Thomas Mann imagined the decadent collapse of poor old Gustav von Aschenbach (no athlete he!), Edschmid's sportsman-protagonist accidently encounters Gagaly and Pista. The three of them resume their complicated affair.

The women find a way to square the triangle. Pista had begun to fall in love with Gagaly the day of their Hungarian tennis match. Each finds the other physically attractive. Driving alone with Pista, Gagaly admires "the long legs of the countess as she reaches for the brakes." She feels another quiver of pleasure "looking at Pista's legs as Pista searched for the Lancia's gas pedals." The mutual attraction becomes even more intense at an automobile race, where one of the drivers dies in a crash and "the countess's passion for [Gagaly] was quickened by the presence of death." Celebrating Cesare's escape from the accident, Gagaly kisses Pista. "From this kiss on, the two loved him in each other."[30] In a neat proleptic inversion of Eve Kosofsky Sedgwick's paradigm of the erotic triangle in which two men seem to be in love with the same woman but actually desire one another,[31] Edschmid offers us two women who desire one another even as they are in love with the same man. Gagaly, who wishes to avoid the social unpleasantness of a divorce, decides that

Cesare should marry Pista and that the three of them should continue to form a triad of lovers. This has unexpected ludic side effects. "The passions of the three gave them tripled strength—and not only in love." Cesare wins automobile races too. As the book comes to a close, Edschmid alludes again to classical prototypes. Of the two women who share Cesare but apparently renounce the pleasures of direct lesbian love, Edschmid writes, "The young men at Olympia also had deeper bonds."[32]

Der Sport um Gagaly, unusual enough in its bold portrayal of female athleticism, stands practically unique in German sports literature in that it comes to what German critics, at a loss for indigenous terminology, refer to as *das Happy End*. It is understandable that literary historians, especially German ones, have hesitated to write about a novel that flirts with Fascism, but it nonetheless does seem a shame that this extraordinary novel has never been translated.

Montherlant and Edschmid were both men of letters respected in their own countries; Hemingway, of course, was a Nobel laureate internationally acclaimed as one of the century's greatest writers. In contrast, Jenifer Levin is hardly known at all, which is a pity because her first novel, *Water Dancer* (1982), is a remarkable dramatization of eros and sports.

All the major characters are swimmers or divers. There is literary as well as psychoanalytic precedence for this aquatic eroticism. In Walt Whitman's sensuous poem, "The Sleepers," the speaker responds powerfully to "a beautiful gigantic swimmer swimming naked through the eddies of the sea." Kate Chopin's *The Awakening* (1899) includes a scene where "the touch of the sea" on the heroine's skin "is sensuous, enfolding the body in its soft, close embrace." In D. H. Lawrence's *The Rainbow* (1915), Ursula, while swimming, is "blinded with passion" at the sight of Winifred's strong legs and shoulders, "the beauty of the fine, white, cool flesh." Levin too exploits to the fullest the sensuality of immersion and the erotic associations of the swimmer's body as it cleaves the water.[33]

In *Water Dancer*, David "Sarge" Olssen was once a top-ranked swimmer and his wife Ilana was a cliff-diver. Their son, for whom they grieve, drowned in a race. Into their lives comes young Dorey Thomas, a woman with a trauma of her own to overcome. Having once dropped out of a race, she has been haunted by the sense that she has failed her vicariously ambitious mother. She comes to Sarge with an appeal: "I want to swim the San Antonio. Will you train me?"[34] Since the San Antonio Strait is where Matt Olssen drowned, Sarge and Ilana are especially reluctant to emerge from the psychic seclusion into which they have retreated. They do agree to watch Dorey run and swim. While they are still undecided, Dorey tells Sarge that Matt was never good enough to have swum the strait. Emotionally jolted, he slaps her—and she punches him. It is the start of a whole series of intimate relationships.

Sarge and Ilana embrace Dorey as a substitute for their lost son. The destructive physical exertions that eventually strengthen the body are implicitly likened to the destructive psychic process that destroys in order to re-create: "Tear things down a little," says Sarge, "they grow back stronger."[35] Sarge and Ilana recruit a friend, Dr. John Gallagher, to aid them. He is an oarsman, an amateur astrologer aptly nicknamed "Tycho Brahe," and exactly the kind of sports physician they need for Dorey. The team is completed when Ann Norton—a swimmer, runner, weight-lifter, archer— agrees to interrupts her graduate study in order to join the adventure as Dorey's pacer. (The *dramatis personae* tallied in this manner seems almost comical; in context, the characters are quite credible.)

None of the action is particularly unexpected in a novel about the challenges of sports and the psychic need to overcome trauma. What sets Levin's achievement apart from more conventional explorations of the theme is her extraordinary openness about erotic physicality.

Merely looking at Dorey, whose body has been shaped by sports, Sarge and Ilana recognize that she is an elite athlete. Her presence acts to heal the psychic wound inflicted by Matt's death—and it stimulates them sexually. The married couple makes love for the first time since their son's death. Their renewed desire for one another is inextricably related to their mutual desire for Dorey, to whom Ilana wants to offer her breast. Sarge is also sexually aroused by Dorey, but makes no move even when he observes her standing shirtless with upraised arms and hands cupped to catch the falling rain. After having decided not to intrude upon that private ritual. Sarge is tempted again when he helps Dorey bathe. " 'You'll be'— he fished for her wrist and held it, rubbed the sponge along her arm—'the strongest lady on earth,' " a status that quite obviously delights and attracts him.[36]

When Dorey enters a race, there is a familiar agony to be overcome: "Below the waist she was numb. Above the waist torn to shreds." It is that strangely masochistic sexualized sensation of mingled pain and pleasure known to every serious endurance athlete. She wins the race and exults to Ilana, "Want to know what put Humpty Dumpty together again?" Since Ilana, too, was an athlete, she understands. As they celebrate, Sarge embraces and kisses her, but Ilana is the first to act on her feelings. She massages the young swimmer, admires the smooth hardness beneath the skin: "All those muscles and you're still very soft, that's remarkable." She is surprised by her own response because "she hadn't expected to be moved by the physical." The two women make love. Sarge finds them together and berates Dorey, who rushes off to New York to be comforted by Tycho. Sarge follows and asks her to return, which she does. At this point, she declares that she loves him too and asks, "Do you want to sleep with me?" " 'The thought,' he said softly, 'has crossed my mind.' " From thought to action they go, but he ejaculates into her hands and she rubs herself with his sperm as she had rubbed herself with handfuls of rain. (The parallel is explicit.)[37]

Now that a one-man–two-women triad has been formed, as it was in Edschmid's *Der Sport um Gagaly*, everyone is ready for Dorey's attempt to swim the strait. Her first effort fails and she has to be pulled from the water in the midst of a sudden storm, but she tries again. Failure seems imminent. After a long night in the icy waters, she becomes delirious and Sarge, frightened by memories of Matt's death, loses faith. Ann screams at him, "Screw you, Sarge, screw you. You're the one who can't make it." He breaks down and weeps, but he doesn't interfere, and Dorey struggles on in an ecstasy of pain and determination. She overcomes her own incubus and swims free of her mother's overly possessive love: "Dorey pulled out the scissors. Sorry, she said, I am sorry. She'd have cried but nothing was left. Sorry, I would carry you now Carol if I had the strength. Except I'm not a giant anymore. Just enough left for me." She perseveres and crawls to shore. "Did it," she says, and that suffices.[38]

These four very different writers are unquestionably a mixed bag, but they share an implicit or explicit recognition of a close association between eros and sports. All four of them imply or assert that death or the possibility of death intensifies this association (which is in accordance with Bataille's theory of eros). Montherlant, Edschmid, and Levin seem to endorse Freud's view of sexuality in that their characters feel homosexual as well as heterosexual desire (and even Hemingway dramatizes the close bonds that develop among male athletes).

FILMS

Films, including those produced by Hollywood's "dream factory," are another source of insight into eros and sports. British films have tended to shy from a focus on the sheer physicality of sports in order to make a statement about the relationship between sports and social class, bitter statements in the case of Tony Richardson's *The Loneliness of the Long Distance Runner* (1962) and Lindsay Anderson's *This Sporting Life* (1963), a sentimental one in the case of Hugh Hudson's *Chariots of Fire* (1981). American films can be just as sentimental. In addition to *The Pride of the Yankees* (1942), *The Babe Ruth Story* (1948), *Damn Yankees* (1958), and many subsequent dramatizations of baseball, there is the extreme instance of sports-related treacle, *Breaking Away* (1979), in which a provincial adolescent passes himself off as a European cyclist in order to coast into his girlfriend's affections.

In addition to their greater willingness to offer movie-goers sentimentalized eroticism, American directors have also been much bolder than their foreign counterparts in the exploration of the sadomasochistic element in sports. From Stanley Kramer's *Champion* (1949) through John Huston's *Fat City* (1972) and the violent nonsense of *Rocky I-V* (1976–1990), boxers have enacted cinematic fantasies of masculinity. These films may not be notable for subtle indirection, but neither are they evasive about hard bodies, sadism, masochism, and the wicked sexual thrill of a knockout punch.

"Hollywood films about sport," comments Pam Cook, "generally centre on the male body."[39] Sharing this insight, Thelma McCormack has anatomized the prizefight film as a form of "jock appeal."[40] No film fits that rubric better than Martin Scorsese's *Raging Bull* (1980), which a poll of American film critics selected as the decade's best film.[41] The screenplay was based on the autobiography of middleweight champion Jake LaMotta, whom Scorsese portrayed as an insanely jealous man obsessed by the constant need to prove his masculinity. When Jake (Robert De Niro) accepts the mob's terms and "loses" a fight in return for a chance at the title, the humiliation is so great that he breaks down into uncontrollable sobs. When his beautiful young wife (Cathy Moriarty) mentions, casually, that a prospective opponent has a pretty face, Jake is not content simply to prove himself the better fighter. He holds his beaten opponent against the ropes and batters him until he is horribly disfigured. When Jake's manager-brother gives his sister-in-law an innocent kiss, Jake accuses her of adultery and then charges—like a raging bull—into his brother's apartment and beats him so badly that the two are permanently estranged. When Jake is at the end of his career and about to lose his title to Sugar Ray Robinson, he lowers his guard, leans back against the ropes, and lets

Robinson punch him again and again. After the fight has ended, Jake staggers across the ring to boast, "You never got me down, Ray. You never got me down." If this scene cannot be interpreted as an instance of erectile pride, then Dr. Freud labored in vain.

Jake's wife is a shapely blonde who attracts his attention when he spots her at the neighborhood swimming pool, but the most obviously erotic moment in the film comes when he lies supinely on their bed, stripped to his boxer shorts, while she covers his torso with kisses. He responds, understandably, with an erection which he then, comically, eliminates with a pitcher of ice water. As Robin Wood has noted, ice water figures again when LaMotta uses it to treat a swollen fist; the penis-fist analogy is hard to miss.[42]

Despite repeated instances of brutally abusive treatment, Jake's wife cannot bear to leave him until he—in retirement—becomes fat and flabby. Without her, without his children, without his brother, without the sport that enabled him to vaunt his virility, Jake descends to the level of entertainer in a sleazy New York bar. His dirty jokes are not funny. Background music from Mascagni's *Cavalleria Rusticana* suggests that he might as well be dead.

Among the most comprehensive cinematic treatments of eros and sports is Leni Riefenstahl's two-part documentary, *Olympia* (1938). Riefenstahl, who was born in Berlin in 1904, was, even as a child, enamoured of sports. At one point in her life, she competed successfully as an alpine skier. Her first professional career, however, was on the stage rather than on the slopes. As a dancer more or less in the tradition of Mary Wigman, with whom she briefly studied, Riefenstahl, who was a very beautiful young woman, was a spectacular success. When an injury ended her dancing career, she turned to acting. Max Reinhardt asked her to play the heroic Amazon queen in his production of Heinrich Kleist's *Penthesilea*, but she preferred to work with motion-picture director Arnold Fanck, then famous for adventurous "mountain films" like *Berg des Schicksals* (1924). Riefenstahl risked her young life and athletic limbs in a number of his films before she ventured to produce, direct, and star in a film of her own: *Das blaue Licht* (1932). She played the role of Junta, a wild girl who lives in the mountains and scales cliffs—with bare hands and bare feet—from which men have fallen to their deaths.

"The most beautiful thing I ever saw in film," commented Adolf Hitler, "was Riefenstahl's dance by the edge of the sea in [Fanck's] *Heiligen Berg*."[43] When Riefenstahl met Hitler, at her request, he was also complimentary about *Das blaue Licht*: "Your film," he told her, "has impressed me enormously, above all because it is unusual for a young woman to make her way against the opposition and the taste of the film industry."[44] Hitler was, for once, apparently sincere. After his fateful seizure of power, he asked Riefenstahl to film the 1934 *Parteitag* at Nuremberg. She produced *Triumph des Willens* (*Triumph of the Will*) (1936), a documentary film so powerful that it can make ruthless dictatorship seem—for a seductive moment—attractive. The spectacular critical success of this prize-winning film was the prelude to *Olympia*, which Riefenstahl has always claimed, perhaps truthfully, was *her* idea and not the result of Goebbels's machinations in the Ministry of Propaganda.

Part I, "Festival of the Nations," begins with a twenty-minute prologue in which Riefenstahl evokes memories of classical Greece. The camera moves from shots of the Acropolis and other romantic ruins to close-ups of ancient statues. After gazing at the strikingly erotic *Sleeping Satyr* (from the Glyptothek in Munich), we see Myron's famous *Discus-Thrower*, a marble form that begins to rotate and then fades into the body of a modern athlete who whirls and releases his discus. With upraised arms, a naked man tosses a shot from hand to hand. Raising and lowering their arms, naked girls dance. (These explicitly erotic scenes have been cut from many of the prints available in the United States.) The camera shifts from these beautiful bodies to an altar where a darkly handsome youth, clad only in a loin-cloth, lights the torch that is then carried, to the swelling sound of Herbert Windt's Wagnerian music, across hilltops, along the seashore, through Greek and Balkan villages, through Sofia, Belgrade, Vienna, and Prague, until the symbolic flame completes the transit from Olympia to Berlin. The torch is carried into the monumental stadium, where it ignites the Olympic flame.

There is an omission that lends credence to Riefenstahl's claim that her only interest in the film was aesthetic; her camera avoids the stadium's absurdly grandiose and unintentionally comic athletic statuary. Produced by Georg Kolbe, Arno Breker, and Josef Thorak, these hulking tributes to Hitler's taste have been characterized as "pin-ups of sexual fantasies" (which is fair enough if one can imagine a two-ton bronze pin-up).[45]

Riefenstahl's prologue to Part II, "Festival of the Peoples," stresses the fraternal interactions of the world's athletes. The opening sequence also dramatizes, rather less melodramatically than in the prologue to Part I, the aesthetics of physicality. Among these lovely scenes, which were shot at the Olympic Village, are an early morning training run through a lakeside wood and a steamy sequence in a Finnish sauna. What, Riefenstahl seems to imply, can be more natural than dewy leaves, morning mists, and our naked physical selves?

Riefenstahl's romantic combination of the aesthetic, the erotic, and the athletic is by no means restricted to the two prologues. Although the narrator names many of the athletes and reports some of the quantified results, *Olympia* is not about winners and losers. What does Riefenstahl offer the viewer? Not an extended newsreel, not even a sports documentary in the usual sense, but rather a lyrical affirmation of the human, especially the male, body. (The emphasis on physical beauty is made explicit in the title of Riefenstahl's book of still photographs taken from her film: *Schönheit im Olympischen Kampf* [1938].) It may be merely accident, but Riefenstahl seems to have selected her images so that the winners, male and female, appear to be more physically attractive than the losers. The huge American shot-putter is no match for his

classically proportioned German rivals. Most famously, Riefenstahl returns again and again to the man whom almost everyone
acknowledged as the hero of the games: Jesse Owens. She shows
his concentration, highlighting the beautifully defined leg muscles
and the swollen temple veins as he crouched and waited for
the starter's pistol. Her camera angle accentuates the uncanny
smoothness of his stride as he seems almost magically to glide
ahead of his awkwardly struggling competitors. The only other
athlete upon whom Riefenstahl lavished such attention was Kitei
Son, the Korean winner of the marathon, another "non-Aryan,"
the symbol of endurance, of sport as masochism. He must have
been weary when he arrived at the finish line, but he seems somehow to be divinely exempt from the exhaustion that disfigures the
faces of the other runners. Ernest Harper, the Englishman who
won the silver medal, looks aged—even ugly—in comparison with
Kitei Son.

The divers are featured in the only sequence to receive as much
critical attention as the images of Jesse Owens and Kitei Son. The
athletes, who are never named, are also stripped of their individu-
ality. They are simply human bodies as they mount to the platform,
prepare for their dives, leap into the air, and descend to the water.
The sequence of images accelerates and the shapes follow one
another with only seconds of interval. The light fades and the
shapes, viewed from below, gradually become dark silhouettes
beneath the sparsely clouded sky. More acceleration. Two bodies
appear at once, three, then a chain of soaring, twisting, turning,
falling demigods. To maintain that this sequence, or the entire film,
is "not about sports" is absurd. To admire the aesthetic dimension
of the sequence and of the film as if it were unrelated to eros is foolishly reductionist. There is no more erotic sports film than
Olympia, a cinematic declaration of love if ever there was one.
(There was also a literal declaration of love; Riefenstahl hoped to
marry Glenn Morris, the American winner of the decathlon, whom
she later accused of jilting her.)

After the release of *Olympia* in 1938, Riefenstahl prepared to play the role of Kleist's Penthesilea (which Max Reinhardt had offered her). She trained hard to become physically credible as Homer's fabulous Amazon queen. Determined to produce an authentic film, and not a despised Hollywood spectacular, she learned to ride bareback, gripping the horse with her thighs. The outbreak of war forced her to abandon the project.

After the war, Riefenstahl suffered from what she has always stubbornly and unconvincingly maintained was a wholly unwarranted political persecution on the part of those who accused her of collaboration with the Nazi regime. Never again was she able to complete a film. She did, however, achieve further fame as the photographer of the Nuba of Sudan. She found the men, especially the ritual wrestlers, immensely attractive. She admired the young women, too, who danced rather than wrestled. Their "overlong, slender, thoroughly trained legs" were proof that "the girls as well as the men have made a cult of the body."[46] Her book of photographs, *The Last of the Nuba* (1973), is a visual declaration of her admiration for these bodies.

Riefenstahl's lifelong love affair with athleticism has been criticized by Susan Sontag and others who see the affirmation of physical strength as proof of Riefenstahl's commitment to Fascism. Love of the strong, the critics argue, must imply a desire to eliminate the weak. Richard Mandell, who lauded *Olympia* in the first edition of his book on the 1936 games, had second thoughts. "It seems clear to me ... that the beautification of mindless, masculine physical power is, in fact, highly supportive and perhaps part of totalitarian ideology."[47] The logic is faulty. It may well be that all Fascists worshipped the body;[48] it is not true that all worshippers of the body are Fascists. If the glorification of physicality numbed Riefenstahl's perception of the horrors perpetrated by Hitler, the fault was in her lack of political awareness and not in her love of powerful bodies black and white. To think otherwise is as illogical as to believe that we should resolutely seek illness because the Nazis were in favor of health.

Politics play a role, although a minor one, in another documentary film made for another celebration of the Olympic Games on German soil. When David Wolper asked eight renowned directors from eight different countries[49] to contribute segments to *Visions of Eight*, a documentary to be filmed in Munich during the 1972 games, there could have been no way for him to have guessed that Palestinian terrorists would make their own unexpected "contribution" to the drama. The masked figures of the gunmen haunt the film that had been intended, like the "cheerful" (*"heitere"*) games themselves, to dispel nightmarish memories of past atrocities.

Except for John Schlesinger, who uses the act of terror to background the story of British marathon runner Ron Hill, the eight directors suppress their awareness of the concurrent horror, which is what one has to do—less crassly—at any sports event on this planet, which has never yet been free of bloodshed. Most of the eight segments express an awed appreciation of the dazzlingly diverse athletes. As they stroll through the Olympic Village, basketball players tower over diminutive gymnasts. Weightlifters thud by and seem to shake the ground under the distance runners and the high jumpers. In the course of the film, these bodies, all shapes and all sizes, perform their various athletic miracles. When the camera belongs to Kon Ichikawa, the segment becomes a visual meditation on the breathless ten seconds of the hundred-meter sprint. When Arthur Penn directs, the focus—now soft, now sharp—is on the soaring, twisting flight of the pole vaulters. Mai Zetterling, who denies any interest in sports, devoted her time to "The Strongest." She shifts back and forth between the huffs and puffs of the weightlifters and the somewhat less strenuous efforts of a German military band. While the lifter marches nervously back and forth, striving to convince himself that he can hoist the enormous weight (which he cannot), the band plays on in unintentional counterpoint. Her section seems to be what media analyst John Fiske refers to (in another context) as women's "subversive carnivalesque mocking of masculinity."[50] Comedy seems to be

Milos Forman's forte too. He accompanies the awesomely strenuous efforts of the decathletes with images of Bavarian women
yodeling and shaking their cowbells and bosoms.

In contrast to these comic statement about inspiration, aspira-
tion, and perspiration, Claude Lelouch chose to film the losers,
among whom are several severely injured wrestlers whose pain, as
they grapple gamely on or writhe helplessly on the mat, must provide him (and us?) with some kind of masochistic pleasure. The
most obviously erotic sequence, shot by Michael Pfleghar, is entitled "The Women." After a panorama of short takes, the segment
concludes with Ludmilla Tourischeva's breathtaking performance
on the uneven parallel bars. As Pfleghar pays tribute to the Russian
athlete's extraordinary strength and regal grace, he seems intentionally to mark the moment when robustly beautiful young
women like Tourischeva were about to be replaced by anorexic children. Tourischeva, whom a bewitched anthropologist and an
enthralled historian both described as a woman endowed with a
"disturbing" sexual attractiveness,[51] was indeed a hauntingly
lovely dark-haired athlete. For me as well, she remains an unusually vivid personification of eros and sports.

Other personifications appeared in Robert Towne's *Personal
Best* (1982). Towne, whose first great success was the screenplay for
Roman Polanski's *Chinatown* (1974), made the film as a tribute to
athletic women. (His friendship with pentathlete champion Jane
Frederick contributed to his desire to make the film.) Aside from
Mariel Hemingway, who plays the role of Chris Cahill, and Scott
Glenn, who plays the part of her coach, none of the principals was
a professional actor or actress. In his quest for authenticity, Towne
filmed real athletes and consulted with them about their métier. He
also studied the techniques employed by Leni Riefenstahl in
Olympia. He chose Michael Chapman as his cinematographer, the
man who had worked with Martin Scorsese on *Raging Bull*.[52]

Personal Best begins with brightly colored indeterminate shapes
that are revealed, as the camera moves away from an extremely

close shot, to be Chris crouched to compete in the hurdles. She runs poorly and is berated by her bullying father, who has acted as her coach. That evening, she drinks too much, weeps in despair, and is comforted by Tory Skinner, the winner of the race (played by Olympic athlete Patrice Donnelly). Tory takes Chris home with her. When Tory expresses doubts about the younger athlete's "killer instinct," Chris indignantly challenges Tory to arm-wrestle. Lying on the floor, the two women clasp hands, strain, pant, sweat—and become sexually aroused. They make love. (The scene is a variation of a segment in Ingmar Bergman's *Sawdust and Tinsel* [1953], in which a female bareback rider boasts that she is stronger than the slender male actor who wants to seduce her. She challenges him to arm-wrestle, loses, and is raped.[53])

Tory persuades her initially reluctant coach to let Chris work out with the team, which she does, but athletic rivalry between the two women disrupts their erotic relationship. When Chris accepts Tory's suggestion for a change in her take-off for the high-jump, she is badly injured, which raises questions about Tory's motivation. Their coach, who is convinced that Tory intended the injury, orders the two women to stay away from each other. (He, too, is sexually attracted by Chris, but he makes no attempt to seduce her.)

While recuperating from the injury, Chris meets and falls in love with Denny, a member of the university's water-polo team (played by marathon runner and *Sports Illustrated* journalist Kenny Moore). The drama comes to a climax at the 1980 Olympic Trials. Despite the erotic transfer from homosexual to heterosexual desire, which some viewers have criticized as a homophobic betrayal, Chris continues to care for Tory. When their coach orders her not to speak to Tory, whom she encounters in the cafeteria, Chris faces him down and walks over to wish her former lover good luck. (To claim that the women in *Personal Best* "never question the manipulative powers of their male coach"[54] is to describe some imagined film other than the one actually screened.) After defying their coach, Chris insists that Tory, who has injured her knee, must not surrender to the pain. She must compete in the 800-meter race and finish the pentathlon. In that race, Chris sprints into the lead and pulls Tory's most dangerous rival with her. The strategy is successful. Tory pushes her way past the fading front runners and wins the race. She and Chris are assured places on the team that should have but did not compete in Moscow. As the two women stand and wait to receive their medals, Tory admits to Chris that her boyfriend Denny is not bad—"for a guy."

Although the film does justice to sports as physical *contests*, Towne never hesitates to underscore the erotic element. In one scene, for instance, Chris and Tory run along a sandy California beach and then struggle their way, gasping and stumbling, to the top of a huge sand dune. While the camera's focus is on the muscles of their legs and the contortion of their faces, the sound track consists of heavy breathing indistinguishable from that characteristic of sexual intercourse. In another scene, Chris meets Denny while both are working out in the gymnasium and she offers to "spot" him in the bench press. He admires the way she does her "reps" and then strains to do as many, a challenge made no easier by the fact that his supine head is placed directly under her crotch.

The bench-press scene is comic. In another scene, one reminiscent of the diving sequence in *Olympia*, the camera frames the thighs and the midsections of the female high-jumpers as they propel themselves upwards and backwards across the bar. In slow motion, the sensuality of the movement is so explicit and so emphatic that some feminist critics have denounced the scene as the most blatantly pornographic sequence in what they condemn as a thoroughly sexist film.

In fact, *Personal Best* has from the day of its release aroused critical passions. In the eyes of some reviewers, the film is a bold statement of a woman's right to use her body in any way that she pleases. *The New Yorker*'s Pauline Kael was enthusiastic about Towne's homage to strong, graceful, athletic bodies[55] and Laurie Stone, writing in *The Village Voice*, raved about the "naturalistic depiction of sport life and its innate eroticism." She went on to say that the film's women "are alluring when they're strong, graceful, accomplished, and rippling with muscle. What a long salubrious way Mariel Hemingway is from the poignantly helpless flesh of Marilyn Monroe, or an anorectic wisp like Audrey Hepburn."[56]

Most reviewers felt that the athleticism did not detract from the women's femininity. Jill Spalding wrote in the British edition of *Vogue* that "Mariel Hemingway crouching to touch her Nikes on the starting line is every bit as feminine as Jean Harlow bending to paint her toenails in the boudoir."[57] In *The New York Review*, Veronica Geng acclaimed Towne's demonstration of "how ideals of independence and strength give rise to a new sense of physical beauty." She denied that the film is voyeuristic: "When [the athletes] are still, the camera never prowls their bodies. When they move, they make their own trajectories."[58]

In the eyes of others, however, *Personal Best* was little better than soft-core pornography. "What gravels me," complained Robert Hatch in *The Nation*, "is its persistent treatment of its large cast of women as sex objects in situations that are unrelated to sex."[59] (The obvious implication of Hatch's criticism is that sports have nothing to do with the erotic.) Reviewing the film for *Jump Cut* magazine, Linda Williams approved of the portrayal of female athletes who are both "tough and compassionate," but she was irked by the voyeurism; the women were presented "as so many trained seals flexing their muscles to male awe and approval."[60] What Williams does *not* acknowledge is the existence of female awe and approval. Among the film's achievements is the recognition that women, too, can find athletic women sexually attractive.[61]

Eros and Psyche:
Masculinity, Femininity, Role Conflict

Karl Marx, Max Weber, Emile Durkheim, George Simmel, and the other founding fathers of modern sociology were principally concerned with social structures and their transformations. They seldom "posed the question of the body as a historical issue."[1] In an essay originally published in 1935 in the *Journal de Psychologie*, the French anthropologist Marcel Mauss noted that "the body is man's first and most natural tool" and he urged attention to *"les techniques du corps,"*[2] but it was not until the late twentieth century that a number of sociologists heeded his advice and began to examine the culturally varied ways that bodies are "socially constructed." An important impetus came in 1971 when Luc Boltanski published "Les usages sociaux du corps" in *Les Annales*.

> The body is, in fact, like all the other . . . objects whose possession sites the individual in the hierarchy of social classes. The body's color (pale or tanned), its texture (soft and flabby or firmly muscled), its size (large or small, plump or slender), its amplitude, its form or the swiftness of its movements through space (gawky or

graceful)—all these are signs of status, perhaps the most intimate and, therefore, the most important of all.[3]

Increasingly now, sociologists realize that men's and women's bodies "reflect back, like the little mirrors on an Indian dress, a kaleidoscope of social meanings."[4]

This dramatic recognition, which has produced the academic equivalent of a gold rush, has been motivated in large part by modern feminism, with its analyses of "sexual politics," and by the work of Michel Foucault.[5] Emphasizing that gendered difference is what society makes of the human body's sexual dimorphism, sociologists have reconceptualized masculinity and femininity as aspects of a "gender regime" that is "constructed within a field of power."[6] The different contours of the male and the female body are perceived as the "inscriptions" of a set of reciprocal but unequal power relations.[7] "The social definition of men as holders of power," writes R. W. Connell, "is translated not only into mental body-images and fantasies, but into muscle tensions, posture, the feel and texture of the body."[8] Inequality is, quite literally, incorporated. (The etymological rightness of this term—corpus = body—can be read from its synonym: embodiment.)[9]

Optimistic scholars believe that we are already well advanced on the difficult path to the utopian goal of ending "masculinity as we know it."[10] Men have allegedly become kinder, gentler, more nurturant. Compared to the men of generations past, they are now less competitive, less aggressive, less violent, in a word, less macho than they were. A Psychology Today survey of some 28,000 mostly single, mostly college-educated young men found that the majority of them "wanted to be warmer, gentler, and more loving, while disdaining competition, aggressiveness, and sexual conquest."[11] The revolution in men's attitudes is, however, less revolutionary than it seems to be. After interviewing sixty-two male undergraduates at an Ivy League college, Mirra Komarovsky concluded, twenty years ago, that these young men wanted to treat women as their equals, but they found it difficult to act upon their idealistic convictions.[12] It is doubtful that today's male undergraduates are any less conflicted. As for their elders, the composition and disposition of the Congress elected in 1994 suggests that there is considerable nostalgia for John Wayne's America, where men were men (i.e., gunslingers) and women were women (i.e., homemakers).

The debate over masculinity has come at a time when modern sports have been severely criticized for their institutionalization of precisely the values from which men are now said to be distancing themselves. In the place of sports, reformist physical educators are advocating a new paradigm that valorizes keeping fit and staying healthy rather than scoring goals and winning prizes. If mention of fitness and health evokes images of grunting bodies in claustrophobic weight rooms, the reformers cheerfully reassure us that "wellness" requires only a few minutes a day of moderate exercise. From the pages of American and European journals like *Quest*, *L'Éducation physique et sport*, and *Sportwissenschaft* comes a call for friendly noncompetitive coeducational egalitarian play, but the call is hard to hear through the roar of the crowds (especially when the ears are blocked by the protective pads of a football or hockey helmet). While it is true that some men have repented and abjured the macho style in the home, the workplace, and the sports complex, I am as skeptical about the proclaimed general disenchantment with modern sports as I am about the alleged widespread shift in conceptions of masculinity. On the contrary, I am convinced that strenuous athletic competition continues to provide today's men, as it did their fathers and grandfathers, with the unmediated physical challenge they cannot encounter in their workaday lives.

This is certainly the impression communicated by Ray Raphael's *The Men from the Boys* (1988), a book composed of vignettes from the lives of a number of socially diversified American men. For most of them, sports continue to be a benchmark of masculinity. "Since professional athletes serve as the most visible models for adult masculinity in American culture," Raphael comments, "the perplexing tasks of personal growth easily get translated into the imagery of sports." The reason seems obvious; sports "offer opportunities for physical expression in a technological world that threatens to deprive us of our sense of bodily strength and well-being."[13]

In Europe and in the United States, the number of male sports participants continues to rise. (The *Deutscher Sport Bund* now enrolls more than one-third of all German men.) Amateur and professional sports leagues—overwhelmingly male—proliferate and expand. Cable networks vie with over-the-air television to bring more and more sportscasts—which are overwhelmingly devoted to men's sports—to more and more European and American homes. The radical critique of men's sports that was a prominent part of the sixties counterculture, especially in France and Germany, has lost most of its force (even as the multinational commercialization of modern sports has spiraled out of control). Increased possibilities for social mobility and a rise in average disposable income have altered the rates of participation in various sports. Soccer and American football, for instance, have become relatively less popular while traditional middle-class sports like tennis and skiing have gained ground,[14] but sports in general still are and will doubtless continue to be demonstrations of masculinity.

Have they also become demonstrations of femininity? A decade ago, Susan Brownmiller asserted sadly that they were not. "How to look feminine while competing is a problem that haunts the psyche of the American female athlete." The dilemma seemed obvious.

> The ambivalence of these [female] athletes is rooted in cultural expectations, for while we have come a long way from the time when riding a bicycle was considered dangerous to the female constitution, the track-and-field star knows that her sweaty tank top does not fit the conventional image of glamour, and the swimmer understands that a poolside bathing beauty in a string bikini cuts a

sexier figure than the rubber-capped winner of the 400-meter freestyle event.[15]

In short, the more a woman achieved as an athlete, the greater was her sacrifice of femininity. There is now reason, however, to doubt the conventional wisdom, which has almost achieved the status of Eternal Truth, that female athletes still suffer from the strains of role conflict. Despite the continued claims of many psychologists to this effect, the evidence of role conflict for today's female athletes is less than conclusive.

Personality tests that routinely discover female athletes are "masculine" cannot be taken seriously as evidence for the loss of femininity because tests like Sandra Bem's widely used Sex Role Inventory are designed to score typically athletic traits—like competitiveness and aggressiveness—as "masculine." This circularity ensures that a woman who admits to the competitiveness and aggressiveness associated with sports is automatically classified as "masculine" or (what luck!) "androgynous."[16] The cultural assumptions behind the tests guarantee anomalous results—such as the "fact" that only 13.6 percent of the female runners tested by the Personality Attribute Questionnaire can be described as "feminine." When the Bem Sex Role Inventory's categories are used in conjunction with one of several measures of body-image satisfaction, the ironic result is that "masculine" women are said to be more satisfied with their physical appearance than "feminine" women.[17]

It may still be a part of folk wisdom that girls and women do sports to compensate for low self-esteem, but most studies have shown, to the contrary, that female student-athletes have a more positive self-image than nonathletes do. In fact, studies inspired by the influential "body-cathexis" research of Sidney M. Jourard and Paul F. Secord[18] have shown that athletic women are more pleased than other women not only with their arms and legs but even with such intractable anatomical details as the shape of their noses. The only reasonable explanation for such results is that involvement in sports raises a woman's self-esteem by enhancing her body image generally.[19] Unfortunately, the research done has not included what might seem an obvious question: "Do you feel that sports have made you more or less sexually attractive?"

Most of these psychological studies of female athletes have been done with that natural prey of the experimenters: undergraduate subjects. When the typical sample is drawn from the undergraduates enrolled in Psychology 101, it is hardly a surprise that "whatever stigma was once attached to females' athletic participation is certainly not present in this study."[20] But what does the American public at large think about the combination of these allegedly discrepant social roles? Sociologists Eldon E. Snyder and Elmer Spreitzer addressed this question directly in an article entitled "Change and Variation in the Social Acceptance of Female Participation in Sports." Respondents in Toledo, Ohio, were asked in 1972 and 1981 if certain specified sports detracted from or enhanced a girl's or woman's femininity. In 1972, 30 percent of the sample had negative feelings about women's track. By 1981 the proportion of those with negative feelings had shrunk to 18 percent. Negative remarks about women's softball dropped from 20 percent to 14 percent (while basketball was unchanged with 21 percent unfavorable responses). More than 50 percent thought swimming, tennis, and gymnastics enhanced femininity, and 19 percent felt the same way about track. When Snyder and Spreitzer put the same questions to Iowans, 23 percent thought track enhanced femininity and only 7 percent thought it detracted.[21]

In another study, 353 Oklahoma City residents were interviewed to discover their reactions to six provocative statements, including the following: "Women are likely to develop unsightly muscles if they exercise regularly" and "A woman cannot be both a good athlete and a truly feminine person." Only 27.2 percent of the sample agreed with the first statement, only 10.8 percent with the second. Not surprisingly, the older and less educated respondents were much more likely to agree with the negative stereotypes. In this, as in a number of other studies, men were found to be more positively disposed to female athletes than women were.[22]

Of all female athletes, the defiant women who have elected to "pump iron" as weightlifters and as competitive body-builders are the ones most likely to elicit negative reactions and nasty aspersions about "masculinization." If power-lifters can deadlift three hundred pounds, benchpress one hundred fifty, and still be considered feminine, role conflict cannot be as severe as claimed. What have social psychologists discovered? The authors of a study of forty-four female power-lifters concluded that the problem of discrepant roles and incongruent body image had been greatly exaggerated. Only 9.1 percent of the lifters experienced great or very great role conflict.[23] When 205 female body-builders were queried about other peoples' responses to their sport, 63 percent of them reported that they had experienced mainly *positive* reactions. The negative reactions came predominantly from other women. The authors of this study concluded that "flex appeal is sex appeal."[24]

Studies of female competitive body-builders have been far more numerous because these women are probably even more distant from conventional notions of femininity than power-lifters are. To put it crassly, the women pictured in *Muscle and Fitness* look more like Arnold Schwarzenegger than like the women on the college tennis team. As demonstrated by the debate over aesthetic standards in the documentary film *Pumping Iron II: The Women* (1984), there is a limit to men's approval of female muscularity. (Especially when there is suspicion that the muscularity is steroid-induced.) When the reduction of body fat by diet and exercise all but eliminates a woman's breasts, when the sharply "cut" muscles resemble the striations of an anatomical chart, when the veins seem to bind the body in a network of knotted cords, most men are repelled. The psychoanalytic explanation of this repulsion is that men suffer from "castration anxiety" or, alternatively, that they are denying to themselves the attractiveness of such "masculine" bodies because they cannot acknowledge their own homosexual impulses.[25]

If one accepts this psychoanalytic interpretation, which I do not, it may came as a surprise that men are in fact more positive about female body-builders than women are. At Brigham Young University, hardly a hotbed of liberal opinion, male and female students were shown slides of female body-builders and asked to rate the women on their physical attractiveness. The men's ratings were significantly higher than the women's. The men were also more likely to see the body-builders as feminine.[26] Another experiment asked male and female undergraduates to characterize two imaginary women who were identically described except that one of them was said to be a body-builder. Female undergraduates rated the imaginary body-builder more masculine and less feminine than the non-body-builder, which was the expected outcome, but male undergraduates thought the female body-builder *less* masculine and *more* feminine. (The female undergraduates were also much more likely to suspect the body-builder of homosexuality.)[27] Role conflict does unquestionably exist for women who "pump iron," but it is actually rather less than expected and it derives more from women's disapprobation than men's.[28]

All of these sports-related studies corroborate the more general psychological research indicating that competence is now more important to most people than "sex-role congruence."[29] What Todd W. Crosset discovered when he interviewed the women of the Ladies Professional Golf Association seems now to be generally true for female athletes: "Most players expressed little difficulty in maintaining their perception of themselves as women in light of their athletic skill."[30] There is no longer any reason to be surprised by the remarks of Patrice Donnelly, the pentathlete who played Mariel Hemingway's lover in *Personal Best*: "Men have always loved my body. My boyfriend loves to show it off. He'll say to friends, 'Hey, watch Patrice flex!'"[31] One can disapprove of Donnelly's boyfriend's manipulative vicarious exhibitionism, but he cannot be accused of fearful hostility to strong women. Additional anecdotal corroboration of these empirical studies comes from some unimpeachable feminist sources. After deconstructing the Reebok advertisement proclaiming that "sweat is sexy," Susan Bordo noted, with some astonishment, "My male students (as well as my female students) almost literally swooned over Linda Hamilton's fierce expression and taut body in *Terminator II*."[32] Hamilton's appearance and performance are said to have inspired thousands of young women to embark on fitness programs.[33]

European attitudes are very similar. In my time spent teaching at various German universities for a total of four years between 1968 and 1982, I was struck by the increasingly athletic female models appearing in cosmetics advertisements on television and in popular magazines like *Der Stern*. It was, moreover, impossible to wait for a trolley and not notice the proliferation of posters urging women as well as men to visit *das Fitness-Studio*. And Jennifer Hargreaves, commenting on British culture, notes that young British women who go in for sports "tend to be mesomorphs with stereotypically 'beautiful' bodies—quite lean and muscular, not overweight and flabby, or underweight and skinny."[34] What is remarkable about this assessment is that lean and muscular female athletes are now described as *stereotypically* beautiful. Ideals have changed. In short, Helen Lenskyj's observation that neither the strong, muscular female sprinter nor the light, graceful male figure skater satisfies the stereotype of heterosexual attractiveness needs to be revised—at least as far as the female athlete is concerned.[35]

In fact, there is strong evidence from a number of psychological studies that the "graceful male figure skater" may feel more, a great deal more, role conflict than the female sprinter does. The boy who is inept at team sports is taunted by his peers to a degree seldom experienced by his athletically talented sister. To be called a sissy is far more humiliating than to be called a tomboy.[36] Psychological studies of children's behavior confirm this. They report data that "strongly support the contention that cross-sex behavior of boys is more highly disapproved of than that of girls."[37] Girls who behave like boys "do not arouse the same disapproval that feminine boys do."[38] Adult women are "relatively free to become more like men in their sex-role attitudes, but men are most unfree to become more like women."[39] Men and women both endorse the presence of "masculine" characteristics in their ideal of desirable femininity, but women who "describe an androgynous ideal for . . . their own sex" prefer "a sex-typed one for a man."[40] Since conclusions of this sort are usually based on studies of the psychologist's own students, hardly a representative cross-section of the American population, caution is advisable, but for the young captives enrolled in Psychology 101, the typical "man's man" turns out to be, ironically, a "woman's man."

While Europeans and Americans of both sexes continue to feel that some sports are more appropriate for men and some for women, the trend is unquestionably toward acceptance of whatever sport a person wants to do. A study of tennis, gymnastics, and soccer clubs in the German *Land* of Hessen, for example, confirmed the hypothesis that the first two sports are considered more appropriately feminine than the third, but fully half the female soccer players practice with the men, which certainly suggests a kind of acceptance by the latter. In fact, only 4.4 percent of the German women who play soccer say that their husbands or lovers disapprove of what is supposedly a serious turf violation. At the same time, however, 26.4 percent of the female gymnasts think that *Fussball* is an inappropriate sport for women and 40 percent of the female soccer players long for the opportunity to add tennis to their sporting repertory.[41]

Alessandro Salvini's *Identità Femminile e Sport* (1982) is an unusually detailed study of 482 teenaged athletes drawn from all parts of Italy, from impoverished provincial Sicily as well as from affluent cosmopolitan Milan. The girls' seriousness is proven by the fact that 72.2 percent of them said they preferred real competition to mere recreational activities. Despite their violation of traditional notions of daughterly behavior ("go to church and pray for a husband"), 97.1 percent of them reported that their parents were supportive. While some Italians still hold that the female athlete is "an exception or a transgression," only 4 percent of these girls believed that *attività sportiva* impeded them in their pursuit of "normal social life and emotional experience"; 13 percent thought sports helped. When asked specifically to name the kinds of criticism they encountered, 35.1 percent were unable to think of *any* negative remarks; 24.1 percent had heard people express the fear that sports destroy a girl's femininity. Did that mean that sports are the product of masculine and not of feminine culture? A resounding 92.3 percent of the girls thought not, and 72.4 percent of them averred that a woman can now participate in whatever sport she wishes.

These committed young athletes were hardly representative of all Italian teenagers. Adolescent opinion, moreover, was unquestionably at odds with that of many older Italians. Indeed, 49 percent of the adult women questioned in a Roman survey explained that they avoided sports because sports cause "an irreversible somatic transformation," that is, masculinization.[42] Nonetheless, this evidence from a Mediterranean culture, where sexual attitudes are far less liberal than in northern Europe, suggests that the old ways have lost some of the suppressive power.

In sports as in other cultural spaces, perceptions of gender appropriateness have changed. Rigid binary classification into male and female roles has given way to more nuanced recognition of "multiple gendered dispositions."[43] In today's reconceptualization of masculinity and femininity, athletic women are no longer seen—by most men—as transgressively masculine. As some men, emulating Robert Bly's "Iron John,"[44] have become a little more like women, many women have begun to act, in their avocations as in their vocations, a lot more like men.

PHYSICAL ATTRACTIVENESS

Alessandro Salvini's exploration of women's sports, Italian style, is a bold exploration of a sensitive area, but not even he was ready to ask directly about the relationship between sports and sexuality. Roles, yes; vibes, no. Similarly, despite the historical tradition of Richard von Krafft-Ebbing and other pioneers of sexual research, German psychologists have restricted themselves for the most part to a *Tanz um den heissen Brei* ("dance around the hot porridge," i.e., they pussyfoot). American researchers have been similarly skittish, preferring, in general, to discuss erotic appeal under the rubric of physical attractiveness, a euphemistic topic that has generated an immense volume of empirical research.[45]

Like other social psychologists, experts in this area are aware that the norms they study are historically as well as culturally specific. "Worship of curves gives way to admiration of muscles; kinky hair gives way to straight hair; legs replace breasts, and vice versa, as the fashion focus moves down or up."[46] Despite this awareness, most experts in the "physical attractiveness phenomenon" have ignored historical studies like Lois Banner's *American Beauty* (1983), which plots the curve of male and female aesthetic ideals from the early nineteenth to the late twentieth centuries. Reports of psychological research are seldom more than still shots from culture's long-running film, but they, too, can be added to our collage.

Relying on surveys, interviews, and a variety of ingenious experiments, psychologists have established scientifically what most people already surmised: since we tend to judge one another, especially during an initial encounter, on the basis of outward appearance, it is a significant advantage for a man or a woman to be considered physically attractive by other men and women.[47] "Having beauty is like having an American Express card. It is good almost anywhere."[48] We expect this to be true when couples meet on a blind date or when individuals describe themselves in "lonely hearts" advertisements,[49] but there is also persuasive evidence that beautiful women are more likely than their less fortunate sisters to marry educated and affluent men (who are not, however, any handsomer than men who are less educated and less occupationally successful).[50]

The advantages of good looks are observable at other sites of social interaction. Within the criminal justice system, men and women accused of misdemeanors (but not those accused of felonies) are treated more lightly if they are conventionally attractive. Those who are thought to be beautiful are also thought to be more talented and professionally competent than their less fortunate peers. Attach to an academic essay or to a job application the photograph of an attractive person and the evaluators will be more favorably impressed than by exactly the same essay or application accompanied by the photograph of a physically unattractive person. Once on the job, the "strikingly handsome" man and the "strikingly beautiful" woman will earn more money than their homely fellow workers. The association between good looks and affluence is so strong that physically attractive men and women are generally assumed to be economically (as well as academically) successful. In general, good looks are a greater advantage for females than for males, but they can also be a disadvantage in some situations. The triumphs of a female lawyer or corporate executive can be dismissively attributed to her winsome features rather than to her assiduously acquired courtroom or boardroom skills. Beautiful women are frequently thought to be vain, spoiled, more likely to tease men with their charms, more likely to commit adultery.[51]

Psychologists have known for some time that the human face, which is by far the most individualized and expressive part of the physical self, is the most important determinant of physical attractiveness.[52] They have recently begun to explore the expressive possibilities of the body and to assess its role in the "physical attractiveness phenomenon."[53] When a team of psychologists analyzed 62,000 responses to a 1973 survey conducted by *Psychology Today*, they were especially impressed when they found that the magazine's mostly upper-middle-class readers were rather satisfied with their physical selves. This unexpected result, more true for men than for women, was communicated in the report's jaunty title: "The Happy American Body." And to what aesthetic standards did these happy bodies conform? Slenderness for women, muscularity for men.[54] Contrary to the vulgate of the locker room, with its focus on the genitals, and contrary to the jargon of Lacanian postmodernism, with its emphasis on "phallocentrism," the *Psychology Today* survey found that the anatomical part most strongly associated with a positive male body image was "a muscular chest," i.e., the *cuirasse esthétique* of the classical nude.[55] It was also quite similar to the masculine ideal articulated by the Goncourt brothers over a century ago: "All the physical beauty, all the strength, and all the development of a woman is concentrated in . . . the pelvis, the buttocks, the thighs; the beauty of a man is to be found in the upper, nobler parts, *the pectoral muscles*, the broad shoulders, the high forehead."[56]

The regnant ideal for women is no surprise, but the feminist debate over "the politics of appearance"[57] has diverted attention from the pressure on men to shape *their* physical selves to cultural expectations. Men, too, labor at compulsory "body work" because, as Seymour Fisher comments, "All kinds of pleasant, good, and rather heroic qualities are ascribed to . . . mesomorphs."[58]

In a typical study of 360 undergraduates, equally divided into groups of black and white men and women, a team of psychologists proved what no sentient observer doubts: "The mesomorph male was perceived significantly more often as masculine."[59] Experimental psychologists have discovered, repeatedly, that mesomorphs are perceived to be good athletes, soldiers, political leaders, friends, and fathers.[60] Indeed, whenever people are asked about their assessment of physical types, there is a cascade of positive characterizations for the privileged mesomorph. The chubby endomorph, on the other hand, is seen as an indolent glutton and the wiry ectomorph as "a friendless bundle of collapsing nerves."[61] The reason for these repeatedly documented associations is not arcane. "We believe," concluded a team of four behavioral scientists in a review of the literature, "that the muscular mesomorph is the ideal because it is intimately tied to cultural views of masculinity and the male sex role."[62] The muscular ideal is, moreover, one that boys internalize in early childhood. For kindergarten children as well as for adults of both sexes, there is a pronounced aversion to obesity. A particularly clever experiment found, as hypothesized, that children of both sexes position themselves spatially much closer to mesomorphic bodies than to chubby endomorphic ones.[63]

Ignoring the plight of the male ectomorph whose "pecs," "abs," and "lats" will never make the grade, Naomi Wolf has lamented that the "beauty myth" compels women to strive for an impossible degree of physical attractiveness.[64] There is no reason to doubt that many women do indeed torture themselves physically and mentally in vain emulation of whoever happens to be the aesthetic ideal of the moment, a serious problem to which I shall return in chapter 8, but there is some evidence that the torture is unnecessary. When American women are asked to compare their own bodies with what they assume to be men's ideal of a woman's body, the average American woman misperceives the relationship. She is actually much closer to men's ideals than she thinks she is. Men, who seem on the whole to have more accurate perceptions of their actual physical selves than women do, are also more likely than women to imagine they approximate the ideal for their sex.[65] In other words, men see their bodies, correctly, as fairly close to what women want; women see *their* bodies, incorrectly, as quite distant from what men want.[66] Since the average male is no closer to Adonis than the average female is to Venus, we can conclude that women demand less of the men in the way of physical attractiveness than men do of women. Feminists are right to assert that women agonize more than men do about how they measure up.[67]

One can learn a great deal from the social psychologists who have specialized in the study of physical attractiveness, but they seem almost comically determined to overlook the issue of sexuality, with which attractiveness is presumably linked in the evolutionary process. "Textbooks on primates," notes Rita Freedman, "always discuss 'attractivity' as a basic part of animal behavior, whereas books on human sexuality and on gender development generally ignore its relevance."[68]

Psychology Today, a commercial venture that needs constantly to hold its readers' attention, has been bolder than the textbooks. The magazine has reported that men and women "who like their bodies have . . . more sexual partners, have more sexual activity, and enjoy sex more than those who have negative body images."[69] This quite plausible correlational finding does not distinguish cause from effect. Does a belief in one's own attractiveness set the sexual merry-go-round in motion or do the passionate advances of interested others gradually dispel the dismal conviction that one is sexually unattractive? In either case, it is a relief to hear from some *bona fide* psychological experts that physical attractiveness has erotic consequences.

Most of the research into physical attractiveness has been silent on the topic of sports, but Fisher has hazarded a cautious generalization. "Muscular movement in the form of athletic activity," he observed, is one way to shape the body into conformity with "an idealized image."[70] To this modest assertion I can add the results of my own comparative analysis of the "personals" advertisements in *Die Zeit* and *The New York Review of Books*, two journals with a highly educated set of subscribers. The male and female professionals and businesspeople who pay by the word in their quest for romance describe themselves and those whom they hope to attract as athletically active and physically fit.[71] Although she has probably not meditated very long on the relationship of sports to eros, the dark-eyed DJF from Los Angeles is clear about her desire for a SWM (25–35, nonsmoker) to share her passion for swimming, boating, tennis, travel, classical music, and gourmet cuisine.

FREUD AND SOME FOLLOWERS

If the readers of *Die Zeit* and *The New York Review* know anything at all about psychoanalysis, and they probably do, they are familiar with "Freudian" symbolism. They are used to assertions like

Michael Balint's: "The whip of the lion-tamer, the pole of the tightrope walker, the sticks of the skier, the baton of the conductor, the sword or rifle of the soldier, the artist's tools and the pilot's joystick are undoubtedly symbols of the erect, potent penis."[72]

Balint's inclusion of sports equipment is no surprise. Leonard Glass, analyzing "hypermasculinity" in the journal *Psychiatry*, mentions bats and balls among the phallic objects with which "the Man's Man surrounds himself."[73] Gill Saunders, a psychoanalytically inclined art historian, is even bolder. Since alterations in the circulation of the blood account for both the engorged penis and the athlete's "pumped" physique, Saunders concludes that the "whole body, muscular, potent, active, may come to represent the phallus."[74] Samuel Fussell, whose *Muscle* (1991) documents the author's obsession with body-building, agrees: "Reduced to his purest form, [the body-builder] symbolizes the penis."[75] Rosalind Miles has made the same point: referring to "pumped" actors like Arnold Schwarzenegger and Sylvester Stallone, she asserts that "each becomes a public phallus, huge, rock-hard, gleaming and veined with blood."[76] The athlete's body becomes his or her ever-present close-at-hand fetish.

Speculations of this sort can easily become a game of unfree association in which every cylindrical object is a penis, every spherical object is an ovum, and every oscillitory motion is a sublimated form of coitus, but sports do provide a plethora of sexually suggestive objects and actions. Consider pool, a game redolent with the aura of working-class masculinity (beautifully captured in Robert Rossen's 1961 film, *The Hustler*). The poolroom has always been a "kind of behind-the-lines or inner frontier, the new no-woman's land, catering to internal refugees from the world of female-imposed gentility, catering to men who wanted to be able to curse and spit tobacco, fight freely, dress sloppily, gamble heavily, get roaring drunk, whore around."[77] In the poolhall's archetype motion, a man grasps the phallic cue in one hand and steadies it with the other. He moves it back and forth three or four times and then thrusts it swiftly forward. The stick propels the ball—is it sperm or egg?—into the yonic pocket.

For those hunting about for sexual symbolism, the bullfighter's arena is an even better venue than the poolhall. In Freudian eyes, the *toro* and the *matador* are two actors in the primal "family drama." The horned bull symbolizes the threateningly potent father whom the son must slay in order to avert castration and achieve mature masculinity. With the thrust of his *spada*, the bull-fighter appropriates his taurine father's virility. Of Freudian inter-preters of the bullfight, and they are numerous enough to fill both *sol y sombra*, Michel Leiris may be the most subtle. As a child, he was sexually stimulated by thoughts of "moist, warm skin, over hard muscles."[78] As an adult, he gravitated to the arena. In his *Miroir de la tauromachie* (1938), which strongly influenced Georges Bataille's *L'Érotisme*, Leiris describes the *matador's* encounter with the bull as an "erotic activity" as well as a tragic drama and a religious ritual. The entire *corrida* is "bathed in an erotic atmosphere." The bull is "essentially phallic" and the move-ments of the deadly contest symbolize the sexual act. The closeness of the man and the animal is like an embrace; their "coming and going" approximates a "sequence of alternating approaches and withdrawals, like the movements of coitus." With the death of the bull comes the crowd's frenzied ovation, an "ejaculation that has bravos for its sperm." This steamy vision of the *corrida* as an orgiastic encounter is illustrated by four drawings done by the author's friend, André Masson. Like Picasso's *Guernica*, which was done at almost exactly the same time, each drawing is a Freudian collage in which images of bulls, *matadors*, rapiers, and naked women interact and intersect.[79]

With ball games as with bullfights, Freudian analysts have had a field day. Helen Deutsch broke new ground with her famous 1926 essay, "A Contribution to the Psychology of Sport," published in the *International Journal of Psychoanalysis*. On the basis of her clinical work with "a patient suffering from impotence, together with anxiety-states and depression," she concluded that ball games allowed her patient to overcome his phobia. Thanks to the feelings of mastery he achieved through sports participation, he rid himself "of part of the dread of castration or the fear of death which is common to all mankind." While this analysis puts the emphasis on what is overcome rather than on the erotic pleasure implicit in the act of overcoming, Deutsch did not entirely ignore the latter, which she referred to as "the pleasurable situation of a game."[80]

If Deutsch's assertion that the soccer ball represents the genital organs of the patient's father is implausible, then total disbelief is the appropriate response to another famous essay, "Psycho-Analytic Reflections on the Development of Ball Games," published in 1955 by the British psychiatrist Adrian Stokes. In his far-fetched analysis, Stokes imagines the lacrosse goal to be "the archetypal vagina" and comments on a rugby game as follows: "Ejected out of the mother's body, out of the scrum, after frantic hooking and pushing, there emerges the rich loot of the father's genital."[81]

Alan Dundes, a psychoanalytically inclined anthropologist, is somewhat more persuasive. Exploiting the many meanings of the word "end" in the context of American football, noting the position of the center when he presents his rump to the quarterback, Dundes argues that the whole game is suffused with sexual significance. "One pats one's teammates' ends, but one seeks to violate the endzone of one's opponents!"[82] In an article published in the *Journal of Psychoanalytic Anthropology*, Marcelo Marió Suárez-Orozco, a student of Dundes, has interpreted the obscene chants of Argentine soccer fans. He documents the fans' use of obscene sexual metaphors to boast of their matchless virility and to sneer at the opposition's alleged homosexuality. The soccer goal is not the symbolic vagina that the lacrosse goal was for Stokes, but rather a symbolic anus, which must be defended from penetration by opponents of the defenders' own sex. The frenzy of the fans and the violence of their language led Suárez-Orozco to conclude that they "are attracted to the soccer field in order to find a therapeutic outlet for their taboo thoughts." Their obsessive references to "faggots" he interprets as "an unconscious and forbidden wish" for a homosexual experience.[83]

In an essay on "The Counter-Phobic Attitude" (1939), Otto Fenichel generalized to all sports the psychoanalytic theories that Deutsch had suggested apropos of ball games. Like Deutsch, Fenichel assumed that sports are essentially *Männersache* (men's business) and that the effort to overcome castration anxiety is a prime factor in men's sports participation. The demonstration of physical skills is a mechanism for the mastery of excessive fears and unconscious wishes. Sports provide "functional pleasure," that is, pleasure derived from a dreaded activity that has been repeated until it is no longer feared.

> No doubt there are erotic and aggressive gratifications in sport, just as they are present in all the other functional pleasures of adults. Certainly not everyone who engages in sport is suffering from an unconscious insoluble fear of castration; nor does it follow that the participant sport for which he shows a later preference must once have been feared. But it will generally hold true that the essential joy in sport is that one actively brings about in play certain tensions which were formerly feared, so that one may enjoy the fact that now one can overcome them.

In short, sports allow us "the belated conquest of an unmastered infantile anxiety."[84]

Similarly, in Heinz Kohut's influential analysis of narcissistic disorders, sports figure as one way to defend the endangered psyche against a fearful sense of fragmentation. One of Kohut's patients, "Mr. K.," found "relief, both from autoerotic body tensions and from dangerous grandiose fantasies, by participating—and with great success—in various athletic activities and sports, in particular those which involved speedy locomotion." Contrary to what one might have expected, Kohut looked positively upon girls who tried to overcome "the narcissistic blow" of a younger sibling by "successes in the realm of athletic, intellectual, and cultural pursuits."[85]

Are athletes aware of this "functional pleasure"? Do *they* experience their athletic performances as erotic? When analyzing the sources of infantile sexuality in the *Three Essays on Sexuality* (1905), Freud touched upon the topic of athletic participation. In a footnote added to the second edition (1910), he wrote, "It is well known that sports are widely used by modern educators to distract youth from sexual activity. It would be more correct to say that sports replace sexual pleasure with the pleasure of movement and push sexual activity back upon its autoerotic components." By referring to replacement, Freud seems to have meant what he more commonly referred to as sublimation. In his original 1905 text, he commented on "the creation of sexual excitement through rhythmical . . . shaking of the body" and on the extraordinary sensual pleasure that accompanies vigorous muscular exertion.[86] Arnold Plack extended these remarks in *Society and Evil* (1969), asserting the existence of an erotic component in running, leaping, riding, and in almost every other kind of human movement. Plack was especially provocative when commenting on equestrian sports: "If one doesn't want to ride one's horse to lameness, one must consciously or unconsciously move with one's back, pelvic, and thigh muscles as in sexual intercourse. . . . It needn't necessarily lead to ejaculation, but the 'passionate rider' always experiences sexual relaxation."[87] As Mariah Burton Nelson says in *The Stronger Women Get, the More Men Love Football* (1994), "Ever since they stopped riding sidesaddle, horsewomen have shared an erotic secret alluded to with smiles, nods, and the phrase 'girls love horses.' "[88]

Very few smiling female equestrians made their way to Freud's couch at Berggasse 19, but a number of his male patients "reported that they experienced the first signs of genital arousal when scrapping or wrestling with their playmates." Freud concluded that it was important in such situations that there be "not only general muscular exertion but also ample skin contact with one's opponent." If there was such contact, the individuals' association ("*Verknüpfung*") of wrestling and sexual arousal could "help to determine the subsequent direction of their sex drive."[89] Referring to what might be called the athleticism of sex rather than the sexuality of athletics, Alphonso Lingis, a writer profoundly influenced by Freud (and by Jacques Lacan), has offered a lyrical interpretation of the similarity between the love of wrestling and the wrestling of love: "My skin and muscles, whose texture and pulp I do not feel, are agitated by the squalls of pleasure across your skin and in your muscles."[90]

Literary examples suggest that these Freudian insights are valid—at least for those sports where the pattern of movement is similar to what is experienced in unquestionably sexual situations, which is certainly the case with wrestling. The best modern dramatization is probably the famous scene in D. H. Lawrence's novel, *Women in Love* (1921), where Gerald and Birkin, both naked, wrestle.

> So the two men entwined and wrestled with each other, working nearer and nearer. Both were white and clear, but Gerald flushed smart red where he was touched, and Birkin remained white and tense. He seemed to penetrate into Gerald's more solid, more diffuse bulk, to interfuse his body through the body of the other, as if to bring it subtly into subjection, always seizing with some rapid necromantic foreknowledge every motion of the other flesh, converting and counteracting it, playing upon the limbs and trunk of Gerald like some hard wind. It was as if Birkin's whole physical intelligence interpenetrated into Gerald's body, as if his fine sublimated energy entered into the flesh of the fuller man, like some potency, casting a fine net, a prison, through the muscles into the very depths of Gerald's physical being.

The men work "into a tighter, closer oneness of struggle" until "Gerald lay back inert on the carpet, his breast rising in great slow panting, whilst Birkin kneeled over him, almost unconscious."

From this sexually suggestive position, Birkin "slid forward quite unconscious over Gerald."[91]

"Wrestling," remarked Gregory Wood in another context, "is the heterosexually acceptable form of homosexual foreplay."[92] Gerald and Birkin seem, rather obviously, to have gone beyond mere foreplay. Ann Hall, an outspoken and prolific Canadian feminist, has discussed this passage from *Women in Love* and has carefully analyzed the sexual language that suffuses it. She asserts that "the Lawrentian wrestle has no relevance for women," but her ability to imagine female equivalence may be hampered by surprisingly conventional assumptions about sexual roles.[93] Perhaps she changed her mind after the release of *Personal Best* (with the steamy scene in which Chris and Tory arm-wrestle and then make love).

Boxers, too, have experienced the impulses mentioned by Freud and dramatized in Lawrence's novel. What else can explain the homoerotic language of nineteenth-century descriptions of the men's bodies?[94] What else explains the impulse that brings two boxers to embrace at the end of a hideously punitive bout? The psychic force of this attraction between athletic opponents is often—perhaps usually—overwhelmed by the contrary, hostile forces of antagonism, but the aggressiveness unleashed in team sports is commonly accompanied by an intense emotional bond among teammates. The experience of fellowship is so intense that memory of it lingers on in nostalgia. No Hall-of-Fame induction is complete without the lachrymose acknowledgement, "And most of all I miss my teammates." Once again, a literary example captures the essence of the phenomenon. In Mark Harris's *Bang the Drum Slowly* (1956), the narrator, a pitcher named Henry Wiggen, says this about his teammates:

> You felt warm towards them, and you looked at them, and them at you, and you were both alive, and you might as well said, "Ain't it something? Being alive, I mean! Ain't it really quite a great thing at that?" and if they would of been a girl you would of kissed them,

though you never said such a thing out loud but only went on about your business.[95]

Team sports not only create an intense emotional bond; they also provide a socially acceptable context for the physical expression of those otherwise repressed homoerotic emotions. "Together, they feel powerful. Together, they act powerful. Together, they fall in love—with power, with masculinity. They also fall in love with each other."[96] Who has not noticed the uninhibited acrobatic embraces of soccer players as they celebrate a score? Their almost universally unchallenged masculinity allows them the privilege of gestures seldom seen in the faculty lounge.

These embraces occur in public. In private, athletes can be even more demonstrative. Rugby players are reputed to be positively orgiastic. Among their raunchy antics is the "elephant walk," performed by a file of naked men, each of whom ambles forward while clutching the penis of the man behind him. To someone who has not experienced the intense male bonding of a rugby match, this might seem too much of a good thing, but it does suggest how much of the macho male's sexual identity is expressed on the athletic field and in its environs.

Concluding Arguments

THE NEO-MARXIST CRITIQUE

Let us return to the criticisms, with which we began, of the erotic element in sports. There may still be clerical voices warning, as Clement of Alexandria once did, that sports are a site of pagan sexuality or that they signify the diabolical exaltation of our sinful bodies, but such voices, no longer much heeded, have grown faint. It hardly seems necessary at the end of the twentieth century to rebut the Roman Catholic bishops who condemned "pornographic" gymnastic meets or the Protestant ministers who fretted about football's sensuality as "a swing back to Olympic Greece and her barbarian ideals."[1]

Although their voices too have faded since their heyday in the Seventies, neo-Marxist criticisms of the erotic element are more substantial and require serious discussion.[2] Neo-Marxism, which I understand to be the effort of Theodor Adorno, Herbert Marcuse, and others to combine the insights of Marx and Freud, affirms eros—but not in the forms given it by modern sports. A reading of

Marx (with an assist from Foucault) leads to the condemnation of sports and the fitness industry for their complicity in the capitalist exploitation of tractable bodies. Body-building, for instance, is interpreted as a "disciplinary regime" that "constructs a body well designed for the complexities of life in late capitalism, which requires a worker's body and a body of workers that are well managed in the way a portfolio is well-managed."[3] A reading of Freud leads these neo-Marxists to a condemnation of sports and the fitness industry for their incubation of "sexual perversions." In the polemics of Ulrich Dix, Gerhard Vinnai, and Paul Hoch, the erotic element in modern sports appears as homosexuality, sadism, masochism, narcissism, and exhibitionism. These appearances the neo-Marxists deplore.

"The erotic life of the [male] athlete," writes Gerhard Vinnai, "demonstrates a strange schizophrenia: in its physiological aspects, it is heterosexual, but in its psychic aspects it corresponds to the erotic dispositions of early childhood, and it is accordingly homosexual."[4] The athlete's wife may satisfy his lust, but his teammates are the true objects of his love. Paul Hoch's thrust is more specific than Vinnai's. He asserts that football is "America's Number One fake-masculinity ritual," an ironic, unconscious display of the very homosexuality that athletes and spectators say they most despise.[5]

There are several ways to respond to this charge. There is no reason to doubt in these post-Freudian days that there is a homosexual component in the heterosexual's responses to athletes of his or her own sex. The frenzy of the mostly male spectators at a boxing match must be more than the excitement occasioned by the demonstration of the manly art of self-defense. The delight felt by figure-skating's mostly female spectators at the sight of Katarina Witt or Kristi Yamaguchi cannot be exclusively aesthetic.

As for the athletes, the best riposte to the neo-Marxist indictment is, once again, simply to acknowledge and affirm the obvious existence of fellowship and affection among athletes of the same sex. The shame—from my point of view—is not that a homoerotic bond unites athletes but rather that this bond unites them, too often, in hostility to others. Sports are, theoretically, a form of competition for which cooperation is a prerequisite. Opponents must agree to have a contest and to have it under certain mutually acceptable rules. Sports, however, can degenerate into bitter conflicts in which camaraderie justifies violence committed against a hated rival. (We love our goons.)

Neo-Marxists have also called attention to the way that celebrations of shared masculinity can degenerate into expressions of misogyny. The psychic mechanism seems simple. Outspoken contempt for women masks the male athlete's anxiety about his own masculinity. In ice hockey as in many other sports, adolescent men (of all ages) make obscene remarks about women in order to demonstrate their solidarity with other men.[6] In *Hockey Night in Canada* (1993), Richard Gruneau and David Whitson—two sociologists closer to the British "cultural studies" approach than to neo-Marxism—provide plenty of evidence for the claim that some sports subcultures are rife with aggressiveness and celebrations of "sexual adventure and conquest as necessary components of masculine identity." They warn that blanket condemnations of misogyny are unfair, but they refer sadly to "initiation rites that rehearse juvenile forms of sexual exhibitionism, the ready circulation of tales of sexual conquest, a latent contempt for groupies and prostitutes, and the sexual innuendo typical in comments made from the bus, the cab, or on the street to women who simply happen to be passing by."[7]

Ice hockey is certainly not unique. In their motivational strategy, basketball coaches like Indiana's Bobby Knight and Catholic University's Bob Valvano implicitly communicate contempt for women. "In response to 'wimpy' performances, male coaches [including Knight] have been known to deposit tampons, sanitary napkins, and bras in young men's lockers."[8] When mere misogyny is not enough to motivate an athlete and reassure him that the surge of love he feels for his teammates is not evidence of latent homosexuality, he can always resort to verbal or physical "queer bashing."

If misogyny is common, misanthropy is not unknown. It is frequently assumed or asserted that female athletes can sing a song of sisterhood without dissonant overtones of nasty hostility to men, but there are clear signs that some sportswomen are expressing their emancipation by denigrating the opposite sex. "Many [women's] rugby teams," writes Mariah Burton Nelson, "are led by women who are openly lesbian or bisexual and openly angry at male sexual dominance." Of men they sing,

> When the prick grows, when the juice flows
> When he's feeling grand
> Just fart in his face and tell him his place
> And that he can use his HAND![9]

Welcome to the club.

There is another twist to the debate over homosexuality in sports. Among gay men, one now sees a "clone culture" of hard bodies, "a reification of the masculine."[10] In *Blueboy* and *Mandate*, two magazines publishing erotica for male homosexuals, the photographs highlight models with "clearly defined musculature."[11] In *The Arena of Masculinity* (1990), Brian Pronger agrees with the neo-Marxist contention that modern sports are a hotbed of homosexual desire—but he reverses all the valences and enthusiastically affirms what Vinnai, Dix, and Hoch condemn. "Within homosexual and gay culture," boasts Pronger, "muscles have become the erotic embodiment of the gay ironic sensibility." The homosexual men Pronger describes are ecstatic about the sexual aspects of sports and they are almost comic in their complaints about the fleshly temptations of the locker room. One has to be a Dickensian prude not to laugh when one of Pronger's informants says, of the locker room's display of male nudity, "It was like having chocolate sauce on your ice cream." Unfortunately, Pronger's welcome *laudatio cupiditatis* devolves into assertions of gay superiority.

Wielding and thrusting a number of weapons drawn from Foucault's well-stocked conceptual arsenal, Pronger argues—with no empirical evidence whatsoever—that the *heterosexual* male's muscular body is "the embodiment of the myth of patriarchal heterosexual masculinity" while the *homosexual* male athlete is a believer in equality who "has no interest in the erotic celebration of [the body's] mythic power over women."[12] In characterizing homosexual athletes as the only authentic egalitarians, Pronger goes to an untenable extreme, but his Foucault-inspired assertions of "gay pride" are a useful counter to neo-Marxist homophobia.

In his campaign against homophobia in sports, Pronger has had a number of lesbian allies. There has always been some empirical basis for the suspicion that aggressively "mannish" or "Amazon-like" female athletes are homosexual. As Susan Cahn notes in *Coming on Strong* (1994), "Lesbian athletes used the social and psychic space of sport to create a shared culture and affirmative identity."[13] A physiological study of 241 lesbians found that they had narrower hips, less subcutaneous fat, and more muscle mass than heterosexual women. These physical differences may be the cause as well as the consequence of a higher degree of sports involvement.[14]

Whatever the causal relationships, for most of the twentieth century, lesbian athletes concealed their sexual orientation and were implicitly encouraged to do so by their coaches and physical-education teachers, who were only too happy to enforce dress and conduct codes that maintained a front of safely heterosexual femininity. Recently, however, a number of uncloseted lesbian athletes have boldly proclaimed their right to be what they are. Birgit Palzkill's manifesto, *Zwischen Turnschuh und Stöckelschuh* (1990), is admirably outspoken (and much more sophisticated than Pronger's opinionated contribution to gay liberation). At moments, Palzkill endorses the typically neo-Marxist critique of "instrumentalized" sports, which "serve to reproduce industrial work" (i.e., sports improve the health and morale of industrial workers and enable their employers to exploit them more fully than if they were sickly and discouraged). To this familiar criticism, Palzkill adds the radical feminist analysis of patriarchy: "The sexual power of men over women represents a central structural characteristic of the distorted hierarchical relationship between the sexes." Although sports have conventionally been treated as a "masculine domain" plagued by patriarchy in one of its most virulent forms, Palzkill argues nonetheless that lesbian women can—if they defy the efforts of prejudiced men and women to stigmatize them—use sports to resist male domination. Lesbians can use sports to become physically strong and mentally confident. They can overcome their self-doubt and the role conflict that tortures them to the point that they feel as if they had somehow been ripped apart. Like Pronger, Palzkill affirms the energizing presence of eros. As one of the nineteen lesbian athletes in her sample comments, "When I was fifteen or sixteen, I was thrilled by female swimmers with broad backs and narrow hips."[15] In the theogony of women's liberation, Aphrodite cleared the way for Artemis and Athena.

Helen Lenskyj has been equally outspoken. Describing her experiences in Toronto's mainly lesbian Notso Amazons Softball League and insisting on "the social, sensual, and sexual pleasures of bodily movement," she acknowledges that feminists have frequently objected to cropped photographs of female athletes when these images appeared in mainstream magazines, but she maintains, in her discussion of the softball league's illustrated calendar, that "it is possible to view [a] woman's muscular forearm . . . and leg . . . as a celebration of women's strength and beauty." Raunchy remarks by lesbians about lesbians ("It's been a pleasure perusing your strike zone") she considers a "nonexploitative celebration . . . of women's bodies from a lesbian perspective." She has no objection to teams with such sexually explicit names as "Dykes on Spikes" and "Lickety Splits."[16] Sports, for Lenskyj as for Pronger and Palzkill are not a perverse sublimation of sexuality; they are a way to experience and affirm the self. Martina Navratilova's continued popularity after her avowal of a lesbian relationship is evidence that the admission of homosexuality is no longer tantamount to the end of an athletic career (although it can still mean the diminution of an athlete's endorsement income).

Condemnations of homosexuality are, however, only one arrow from the neo-Marxist bow. Expanding upon Freud's analysis in "Drives and Their Fates" (1915), Dix, Vinnai, and Hoch characterize modern sports as sadistic and masochistic. As a generalization, this will not do because there are certainly many sports—bowling, croquet, curling, golf, diving, tennis, yachting—that cannot reasonably be categorized as sadistic or masochistic (unless one goes metaphoric and adduces the psychic pain of gutter balls, bogeys, and double faults). Still, as an observation about *some* modern sports, the truth of the neo-Marxist accusation has to be admitted. The football players (of various codes) who celebrate a score by embracing their teammates and toppling into a human heap of exuberant affect are also the men who, a moment later, will hurl their bodies at those of their opponents in an aggressive effort to block, tackle, punish, and—with a little bit of luck—maim them. The opposing side returns the favor. In these as in most combat sports, we can observe sadistic and masochistic impulses, the sexually motivated desire to inflict and to experience pain. Few of the athletes who pride themselves on their ability "to take it and to dish it out" are likely to acknowledge that the pleasure they feel is erotic, but Peter Fuller, who may be the only professionally ranked boxer to have benefitted from a Harvard education, admitted that the sensation he felt when delivering a solid knock-out punch went "directly . . . to the genitals."[17] And who doubts that hysterically screaming fight fans are as vicariously sadistic as the men and women who lusted for blood in the Roman arena?

The comparison to the Roman arena deserves a moment's thought. In *The Sorrows of the Ancient Romans*, Carlin Barton comments that the "gladiator's love of death (*amor mortis*), his enthusiastic cooperation in his own death, redeemed both himself and the audience." Citing lines from Juvenal's satires and Martial's epigrams, Barton argues convincingly that "the closeness of the blade, the closeness to death and violation . . . rendered the gladiator beautiful."[18] The *munera* of the Roman Colosseum are an extreme case, a magnifying glass that enables us to detect the less obvious sadomasochistic emotions of the modern boxing fan. What ringside spectator is unaware of the delicious possibility that one of the two physically powerful men—so *alive*—who touch gloves at the start of a bout might, fifteen minutes later, be as dead as the deadest Roman gladiator? "The excitement of sports," write Gerd Hortleder and Gunter Gebauer, "is enacted against a backdrop of death."[19] For this excitement, as for almost all others, Freud posited a sexual origin.[20]

In addition to a vocal minority advocating the acceptance of S/M for consenting sadists and masochists, there is probably a silent majority—and not just within capitalist economies—in favor of *some* of the pain experienced in sports. Boxers experience perverse pleasure in the physical punishment they endure. Football and basketball players who "play hurt," that is, who continue in the game despite an injury, sometimes complain of the coaches who coerce them to risk permanent disabilities, but resentment at the coercion is frequently accompanied by the athlete's pride in his or her Spartan ability to overcome pain. "Injuries are listed like accomplishments: cracked ribs, herniated disks, bruised shoulders. Rugby players even wipe their teammates' blood onto their own uniforms."[21]

Male rugby players are notorious for sadistic fantasies like "The Engineer's Song," which celebrates the achievements of a man who punished his sexually insatiable wife by building a mechanical dildo that ripped her to shreds. Female players have begun to reply with obscene lyrics of their own, which are said by some to encourage "resistant practices" and a "feminist sensibility."[22] The pleasures of the songs, such as they are, cannot be wholly unrelated to the pleasures of the game.

Homosexual athletes are as prone as heterosexuals to affirm the pleasures of pain. "The pain is worth it," says Brian Pronger, "because masculinity is worth it."[23] No one who has experienced the tremulous spasm of the fifteenth repetition of the third set of a benchpress can doubt the masochism of the body-builders. "My attitude is to make friends with the pain and ride it to the top," explained one body-builder to an anthropological investigator. "The more it hurts to keep pushing in a set, the more the workout improves my muscle mass and density, and the more I enjoy the pain."[24] The masochism of the long-distance runner is equally obvious. "To run with pain," cries Mike Frankfurt, "is the essence of life."[25] The postmodernist guru Jean Baudrillard labeled the New York marathon "a form of demonstrative suicide."[26] Every language seems to have some equivalent of "no pain, no gain." (Germans speak of overcoming *den inneren Schweinehund.*) Whether the sadism and masochism evident in many sports are admirable or deplorable can be, has been, and will continue to be debated.

And then there is that other pair of notorious psychoanalytical twins: narcissism and exhibitionism. Examining narcissism and exhibitionism in *Sport und Sexualität* (1972), Ulrich Dix explained that the athletes who suffer from these neuroses have had their psyches so distorted by capitalism that their libido is regressively misdirected toward their own bodies.[27] Body-builders are, once again, an obvious case in point. Their workouts are incomplete without a series of poses before the gym's ubiquitous mirrors. At the very start of his exploration of the "body-building subculture," Alan Klein was shocked by the raw sexuality of the gym. "The whole place seemed caught up in one large orgasm, and in that first encounter I did not want to be the dreaded interruption of the erotic scene between humans, mirrors, and metal."[28] Mirrors provide opportunities not only for self-satisfaction but also for reality checks. "If I didn't look in the mirror and I just felt myself," explained a female body-builder, "I'd think I was the most beautiful, strongest person in the world."[29]

Mirrors are necessary but hardly sufficient. Progress toward the maximum possible hypertrophy is accompanied by anatomical measurements that evoke sighs of pleasure (girth increased by a centimeter) or of disappointment (still smaller than Arnold). From the mirror-mirror-on-the-wall atmosphere of the gym, the body-builder moves to the stage to flex and smile for the title of Mr. Universe or Ms. Olympia, at which point narcissism becomes exhibitionism. When the tanned, oiled contestants segue into their routines, "whole anatomies are pumped like priapic erections, contracting poses and shifting with held violence from one pose to the next with the vaginal contractions of labor pains."[30]

The Angeleno denizens of Gold's Gym are certainly not the only narcissists in sight. Less egregious and less suspect forms of self-presentation can be observed at ball games, where players who miss an opportunity to score because they are too preoccupied with their appearance are disparaged as "showboaters." And every athlete understands the emotional difference between playing a game in an empty stadium and performing before a hundred thousand cheering spectators. Champions who strut across the world's electronic stage were once little boys and girls who proudly "made a muscle" at Daddy's behest and rode "no hands" to impress Mommy with their cycling skills.

Behind the tensed muscles, however, there palpitates a fearful heart. This, at least, is the conclusion of Klaus Theweleit's two-volume anatomy of the German officer corps in the years between 1871 and 1933, a group of men whom he excoriates as rigidly hysterical martinets so fearful of their own inner softness that they were ready to murder anyone upon whom they projected their anxieties. Hypermasculinity was the grotesque mask they wore to disguise the humiliating traces of effeminacy. The real woman out there, and the metaphorical woman within, are the twin threats to masculine hegemony. Hardened muscles are the male body's defensive armor. Theweleit's historical dissection of the *Freikorps* (and a vast number of related institutions) might well be cited by the sociologists who seek to "read" today's muscular body. After all, liberated women now storm America's ideological barricades just as the "Communist whores" of 1917 "swarmed" and "swirled" against the fragile psychic defenses of Kaiser Wilhelm's Germany.[31]

In the strikingly similar language of his autobiographical novella, *Confessions of a Mask*, Yukio Mishima, the Japanese writer, body-builder, and nationalist political activist, described his homosexual obsession with Guido Reni's sadomasochistic portrait of Saint Sebastian: "His white and matchless nudity gleams against a background of dusk. His muscular arms, the arms of a praetorian guardian accustomed to bending of bow and wielding of sword, are raised at a graceful angle, and his bound wrists are crossed directly over his head."

The sight of the arrows that have "eaten into the tense, fragrant, youthful flesh" fills the narrator with "pagan joy," produces an erection, and induces his hands to begin "a motion they had never been taught" (i.e., masturbation).[32] For him as well as for Theweleit's rigidly erect military men, narcissism and exhibitionism had sexual origins.

In "Reading the Muscular Body," a pair of sociologists make this point without the benefit of Theweleit's medley of metaphors or Mishima's bathos. They write that "the resurgent cultural ideal of the muscular body . . . and the increased popularity of bodywork practices are symptomatic of a trend in our culture seeking to reestablish an ideology of gender difference in the face of emancipatory forces." The muscular body is "compensation for an erosion of power in a world where masculine privilege is often denied."[33] Similar conclusions were reached by Alan Klein, after years of participant-observation in body-building studios, and by Samuel Fussell, whose memoir of his quest for the appearance of strength is a painful revelation of psychic weakness. More drastic still is the judgment of J. J. Courtine, one of the many French sports sociologists influenced by Michel Foucault. Alluding cleverly to the USSR's "heroes of labor," he characterizes body-builders as "stakhanovites du narcissisme," men driven not by hedonism but rather by disciplinary control and a "repuritanization" of the body.[34]

Male athletes are obviously not the only ones to flaunt tight bodies and muscular definition. Female athletes can be just as narcissistic. They too mix play and display[35] and some of them have second thoughts about deltoids and quadriceps as a fetish. "When I was busy being strong, and vain about that strength," admitted a female body-builder interviewed by Mariah Nelson, "I let people feel my thighs, but I'm not sure I let them know me."[36]

The presence in sports of narcissistic and exhibitionistic traits and behaviors is unquestionable. Am I therefore ready to join the neo-Marxists in lamenting them as infantile psychic disorders? Not quite. There must be at least a trace of narcissism and exhibitionism in any sports performance that attracts spectators, which is why preseason contests are fittingly referred to as exhibition games. Given the pejorative connotations of these terms in psychoanalytic literature and in ordinary speech, not many people want to admit that they are narcissists or exhibitionists, but how else can we explain the craze for sports and physical fitness, which holds millions in its spell, if these millions do not want to inhabit and make visible bodies which are, if not perfect, at least more nearly perfect than they were before they took up sports and exercise? "Fame is the spur," wrote John Milton in "Lycidas," "that last infirmity of noble mind." Vanity is the spur for those of us without Miltonically noble minds. What else, if not vanity, if not a harmless form of narcissism and exhibitionism, can explain the efforts we make to compete, to demonstrate our physical skills, to remain agile and youthful, and—let us admit it—to be as sexually attractive as possible for as long as possible?[37] Why should anyone fulminate against what, in moderation, is an innocent pleasure?

There are signs that at least some psychoanalysts are ready to revise their profession's previously negative interpretation of narcissism and exhibitionism. With little indication of animus against these alleged neuroses and with a positive view of sports participation, Daniel Dervin published an unusually interesting article in *The Psychoanalytic Review*. He maintained that "the perfect self is on exhibition [in athletics] as in no other comparable performance. The athlete's goal of winning comprises a narcissistic triumph, accompanied by restored self-esteem and elation."[38] We may, if Dervin is representative of his profession, be on our way to a psychoanalytic view of sports that goes beyond the therapeutic insights of Fenichel and Kohut. Sports may yet be reclassified and elevated to the level of the arts—as one of humankind's happier sublimations.

FEMINIST CRITIQUES

The more time one spends studying the work of Vinnai, Dix, Hoch, and the other neo-Marxists, the more their root-and-branch critique of the erotic element in sports appears to be a flimsy affair constructed from weatherbeaten prejudice against homosexuality, propped by some justified concern about sadomasochism, and finished with overwrought worry about narcissism and exhibitionism. Other critics have built sturdier arguments. The most sustained and forceful attack on the erotic element in sports comes from the radical feminist camp. Many of the theoretical weapons employed in the onslaught have been forged by Michel Foucault and Jacques Lacan. Freud, who tends to be a feminist *bête noir*, contributes little to their criticism of eros and sports.

It should be emphasized that *liberal* feminists have, as a rule, *not* participated in the attack. Equality is their watchword and they are generally positive about women's participation in modern sports and in fitness programs. In fact, they are adamant about their right to participate in all aspects of the very same physical regime that many radical feminists characterize as "dehumanizing." It should also be emphasized at the outset that radical feminists vary greatly among themselves. Some vehemently denounce modern sports while others maintain that sports—once liberated from "patriarchal disciplinary controls"—can be a domain of female autonomy.

Despite their disagreements, most radical feminists unite in adamant condemnation of the "sexualization" of women's sports.

Crucial to their radical critique is the concept of voyeurism, a "perversion" that also plays a minor role in neo-Marxist polemics. In the development of the case against "lookism," many British and American feminists have drawn upon an influential book of art criticism by John Berger. In *Ways of Seeing* (1972), which was originally a BBC series, Berger argued that "a naked body has to be seen as an object in order to become a nude." Western art has a plethora of female nudes because this objectification of the body is something that happens, typically, to women rather than to men. "Men look at women," wrote Berger, and women experience themselves as the objects at which men look.[39]

Berger's rather mild remarks led to a heated discussion of "the male gaze." Radical feminist horror of this gaze eventually intensified to the point where M. A. Doane asserted that "the simple gesture of directing a camera towards a woman has become a terrorist act."[40] Somewhat less extreme is the film theorist Laura Mulvey. Her seminal article, "Visual Pleasure and Narrative Cinema," has been hailed as "the single most influential feminist-psychoanalytic analysis of women's representation in the Hollywood cinema and of male spectatorial response."[41] Mulvey's article, which has its origins in Freud's discussion of "scopophilia" (in the *Three Essays on Sexuality*), is a Lacanian denunciation of the "phallocratic" male gaze. "The paradox of phallocentrism in all its manifestations," argued Mulvey, "is that it depends on the image of the castrated woman to give order and meaning to its world."[42]

In "Fabricating the Female Body," which includes an explication of Mulvey's theories, Jane Gaines explains that women's terrifying, castrating bodies are transformed by the overtly bold but covertly fearful narcissistic male gaze "into the comforting image of the male phallus."[43] Adam has a phallus; Eve is one. Although articles such as these are often unintelligible to readers who have not yet learned to abjure "phallocratic" logic, this much is clear: Mulvey and quite a number of other radical feminists believe that women are objectified and victimized by the voyeuristic male gaze.

To the argument that male nudes also appear in works of art and that feature films now include male as well as female nudity, there is a curt reply. "That which can be signified by the male figure is . . . curtailed by the historical specificity of the sign 'man' within patriarchal ideology." In other words, effective reversal of gender conventions is an "impossibility."[44] Men are too powerful, and women too powerless, for the ideological tables to be turned.

Not all radical feminists agree. Margaret Morse, whose interest in Lacan seems to be as intense of Mulvey's, thinks that the fitness fad has real possibilities: "The *phallus* or symbol of perfection and sign of exchange value is what we create with our aerobic muscles."[45] Suzanne Moore takes issue directly with the Mulveyan analysis of voyeurism and comments, in the midst of a discussion of "the male body on display," that "women *can* and *do* look actively and erotically at images of men." The male body is also an object of "scopophilic" pleasure. To deny this is to succumb to "the stifling categories of a theory."[46] Men, it seems, can also be (as well as have) a phallus.

A dismayingly large number of radical feminist sports sociologists have adopted Mulvey's views. Evidence for their contention that there is an obvious similarity between the voyeurism of the art collector or movie-goer and that of the male sports spectator does not come, although it might have, from the comments of male sports spectators. Instead, their evidence consists largely of photographs in newspapers and popular magazines. "Sports photography has become a significant part of the mass market in pornography," comments Jennifer Hargreaves, a leading sociological authority on women's sports. "Sportified images of female sexuality are metaphors for male desire."[47] After warning in an article that *all* sports are potentially voyeuristic, Margaret Carlisle Duncan has written a sharply focused attack on the alleged "soft-core pornography" in media coverage of women's sports. Analyzing 186 photographs from the 1984 and 1988 Olympic Games, she notes the intense media interest in sexually attractive athletes like Katarina Witt and Florence Griffith-Joyner. Such athletes are portrayed in ways that emphasize the sexual difference between men and women. Witt, for instance, was shown with "her lipsticked lips drawn up in an exaggerated pout" while four Romanian gymnasts were photographed from behind as they bent over to congratulate their Chinese rivals—a pose which, according to Duncan, accentuated the gymnasts' small stature and made them seem submissive and sexually vulnerable. "This is a potentially dangerous combination because it sexualizes a child image and gives viewers visual power over that image."[48] In an attempt to combine Mulvey's analysis of voyeurism with Foucault's theory of the "panopticon," Duncan writes, "The gaze is not only a visual act, it is an economy of surveillance." The most unfortunate consequence of male power is that "women internalize the gaze and turn it against themselves." They become narcissists, "objects for their own gaze."[49]

Although German feminists seem less enthralled than their American sisters by postmodernist theory, they too have deconstructed the "gestures of submission" that "constitute the [female] gymnast as sexual object."[50] In an unusually thorough and careful analysis of Germany's most popular tabloid, the *Bild-Zeitung*, Marie-Luise Klein and Gertrud Pfister documented the sexual exploitation of female athletes who appear more often than not as sylph-like creatures "with long hair and slender bodies, but without muscular definition." Of a soccer player, *Bild-Zeitung* notes, typically, "Her black hair is flying and there's also something moving under her shorts."[51] When Klein broadened the survey to include a number of other German newspapers, she found that some papers, like the left-wing *Frankfurter Rundschau*, were fairly objective in reporting on women's sports while other publications used photography to awaken "the reader's erotic fantasies by means of nakedness thinly concealed by skin-tight clothing." Fantasy was also induced "by graceful poses, stretched bodies, and spread legs."[52]

Although newspapers and magazines have been studied more intensively than television (which was much harder to analyze before the easy availability of videotapes), the electronic medium has recently come in for its share of criticism. Margaret McNeill has condemned television's manipulation of the images of female body-builders, whose sexuality is accentuated by voyeuristic camera angles. Like Duncan and Klein, McNeill attributes this mistreatment to "patriarchal capitalism."[53]

The indictment continues. In addition to the media's (and the male spectators') selective focus on erotic bodies, there is the exploitation of these bodies in contexts that are only peripherally related to actual sports competitions. During the frantic attempt to keep the failing Women's Basketball League alive, promoters marketed posters of Molly Bolin in shorts and a tank top.[54] Similarly, the women's basketball team at Louisiana's Northwestern State University were asked to don Playboy bunny outfits to pose for their school's 1987–1988 media guide.[55] In 1981, the Ladies Professional Golf Association hired Ray Volpe to improve the appeal of women's golf with photographs of Laura Baugh and other beautiful drivers and putters. Another female golfer, Australia's Jan Stephenson, suddenly appeared in *Fairway*—in bed with a seductive display of leg.[56] *Fairway* followed this promotional ploy with facsimile scenes from sexy films.[57] To bring Tammie Green and Deborah McHaffie to the Hennessey Ladies Cup in Paris in 1991, the promoters offered them seven thousand pounds—despite the relatively inferior level of their play. Lionel Provost defended this lavish expenditure of funds by observing that "they are exceptionally attractive."[58] More abysmal yet was *Vogue*'s April 1990 issue, in which Steffi Graf posed in "a black Norma Kamali maillot dress, adjusting her high heel and aiming her décolletage lensward."[59]

What the perpetrators of these travesties have in common (apart from their commercial instincts) is their failure to understand that *the erotic appeal of the female athlete is to a large degree sport-specific*. In an astute analysis of the dancer's body, Elizabeth Dempster describes the way that practice and performance mold the contours of the body. "It is through participation in the given discourse of a genre, constituted by dance classes, rehearsals and performances, that the body characteristic of the genre is constructed and inscribed."[60] Terry Todd makes a similar point about the movements of athletic women. Their special attraction "springs from the fact that . . . their bodies must move free of wasted motion; this beautiful movement creates the sort of form we regard as an aspect of beauty."[61] In other words, these allegedly sexualized female athletes are unusually attractive simply because of the way they move and have moved—*as athletes*. In the last analysis, we can no more separate the athlete from his or her performance than William Butler Yeats was able to tell the dancer from the dance. The excellence of their athletic performances eroticizes them as a maillot dress cannot. Is it necessary to add that the erotic attraction of the male athlete is also attributable to his marvelous movements and the way that they have shaped his body?

From a radical feminist perspective, the success or failure of the pose is not the issue. Ire is aroused even if the putative male viewer is not. But is the critique justified? In part, yes. If sports spectators are interested *only* in the erotic appeal of the athlete's body, then they have foolishly circumscribed their emotional involvement in the excitement of the physical contest. They *have* separated athletes from their performances. It is their loss and they are impoverished by it. In part, however, the radical critique is misguided. Its hostility to the erotic element in sports is so extreme that liberal feminists have had cause to worry, in Margaret Hunt's apt phrase, about "the de-eroticization of women's liberation."[62] As Kathy Myers has argued, there must be a way for feminists "to account for women's pleasure in looking at images of women" and to "reintroduce the notion of the erotic."[63] Rather than condemning the men who have admired physically fit women and their sports performances, should not radical feminists, more logically, defend women's right to admire—and even to be erotically stimulated by—physically fit men and *their* sports performances? Although thoughtful scholars are properly leery of efforts to legitimize culture by references to nature, Charles Darwin did seem to have a point when he found biological justification for mutual attraction between men and women.

My plea for the acceptance of mutually admiring male and female gazes (and for gay and lesbian ones as well) will not persuade feminists who see imbalances in political, economic, social, and physical power as permanent impediments to gender equality. In their eyes, male voyeurism is a prelude to physical aggression against women. They argue that voyeurism leads to lust which leads to rape and other violently transgressive misogynist acts. Since the erotic component in men's and women's sports is ineradicable, this reductionist line of argument seems to lead to the neo-Marxist conclusion that sports ought to be abolished—along with ballet, modern dance, and most other public forms of physical expression. But is there any reason to believe that sports fans who find female athletes physically attractive are therefore more likely to commit violence against them or against any other woman? Decades of research by Jennings Bryant, Edward Donnerstein, Daniel Linz, Neil M. Malamuth, Dolf Zillmann, and a number of other social psychologists have shown conclusively that the relationship between erotica and violence against women is far from simple.[64]

In seeking to understand this complex relationship, psychologists have exposed male and female undergraduate subjects to films, photographs, slides, audiotapes, and/or written accounts of violent and nonviolent sexual behaviors. Many experiments have been variations on one of two paradigms. In the first, subjects were (1) provoked by the experimenter's confederate, (2) exposed to violent or nonviolent erotica, and then (3) placed in a position to retaliate against the provoker (usually by administering noxious noise or what the subject believed was electric shock). In the second paradigm, subjects were (1) provoked, (2) exposed to violent or nonviolent erotica, (3) shown a film of a rape trial, and (4) asked what sentence should be meted out to the rapist. On the basis of such experiments, most psychologists agree that exposure to visual or verbal images of sexual violence is like exposure to images of non-sexual violence; it increases aggressiveness[65] and the acceptance of rape.[66] This is especially true if the subjects are shown materials implying that the rape victims really enjoyed their sexual victim-ization. At least one study found, however, that repeated exposure to violent and nonviolent pornography had no "significant effect on laboratory aggression against women"[67] Some experts in the field went a step farther. Their experiments convinced them that men and women exposed to *non*-violent erotica are *less* prone than others to commit acts of aggression or to condone rape. Exposure to mild erotica actually reduced the likelihood and the level of aggres-sive behavior.[68] Donnerstein concluded on the basis of such results, that "it is the aggressive content of pornography that is the main contributor to violence against women."

Zillmann and his collaborators have been critical of Donnerstein and *his* collaborators. In their view, "erotic communications . . . tend to intensify post-exposure aggressiveness to a higher degree than communications depicting aggressive and violent acts."[69] While admitting that erotic materials with "positive hedonic valence" may sometimes lessen annoyance and the propensity to commit acts of violence,[70] they warned that it is unreasonable to expect that exposure to mild erotica can do much to "control intense reactions of anger to strong provocation."[71] In response to such criticism, Donnerstein and Linz seemed to agree that long-term exposure to nonviolent erotica can increase callousness,[72] but they subse-quently reiterated that they were unable to find "antisocial effects for exposure to pornographic material that is not overtly violent."[73]

What do these results say about sports spectatorship and the problem of voyeurism? While I am convinced that the habitual consumption of violent erotica degrades men as well as women and desensitizes the consumer to violence of all sorts, I doubt that any reasonable person can compare the "male gaze" at a track meet or a tennis match to the rapist's addiction to "slasher" films and photographs of sadomasochistic bondage. It seems perverse to liken female athletes to the bound, beaten, and raped women who appear in hard-core pornography. Unlike these victims, female athletes are physically active women and most of them have high self-esteem and a strong sense of personal autonomy. I am aware that men have committed acts of violence against female athletes, but I am not convinced that these acts were facilitated by the women's erotic appeal. Ironically, if "aggressive images are the issue, not sexual images,"[74] then radical feminists who believe that sports voyeurism instigates violence against women should worry more about the fans of women's judo and rugby and less about spectators who are excited about diving, gymnastics, and figure skating.

Although none of the intriguing laboratory experiments conducted by Zillmann and others asked directly about the alleged association between sports spectatorship and violence against women, at least one field study has answered the question. In the course of investigating the association between athletic *participation* and sexual aggression, Mary P. Koss and John A. Gaines discovered in a careful survey of 530 University of Arizona students that membership on a varsity team correlated weakly with an anonymously admitted propensity to commit acts of sexual aggression against women, but *spectatorship* did not.[75] The evidence is scanty, but there is no good reason to take the violent actions of some male athletes as a predictor of similar behavior on the part of male sports spectators. The gaze-leads-to-rape argument reduces all men to the status of a single litter of Pavlovian dogs.

The voyeurism of the "male gaze" has occasioned the most vehement rejections of the erotic element in sports, but there has also been strenuous feminist opposition to the coercive power of men's media-propagated images of ideal female bodies. Is it ethically responsible to tantalize women with images of physical perfection more appropriate, genetically, for men? In *The Obsession*

(1981), Kim Chernin remembered comparing her body, unhappily, to that of an athletic young male:

> I reverted to a fantasy about my body's transformation from this state of imperfection to a consummate loveliness, the flesh trimmed away, stomach flat, thighs like those of the adolescent runner on the back slopes of the fire trail, a boy of fifteen or sixteen, running along there one evening in a pair of red trunks, stripped to the waist, gleaming with sweat and suntan oil, his muscles stretching and relaxing as if he'd been sent out there to model for me a vision of everything I was not and could never be.

She lamented that "none of us can identify with the hated flesh we are so determined to alter and shape."[76] A decade after Chernin published *The Obsession*, a feminist student lamented her "deep fear of having a womanly body, round and fully developed. I want to be tight and muscular and thin."[77] More recently still, Susan Douglas has satirized the mass media for demanding that "a forty-year-old woman should have thighs like a twelve-year-old boy's."[78] In the heated debate over "the obsession," the condemnation of the fitness craze is even more severe than the critique of the cosmetics industry (which is dominated by female-owned companies). Susan Birrell and Nancy Theberge, two leading sports sociologists, are especially firm: "The fitness industry relies heavily on conventions of soft-core pornography to promote and sustain the boom and to represent to female consumers the true feminine ideal they must strive to approach through fitness regimes."[79]

Susan Bordo's philosophically informed analysis of the "elicitation of desire" for just such an impossibly perfect body is among the most perceptive contributions to the feminist debate. She agrees with Susan Orbach that "a constellation of social, economic, and psychological factors have combined to produce a generation of women who feel deeply flawed, ashamed of their needs, and not entitled to exist unless they transform themselves into worthy new selves." Bordo laments that the film goddesses of the seventies who once seemed "fit and slender now [appear] loose and flabby" even to her feminist eyes. In the eyes of her students, Marilyn Monroe, whom Bordo describes as "the dominant ideal of female beauty" for the fifties, is "a cow."[80] While Miss America contestants, Hollywood starlets, and *Playboy* centerfold nudes are all more slender than they were a generation ago, the average American woman now weighs approximately five pounds more than her mother did, which is taken to mean that the gap between the actual and the ideal is even harder to bridge than it was.[81] It does not seem to matter to women suffering from the tyranny of slenderness that "a thin ideal of female body attractiveness is held by females but not by males."[82]

Bordo also expresses her dismay at the depredations of anorexia and bulimia, eating disorders common among young women. She attributes both illnesses, in part, to the obsessive pursuit of slender "flablessness."[83] She comments insightfully on the parallel between these disorders and compulsive exercise, two related forms of neurotic behavior expressing an obsessive need to control the body. The beguiling fantasy of impossible physical perfection can seduce a woman to starve herself into emaciation or to ingest anabolic steroids in order to shape a weight-trained body so sinewy, vascular, and breastless that most people are appalled by it. For women subjected to the mass media's daily dose of unreal images, there is what Jane Gaines describes as a forced choice between "the deformed anorexic body or the reformed muscled body."[84] When *haute couture* provides the models, women compare themselves to air-brushed images of surgically altered bodies and then diet to emaciation or undergo the horrors of liposuction. When athletes like Florence Griffith-Joyner or Fatima Whitbread are the models, women become addicted to exercise and resort to performance-enhancing drugs. In either case, as Helen Lenskyj sees it, "a woman's conformity to male-defined standards of heterosexual attractiveness signifies her acquiescence to men's rules."[85] When insurance companies revised their standards for height and weight in the fifties, they defined the majority of women as overweight, which led to "an epidemic of self-rejection."[86]

All things considered, how persuasive is the radical feminist critique of "sexualized" sports and the fitness industry? What can one say about "sexualization"? Complaining that the media have portrayed Katarina Witt "as a sexy female" rather than as "a serious, committed athlete with a discipline and a desire for athletic excellence," Mary Jo Kane and Susan L. Greendorfer fail to acknowledge that Witt—like thousands of other women—is a serious athlete *and* a sexy female (who is very obviously aware of her physical attractiveness).[87] The media can be faulted whenever they focus mainly or exclusively on a female athlete's erotic appeal, which is what they often did in the past, but it is time to recognize that most of today's journalists are more than willing to acknowledge the strength, endurance, toughness, and skills of women like Witt. (Neanderthals still roam the airwaves, but they are a dying species.)

And the manipulation of women by the male-dominated fitness industry? While it is undeniable that the quest for men's approval drives many women to "pump iron" or to enter marathons, it is a mistake to describe these women as if they had no motivation other than the desire to please the opposite sex. Innumerable women have testified proudly that sports participation has enhanced their self-esteem and granted them a hitherto unknown sense of autonomy and empowerment. Numerous studies have documented the fact that athletic women have a more positive body image than their sedentary sisters do[88] and that adolescents involved in sports are a striking exception to the rule that teenage girls are extremely unhappy about their physical selves.[89] Psychologists can be accused of bias and the testimonials of older women—on talk shows, in fitness journals, and in books like Trix Rosen's *Strong and Sexy* (1983)—can be dismissed as part of a patriarchal media campaign, but there are also feminists who insist that the athletic ideal has contributed to women's liberation. Mariah Burton Nelson, who has been adamant (and funny) in her critique of men's "appropriation of women's sports images as sexy [and] seductive," nonetheless admits that "the athletic act" can become "a feminist act," especially when it involves "enjoying one's female body as it moves with and against other female bodies."[90]

Anne Bolin makes a similar point about the extreme case of women's body-building. After all, it is an activity that challenges "the Western gender schema and its biology of difference, [its] paradigm of patriarchy and inequality."[91] Laurie Schulze agrees. Female body-builders are a threat not only to current "socially constructed definitions of femininity and masculinity" but also to "the system of sexual difference itself." As an "erotic spectacle," women's body-building may actually undermine rather than buttress "patriarchal and heterosexist ideologies."[92] Susan Douglas puts the paradox into vernacular terms; female muscles are meant "to serve simultaneously as a warning and as an enticement to men. Buns of steel [mark] a woman as a desirable piece of ass, and as someone who [can] kick ass when necessary."[93] For the female athlete, Juvenal's poetic tag requires only a slight modification: a strong mind in a strong body.

As for television's power to inflict an impossible ideal upon an audience of women depressed by comparing themselves with the incomparably beautiful images displayed on the screen, there is at least some empirical evidence that the effects of the medium are the opposite of what was anticipated. Young women who were exposed to videotapes of "body image commercials" were *less* likely to overestimate their own physical dimensions than women exposed to "neutral" footage and they experienced "a light euphoria, a lessening of depression."[94] Because they identified with the models in the advertisements? Because they were convinced that they had the ability to shape themselves to the same ideal? However one explains the intriguing result, it is not what Cassandra expected from observations of Helen.

Finally, in the heat of the debate over men's coercive expectations, it is easy to forget what women expect of men. Every educated person knows about Ibsen's Nora and her door-slamming departure from the doll's house. How many people remember the sad fate of Ibsen's Halvord Solness, the protagonist of *The Master Builder* (1892), who plunges to his death in a desperate attempt to climb the tower that symbolizes young Hilda Wangel's vicarious ambition? Are the men who wish they were Michael Jordan fewer than the women who wish they were Nancy Kerrigan? The wall flower at the dance (too heavy) has her counterpart in the wimp who didn't make the team (too light). Susan Bordo acknowledges as much when she writes that "far fresher insights can be gained by reading the male body through the window of its vulnerabilities rather than the dense armor of its power."[95]

It is easy to forget that "athletic ability and a muscular development have long been routine obligations imposed on every American male."[96] Focus on coercive images of female slenderness and fitness and what they do to a woman's consciousness has drawn attention away from the plight of men who are tormented by daily exposure to the spectacular performances of their athletic heroes, embodiments of a physical ideal attainable by a minuscule number. The message addressed to men is loud and clear, deafeningly amplified by the mass media. The effects of print advertisements celebrating "the young, lean, muscular male body" and of fashions requiring "a more muscular and trim body"[97] are reinforced by the megaton impact of the hundreds of hours of men's sports seen every week of the year on over-the-air and cable television networks.

Men get the message. For the athletically inept male, sports—whether part of a physical-education requirement or a company picnic—are a "degradation ceremony."[98] The devastation of a man who fails in an attempt to demonstrate his athletic prowess is dramatized in a poignant scene from F. Scott Fitzgerald's *Tender Is the Night* (1934). The hero, Dick Diver, struggles to repeat an aquatic stunt he had performed in the past. He tries to rise to an erect position, with a man on his shoulders, while balancing on a board towed by a motorboat.

> Nicole [his wife] saw him shift his position and strain upward again but at the instant when the weight of his partner was full upon his

shoulders he became immovable. He tried again—lifting an inch, two inches—Nicole felt the sweat glands of her forehead open as she strained with him—then he was simply holding his ground, then he collapsed back down on his knees with a smack, and they went over, Dick's head barely missing a kick of the board.

As Nicole stares at her husband, "floating exhausted and expressionless," she feels only contempt. She betrays him with a younger man who is "roped" with muscle.[99] Is there a middle-aged man anywhere who can read this scene and calmly go about his (probably sedentary) business?

And it is not just the middle-aged man who is glum about his physical self. A psychological study of eighty-eight male undergraduates, adolescents who were presumably blessed with a degree of youthful vigor, found that most of them "wanted to be more muscular or mesomorphic than they were."[100] The male undergraduates sampled in two subsequent surveys expressed the same wish; over 90 percent of them wished to be more muscular.[101] In these and similar studies, one unmistakable motive was men's desire to be more sexually attractive. The puny lover risks the beloved's ridicule at the moment when he most vulnerable. She chuckles at the sight of his scrawny body and he feels "as if someone had run me over with a Mack truck."[102] A comic moment—if you are not the man run over by the truck. It is true that dissatisfaction with one's imperfect body is more common among women than among men,[103] but reported differences in the rate of dissatisfaction—38 percent of the women versus 34 percent of the men or 24 percent of the men versus 31 percent of the women—hardly justify broadbrush assertions about male self-love and female self-hate.[104]

There is a curious symmetry at work. Athletic women are more likely to seek athletic men,[105] which means that men who lust for hard bodies had better shape up. To avoid embarrassment, to fulfill a culturally imposed ideal of masculinity, to attract the "girl of their dreams," men are far more likely than women to resort to drugs. A team of authors estimated, in an article published in the *Journal of the American Medical Association,* that as many as 500,000 high-school students use anabolic steroids.[106] The users frequently attempt to justify their behavior by saying that they want to improve their sports performance *and* to make themselves physically more attractive to the opposite sex. In short, horror stories about anorexia and the destructive effects of steroids on female athletes can be matched, story for story, by reports of male athletes whose bodies have been ravaged by substance abuse. The German heptathlete Birgit Dressel died after years of drug-enhanced sports achievement; male body-builders have also died when their pathetic lack of self-esteem drove them to compulsive, compensatory, steroid-assisted workouts.[107] Their stories seem equally tragic. What's bad for the goose is bad for the gander.

In the last analysis, however, one has to balance the depressing reports of exploitative, obsessive, compulsive, and addictive behaviors against the evidence—which is overwhelming—that sports are, for most men and women, a positive experience. They are a harmless distraction, a source of innocent amusement, a chance to socialize, an opportunity to free one's body from mundane constraint, an occasion to match one's physical prowess against that of others, and—sometimes—a form of ecstatic *jouissance.*[108] The historical record, the evidence of literature and the visual arts, the results of sociological and psychological investigations, the blatant manifestations of European and American popular culture, and the instinctive testimony of our senses all agree that men's and women's sports experiences can be and often have been suffused with a sense of erotic pleasure. The Greeks who gathered at Olympia for athletic festivals in honor of Zeus and Hera were candid about this pleasure. Perhaps, after two millennia of disavowal and denial, it is time for us to be as candid as they were.

Definitions

No important question about eros and sports can be posed, much less answered, without some definitions. Sports, in their ideal form, I define as I have in my previous work: autotelic physical contests.[1] They have intrinsic rather than extrinsic goals. They involve the body as well as the mind. They are competitions, not merely recreational activities. Needless to say, sports do not always occur in their ideal form. Major-league baseball, for instance, ceases to be a sport for players who are motivated *solely* by their salaries. Strict definition enables us to perceive and to evaluate such lamentable divergences from the ideal. Mine is obviously not the only possible definition of sports, but it is the one that I have found most useful. Within my admittedly abstract definitional frame, there is room for a myriad of different sports, each the product of its time, place, and cultural milieu.

Eros is a much more problematic concept. If one defines the term very broadly, as Freud did, eros becomes much more than a mere desire for sexual intercourse. In *Beyond the Pleasure Principle*

(1920), the "sex drive" ("*Sexualtrieb*") appears as "all-encompassing eros."[2] In *Group Psychology and the Analysis of the Ego* (1921), eros is the mighty force that "holds all the world together."[3] Eros is very similar, as Freud himself noted, to Arthur Schopenhauer's concept of the will to live.[4] When civilized society, internalized as the Super-Ego, blocks the path between initial desire and final fulfillment, erotic energy is either repressed or redirected (i.e., "sublimated") into other forms of expression. For Freud, art was the most interesting form of sublimation, but at least a few of his followers have written about sports as sublimated eros.

Freud may have introduced the notion of a "death drive" ("*Todestrieb*") in *Beyond the Pleasure Principle* in order to deflect the criticism that his increasingly expansive conception of eros left little room for any other drive. Georges Bataille, the influential author of *L'Érotisme* (1957) and *Les Larmes d'éros* (1965), trumps Freud by defining eros so broadly that it encompasses death as well as life. For Bataille, eros is the product of a universal human desire to escape the anxious solitude of the embodied self's "discontinuity" and briefly to experience the "continuity" lost at the moment of birth and recovered at the moment of death. Christoph Wulf offers a reasonably lucid gloss of Bataille's complicated argument: "As death is the [final] dissolution of the discontinuity of Being into the continuity for which it longs, the eroticism of the body is its demand to overcome its discontinuity in the [temporary] ecstasy of sexuality."[5] Eros can be observed, according to Bataille, not only in the Dionysian orgies depicted on Greek vases and in the ecstatic mysticism of Bernini's Saint Theresa but also in the human sacrifices of Aztec religion and in the act of murder lovingly described by the Marquis de Sade. In support of his assertions, Bataille cites the French idiom that refers to sexual orgasm as *la petite mort*. He might also have cited Freud's *The Ego and the Id* (1923) on the orgasm's resemblance to death; both reduce the organism's level of excitation (the latter rather drastically).[6] It is sufficient for my purposes to define eros less expansively than

Bataille does and more in line with Freud's early speculations in the *Three Essays on Sexual Theory* (1905). By eros I mean simply the force or drive that begins with a sense of physical attraction to another person and concludes, ideally, with the consummation of sexual union. It is important to understand the word "attraction" in its literal sense—to attract is to pull toward (Latin: *ad* + *trahere*). To say that someone is attractive is to imply that one feels physically drawn toward that person. To make oneself attractive is therefore—consciously or unconsciously—to wish to attract.

In this narrower, more literal sense, "eros" is a synonym for what Freud referred to in the *Three Essays* as "libido." In fact, at the time that he wrote *Group Psychology and the Analysis of the Ego*, Freud thought of these two terms as more or less identical. He scornfully ridiculed those who timidly prefer the genteel Greek term "eros" to the more clinical expression "libido" and the ordinary German word "*Liebe*." "As for those who consider human sexuality . . . shameful and degrading, they are free to use the more delicate terms eros and the erotic."[7] Despite Freud's sarcasm, "eros" seems the best word to describe the sexual force that pulls one person toward another. "Libido" seems excessively clinical. Although I shall sometimes refer to love, that concept usually suggests too much spirituality.

How Does the Erotic
Differ from the Pornographic?

What I have called the erotic element in sports others have classified as pornography. Some readers may want these appended
thoughts on the difference between the erotic and the pornographic.

How can we deal with the alarming fact that some people take
Fanny Hill in their stride while others are outraged by the sexual
explicitness of *Romeo and Juliet*? One approach is to distinguish
between the erotic and the pornographic, but this is a difficult task
to perform because definitions of pornography vary. Some scholars
define pornography by its effects. Catherine A. MacKinnon, for
instance, sees it as a harmful act, an assault upon the women
depicted, and an instigation to misogynist violence. In her polemics
she obscures not only the important distinction between the production and the consumption of pornography but also the even
more important distinction between action and the representation
of action. The result is confusion.[1]

A second approach is to emphasize intentions rather than consequences. "Pornography," writes Rosalind Coward, "is an industry

of images aimed at sexual arousal."[2] To define pornography by intentionality—it is meant for no purpose other than the sexual arousal of its consumers—will not do because we have no way accurately to assess intentionality. What *were* D. H. Lawrence's intentions when he wrote *Lady Chatterley's Lover*?

A third approach stresses the integrity of the person, which pornography violates. Harry Brod has tried this definitional tack: "Erotica, as sexual art, expresses a self, whereas pornography, as a sexual commodity markets one."[3] To define pornography as words or images that treat a man or woman as other than a self seems, initially, to make sense, but this definition will not do either. The difficulty, aside from the fact that it too seems to reduce the question to economics (erotica for sale = pornography), is that it displaces rather than eliminates the uncertainty and reintroduces the problem of intentionality. Did Robert Mapplethorpe intend his photographs as an expression of the erotic self or did he violate the integrity of those whom he photographed in order to enrich himself as a purveyor of smut? A focus on content rather than on intentions fails to solve the problem of definition.

A number of social psychologists have attempted to operationalize the distinction between erotica and pornography by defining the latter as sexually stimulating materials that are physically violent.[4] In many contexts, this distinction between violent and nonviolent erotica is unquestionably important, but the Christian Coalition is not likely to be satisfied by images of naked men and women in consensual mutually enraptured nonviolent carnal embrace. Other social psychologists have combined the criteria of content and intentionality. Citing the Meese Commission (1986), they define pornography as "any material that is predominantly sexually explicit and intended primarily for the purpose of sexual arousal."[5] The difficulty here is that this approach may require us to categorize the Song of Solomon, Hindu temple statuary, and Ravel's *Bolero* as pornography. Similar problems arise when we ask about the erotic element in sports.

Since the search for objective criteria distinguishing the erotic from the pornographic has led to interminable haggles, ill will, legislative stalemate, split hairs, and a divided judiciary, the best way out of the definitional *cul de sac* seems to be the frank acceptance of subjectivity: if someone believes that the sexuality represented in a work of art (or embodied in an athletic performance) is morally or aesthetically objectionable, then the work (or performance) is— for that person—pornographic rather than erotic. It is "beyond the pale of socially acceptable representations of sexuality."[6] And no argument is likely to persuade him or her to the contrary or to dissuade legislatures from attempts at censorship.

1. Introduction: Candor, Euphemism, and Denial

1. James C. Whorton, *Crusaders for Fitness* (Princeton: Princeton University Press, 1982), pp. 318–19.
2. *Wesleyan Christian Advocate*: quoted by Andrew Doyle, " 'Foolish and Useless Sport': The Southern Evangelical Crusade against College Football" (unpublished paper, 1994). See also William R. Hogan, "Sin and Sports," *Motivations in Play, Games and Sports*, eds. Ralph Slovenko and James A. Knight (Springfield, Ill.: Charles C. Thomas, 1967), pp. 121–47.
3. Douglas Booth, "Swimming, Surfing and Surf-Lifesaving," *Sport in Australia*, eds. Wray Vamplew and Brian Stoddart (Cambridge: Cambridge University Press, 1994), pp. 236–38.
4. Jennifer Hargreaves, *Sporting Females* (London: Routledge, 1994), pp. 128–29.
5. Villeneuve: quoted in Jean Harvey, "Sport and the Quebec Clergy, 1930–1960," *Not Just a Game*, eds. Jean Harvey and Hart Cantelon (Ottawa: University of Ottawa Press, 1988), p. 74. See also Jan Tolleneer, "Die Belgische Katholieke Turnbond," *Voor Lichaam &*

Geest, eds. Mark D'hoker, Roland Renson, and Jan Tolleneer (Leuven: Universitaire Pers, 1994), pp. 130–31.

6. Sigrid Block, *Frauen und Mädchen in der Arbeitersportbewegung* (Münster: LIT-Verlag, 1987), p. 333.

7. Gertrud Pfister, "Demands, Realities and Ambivalences—Women in the Proletarian Sports Movement in Germany (1893–1933), *Women in Sport and Physical Activity Journal*, 3(2) (Fall 1994): 53.

8. Franz Blei, "Wandlung der Oberfläche": quoted in Frank Becker, *Amerikanismus in Weimar* (Wiesbaden: Deutscher UniversitätsVerlag, 1993), pp. 320–21.

9. Richard Mandell, *The Olympics of 1972* (Chapel Hill: University of North Carolina Press, 1991), p. 123.

10. Gregory L. White, Sanford Fishbein, and Jeffrey Rutstein, "Passionate Love and the Misattribution of Arousal," *Journal of Personality and Social Psychology*, 41 (1981): 56–62; James B. Allen, et al., "Arousal and Attraction," *Journal of Personality and Social Psychology*, 57 (1989): 261–70. The effects of sexual intercourse on athletic *performance* have occasionally been studied; see April Carlin, "Athletic Performance and Sexuality," *Modern Athlete and Coach*, 32(3) (1994): 34–36.

11. Donald Sabo and Michael A. Messner, "Whose Body Is This?" *Women in Sport*, ed. Greta L. Cohen (London: Sage, 1993), pp. 18, 22. My disagreement on this point implies no lack of respect for the important work done by Sabo and Messner.

12. Elliott J. Gorn and Michael Oriard, "Taking Sports Seriously," *Chronicle of Higher Education*, March 24, 1995.

13. Margaret Walters, *The Nude Male* (New York: Paddington Press, 1978), p. 14.

14. Ulrika Prokop, *Soziologie der Olympischen Spiele* (Munich: Hanser Verlag, 1971), p. 21.

15. Christine Kulke, "Emanzipation oder gleiches Recht auf 'Trimm Dich'?" *Sport in der Klassengesellschaft*, ed. Gerhard Vinnai (Munich: Fischer, 1972), p. 101.

16. Nancy Theberge, "Sport and Women's Empowerment," *Women's Studies International Forum*, 10(4) (1987): 389.

17. Coubertin: quoted in Richard D. Mandell, *The First Modern Olympics* (Berkeley: University of California Press, 1976), p. 69.

18. Alphonso Lingis, *Foreign Bodies* (New York: Routledge, 1994), p. 128.

19. Christian Messenger, "The Inscription of Women in American Sports Fictional Narrative," *Heldenmythen und Körperqualen*, ed. Nanda Fischer (Clausthal-Zellerfeld: DVS, 1989), p. 83.

20. David M. Halperin, *One Hundred Years of Homosexuality* (New York: Routledge, 1990), p. 9.

21. Thomas Laqueur, *Making Sex: Body and Gender from the Greeks to Freud* (Cambridge: Harvard University Press, 1990), p. 16.

22. Sander L. Gilman, *Sexuality* (New York: John Wiley & Sons, 1989), p. 16. Gilman is a true polymath whose work combines the histories of science, art, and literature.

23. Chris Schilling, *The Body and Social Theory* (London: Sage Publications, 1993), p. 11.

24. Robin Tolmach Lakoff and Raquel L. Scherr, *Face Value: The Politics of Beauty* (London: Routledge & Kegan Paul, 1984), p. 64.

25. April Fallon, "Culture in the Mirror: Sociocultural Determinants of Body Image," *Body Image*, eds. Thomas F. Cash and Thomas Pruzinsky (New York: Guilford Press, 1990), p. 82; see also Allan Mazur, "U.S. Trends in Feminine Beauty and Overadaptation," *Journal of Sex Research*, 22(3) (August 1986): 283.

26. Mark Elvin, "Tales of *Shen* and *Xin*: Body-Person and Heart-Mind in China during the Last 150 Years," *Fragments for a History of the Human Body*, eds. Michel Feher, Ramona Naddaff, and Nadia Tazi, 3 vols. (New York: Zone, 1989), 2:267.

27. Kenneth R. Dutton, *The Perfectible Body* (New York: Continuum, 1995), p. 30.

28. Dolf Zillmann, *Connections between Sex and Aggression* (Hillsdale, New Jersey: Lawrence Erlbaum, 1984).

29. L. M. Bartoshuk and G. K. Beauchamp, "Chemical Senses," *Annual Review of Psychology*, 45 (1994): 419–49.

30. Margaret Morse, "Artemis Aging," *Discourse*, 10(1) (Fall–Winter 1987): 33.

31. On the epistemological difficulties to which I allude, see Richard Rorty, *Philosophy and the Mirror of Nature* (Princeton: Princeton University Press, 1979).

2. *Antiquity*

1. The three volumes of a massively comprehensive history of the body,
    which includes countless discussions of sexuality, have hardly a word
    about sports. See *Fragments for a History of the Human Body*, eds.
    Michel Feher, Ramona Naddaff, and Nadia Taxi, 3 vols. (New York:
    Zone, 1989). *The Body Reader*, a collection of anthropological writing
    edited by Ted Polhemus (New York: Pantheon, 1978), was similarly
    silent.
2. Arthur Brittan, *Masculinity and Power* (Oxford: Basil Blackwell,
    1989), p. 99.
3. I have resisted the temptation to explore the anthropological argu-
    ment for a ubiquitous consensus on the nature of masculinity. See
    David Gilmore, *Manhood in the Making* (New Haven: Yale
    University Press, 1990).
4. David Sansone, *Greek Athletics and the Genesis of Sport* (Berkeley:
    University of California Press, 1988).
5. Nicole Loraux, "Herakles: The Super-Male and the Feminine," *Before
    Sexuality: the Construction of Erotic Experience in the Ancient
    Greek World*, eds. David M. Halperin, John J. Winkler and Froma I.
    Zeitlin (Princeton: Princeton University Press, 1990), p. 31. The most
    accessible acount of the origins of the Olympic Games is Ludwig
    Drees, *Olympia*, trans. Gerald Onn (New York: Praeger, 1968), pp.
    7–38; see also Ludwig Deubner, *Kult und Spiel im alten Olympia*
    (Leipzig: Verlag von Heinrich Keller, 1936); Hans-Volkmar
    Herrmann, *Olympia: Heiligtum und Wettkampfstätte* (Munich:
    Hirmer Verlag, 1972), pp. 7–59; Ulrich Sinn, "Olympia," *Nikephoros*,
    4 (1991): 31–54; Benny Josef Peiser, *Das dunkle Zeitalter Olympias*
    (Frankfurt: Peter Lang, 1993).
6. Plato, *The Dialogues* [*Laws* 832–33], trans. Benjamin Jowett, 2 vols.
    (New York: Random House, 1937), 2:582.
7. Thomas Yiannakis, "The 'Oplitidromia' (or 'Armour Bearing Race')
    of Ancient Greeks . . . ," *Canadian Journal of History of Sport*, 25(2)
    (December 1994): 37.
8. K. J. Dover, *Greek Homosexuality* (Cambridge: Harvard University
    Press, 1978), p. 70. If Aristophanes was a reliable spokesman for pop-
    ular opinion, this configuration remained the ideal in 423 B.C.; see

The Clouds, trans. William Arrowsmith (Ann Arbor: University of Michigan Press, 1962), p. 75.

9. Mario Perniola, "Between Clothing and Nudity," *Fragments for a History of the Human Body*, 2:243.

10. Matthew W. Dickie, "Callisthenics in the Greek and Roman Gymnasium," *Nikephoros*, 6 (1993): 105–51.

11. Margaret Walters, *The Nude Male* (New York: Paddington Press, 1978), p. 39.

12. Dickie, "Callisthenics in the Greek and Roman Gymnasium," p. 149.

13. Ibid., p. 106. The term comes from *palaestra* ("wrestling hall").

14. Dover, *Greek Homosexuality*, pp. 54–55. See also John Boardman and Eugenio LaRocca, *Eros in Greece* (New York: Erotic Art Book Society, 1975), p. 42; Rosalind Miles, *The Rites of Man* (London: Grafton Books, 1991), p. 146.

15. Stephen G. Miller, "The Stadium at Nemea and the Nemean Games," *Proceedings of an International Symposium on the Olympic Games*, eds. William Coulson and Helmut Kyrieleis (Athens: Deutsches Archäologisches Institut, 1992), p. 85; Charlotte Roueché, *Performers and Partisans* (London: Society for the Promotion of Roman Studies, 1993), p. 107.

16. Eva C. Keuls, *The Reign of the Phallus: Sexual Politics in Ancient Athens*, revised edition (Berkeley: University of California Press, 1993), p. 284.

17. Northrop Frye, *The Secular Scripture* (Cambridge: Harvard University Press, 1976), p. 104.

18. Alain Schnapp, "Eros the Hunter," *City of Images*, ed. Claude Bérard, trans. Deborah Lyons (Princeton: Princeton University Press, 1989), p. 71.

19. Aristophanes, *Peace* [762–63], trans. Alan H. Sommerstein (Chicago: Bolchazy-Carducci, 1985), p. 77.

20. Aeschines, *Speeches*, trans. Charles Darwin Adams (London: Heinemann, 1919), p. 109.

21. Theognis, *Elegies* [1335–36], trans. Dorothea Wender (Harmondsworth: Penguin Books, 1973), p. 145.

22. For a reasonably up-to-date introduction to the debate, see David M. Halperin, "Why Is Diotima a Woman? Platonic *Eros* and the

Figuration of Gender," *Before Sexuality*, pp. 257–308. See also John J. Winkler, *The Constraints of Desire* (London: Routledge, 1990).

23. Plato, *Dialogues* [*Phaedrus* 255], 1:259.

24. Ibid [*Charmides* 154–55], 1:4–5.

25. Sigmund Freud, *Drei Abhandlungen zur Sexualtheorie* [1920], *Werkausgabe*, eds. Anna Freud and Ilse Grubrich-Simitis (Frankfurt: Fischer, 1978), 1: 238.

26. Freud, *Massenpsychologie und Ich-Analyse* (1921), *Werkausgabe*, 2:443.

27. In addition to the two references just given, see *Jenseits des Lustprinzips*, (1920), "Die Widerstände gegen die Psychoanalyse" (1925), and "Warum Krieg?" (1932) (*Werkausgabe*, 1:221–22; 2:56, 2:489).

28. Plato, *Dialogues* [*Republic* 217], 1:340.

29. Aristophanes, *Peace*, [894–905], p. 89. These lines, which I have slightly revised, can be compared to the comic scene in Robert Coover's *Universal Baseball Association* (New York: Random House, 1968), where sexual intercourse between Henry Waugh and "a neighborhood B-girl named Hettie" (p. 21) is described at some length as if it were a baseball game.

30. Longus, *Daphnis and Chloe* [3.19], trans. George Thornley and J. M. Edmonds (London: William Heinemann, 1916), p. 157.

31. Amy Richlin, *The Garden of Priapus* (New Haven: Yale University Press, 1983), p. 50. Since the marathon is a modern race, Richlin's translation is clever but anachronistic. Translated literally, *Kypridos dolichon* is "the Cyprian's twelve-lap footrace." (Aphrodite was born from the sea near Cyprus.)

32. K. J. Dover, "Classical Greek Attitudes to Sexual Behaviour," *Women in the Ancient World*, eds. John Peradotto and J. P. Sullivan (Albany: State University of New York Press, 1984), p. 152.

33. H. A. Harris, *Greek Athletes and Athletics* (Bloomington: Indiana University Press, 1967), p. 28; see also Waldo E. Sweet, *Sport and Recreation in Ancient Greece* (New York: Oxford University Press, 1987), p. 210.

34. *Pindar's Victory Songs* [*Pythian* 10:54–60], trans. Frank J. Nisetich (Baltimore: Johns Hopkins University Press, 1980), p. 218. I have altered the translator's spacing of the lines.

35. Xenophon, *Minor Works*, trans. J. S. Watson (London: Henry G. Bohn, 1857), pp. 150, 188.

36. Richlin, *Garden of Priapus*, p. 37.

37. Walters, *The Nude Male*, p. 35. See also Aline Rousselle, *Porneia: On Desire and the Body in Antiquity*, trans. Felica Pheasant (Oxford: Basil Blackwell, 1988), p. 2: "All our information about the men and women of antiquity comes from male sources."

38. Gilmore, *Manhood in the Making*, pp. 89–91.

39. David D. Gilmore, "The Beauty of the Beast," *The Good Body*, eds. Mary G. Winkler and Letha B. Cole (New Haven: Yale University Press, 1994), p. 202.

40. Homer, *The Odyssey* [8:20–23, 455–59], trans. Richmond Lattimore (New York: Harper, 1967), pp. 121, 133.

41. Plato, *Dialogues* [*Republic* 458, 461], 1:720, 723.

42. Ibid [*Laws* 835, 839], 2:585, 589. On the ancient assumption that athletes should be abstinent, see Wilfred Fiedler, "Sexuelle Enthaltsamkeit Griechischer Athleten und Ihre Medizinische Begründung," *Stadion*, 11(2) (1985): 137–75.

43. Theocritus: quoted in Peter Bing and Rip Cohen, *Games of Venus* (New York: Routledge, 1991), pp. 150, 152–53, 155.

44. Claude Bérard, "The Order of Women," *City of Images*, p. 92. The vase is reproduced in color on p. 94, fig.127.

45. Claude Bérard, "L'impossible femme athlète," *Annali*, 8 (1986): 197.

46. Dover, *Greek Homosexuality*, p. 70.

47. Walters, *The Nude Male*, p. 36.

48. Françoise Frontisi-Ducroux and François Lissarrague, "From Ambiguity to Ambivalence: A Dionysiac Excursion through the 'Anakreontic' Vases," *Before Sexuality*, p. 217, n. 34.

49. Lilly Kahil, "L'Artémis de Brauron: Rites et Mystère," *Antike Kunst*, 20 (1977): 97. For other contributions to the scholarly debate, see Lilly Kahil, "Mythological Repertoire of Brauron," *Ancient Greek Art and Iconography*, ed. Warren Moon (Madison: University of Wisconsin Press, 1983), pp. 231–44; Erika Simon, *Festivals of Attica* (Madison: University of Wisconsin Press, 1983), pp. 83–88; Paula Perlman, "Plato Laws 833c-834d and the Bears of Brauron," *Greek, Roman and Byzantine Studies* 24 (1983): 24:123; Scanlon, "The

Footrace of the Heraia at Olympia," *Ancient World,* 9(3–4) (1984): 77–90; Giampiera Arrigoni, "Donne e Sport nel Mundo Greco," *Le Donne in Grecia,* ed. Giampiera Arrigoni (Bari: Editori Laterza, 1985), pp. 101–5; Pierre Vidal-Naquet, *The Black Hunter,* trans. Andrew Szegedy-Maszak (Baltimore: Johns Hopkins University Press, 1986), p. 146; Thomas F. Scanlon, "Virgineum Gymnasium: Spartan Females and Early Greek Athletes," *The Archaeology of the Olympics,* ed. Wendy J. Raschke (Madison: University of Wisconsin Press, 1988), pp. 185–216; Christiane Souvinou-Inwood, *Studies in Girls' Transitions* (Athens: Kardamitsu, 1988), pp. 15–105; Steven H. Lonsdale, *Dance and Ritual Play in Greek Religion* (Baltimore: Johns Hopkins University Press, 1993), pp. 171–93.

50. Kahil, "L'Artémis de Brauron," p. 91.

51. Pausanias, *Description of Greece,* trans. W. H. S. Jones, 4 vols. (London: William Heinemann, 1918–35), 2:473.

52. Claude Calame, *Les Choeurs de jeunes filles en Grèce archaïque,* 2 vols. (Rome: Edizione dell'Ateneo e Bizzarri, 1977), 2:45–133.

53. Arrigoni, "Donne e Sport nel Mundo Greco," p. 83; Scanlon, "The Footrace of the Heraia at Olympia," p. 90; see also Scanlon, "Virgineum Gymnasium," p. 201.

54. And his admiration, speculates I. F. Stone, was one reason why the Athenians treated Socrates as harshly as they did; see I. F. Stone, *The Trial of Socrates* (Boston: Little, Brown, 1988).

55. Xenophon, *Constitution of the Spartans* [I.4], trans. H. G. Dakyns, *The Greek Historians,* ed. F. R. B. Godolphin, 2 vols. (New York: Random House, 1942), 2: 658–59.

56. Plutarch, *Lives,* trans. John Dryden and Arthur Hugh Clough (New York: Random House, 1932), pp. 59–60. In line with modern scholarship, I have substituted "discus" and "javelin" for "quoit" and "dart."

57. Euripides, *Andromache* [595–600], trans. John Frederick Nims, *The Complete Greek Tragedies,* eds. David Grene and Richmond Lattimore, 4 vols. (Chicago: University of Chicago Press, 1959), 3:582.

58. Plutarch's *Lives,* p. 60. The reference to Plato is presumably to the passage in *The Republic,* discussed above, where Socrates and Glaucon agree that "coeducational" gymnastics and other intimate interactions of men and women should lead "by necessity" to matrimony.

59. Arrigoni, "Donne e Sport nel Mundo Greco," p. 66.
60. Propertius, *The Poems of Propertius* [3.14], trans. John Warden (Indianapolis: Bobbs-Merrill, 1972), pp. 166–67. In another poem, Propertius describes how Atalanta's lover "brought that swift-footed girl to heel" (p. 3). On Propertius and other Latin love poets, see R. O. A. M. Lyne, *The Latin Love Poets* (Oxford: Clarendon Press, 1980).
61. Martin Dolch, "Wettkampf, Wasserrevue oder diätetische Übungen?" *Nikephoros*, 5 (1992): 163.
62. Michael Hofmann and James Lasdun, eds., *After Ovid* (New York: Farrar, Straus, 1994), pp. 250–51. The translation is by Ted Hughes. The swallows and swifts are his additions; otherwise, he is close to the original.
63. Hugh Lee, "Athletics and the Bikini Girls from Piazza Armerina," *Stadion* 10 (1984): 45–76; Dolch, "Wettkampf, Wasserrevue oder diätetische Übungen?" pp. 53–92.
64. Juvenal, *Satires*, trans. Rolfe Humphries (Bloomington: Indiana University Press, 1958), pp. 72–73.
65. Carlin A. Barton, *The Sorrows of the Ancient Romans* (Princeton: Princeton University Press, 1993), p. 47.
66. Ovid, *The Art of Love*, trans. Rolfe Humphries (Bloomington: Indiana University Press, 1957), p. 110. For the sake of alliteration, Humphries substituted "Cupid" for "Venus."
67. Barton, *The Sorrows of the Ancient Romans*, p. 47.
68. Arthur Maria Rabenalt, *Mimus Eroticus: Die erotische Schauszenik in der antiken Welt*, 5 vols. (Hamburg: Verlag für Kulturforschung, 1965–67), 1:374.
69. Keith Hopkins, *Death and Renewal* (Cambridge: Cambridge University Press, 1983), p. 22.
70. Barton, *The Sorrows of the Ancient Romans*, p. 48.
71. Petronius, *The Satyricon*, trans. William Arrowsmith (Ann Arbor: University of Michigan Press, 1959), p. 153.
72. Barton, *The Sorrows of the Ancient Romans*, p. 81
73. Juvenal, *Satires*, pp. 66–67.
74. J. P. V. D. Balsdon, *Life and Leisure in Ancient Rome* (London: Bodley Head, 1969), p. 253.

75. Apuleius, *Metamorphoses*, ed. and trans. J. Arthur Hanson, 2 vols. (Cambridge: Harvard University Press, 1989), 1:89.

76. Dickie, "Callisthenics in the Greek and Roman Gymnasium," p. 109.

77. Richlin, *Garden of Priapus*, p. 44; see also Aline Rousselle, "Personal Status and Sexual Practice in the Roman Empire," *Fragments for a History of the Human Body*, 3:313.

78. On the "Blues" and the "Greens," see Alan Cameron, *Circus Factions: Blues and Greens at Rome and Byzantium* (Oxford: Clarendon Press, 1976).

79. Alan Cameron, *Porphyrius the Charioteer* (Oxford: Clarendon Press, 1973), p. 251.

80. Eric Alliez and Michel Feher, "Reflections of a Soul," *Fragments for a History of the Human Body*, 2:48.

81. Augustine, *Confessions*, trans. E. B. Pusey (London: J. M. Dent, 1907), pp. 106–07.

82. Peter Brown, "Bodies and Minds: Sexuality and Renunciation in Early Christianity," *Before Sexuality*, p. 483.

83. Rousselle, *Porneia*, p. 152.

84. Clement of Alexandria, *Stromateis*, trans. John Ferguson (Washington: Catholic University of America, 1991), p. 2391. Modern attempts to absolve early Christianity from the taint of extreme hostility to the body are not persuasive; see Alois Koch, *Die Leibesübungen im Urteil der antiken und frühchristlichen Anthropologie* (Schorndorf: Karl Hofmann, 1965).

85. Peter Brown, *The Body and Society: Men, Women and Sexual Renunciation in Early Christianity* (New York: Columbia University Press, 1988), pp. 437–38.

3. From the Middle Ages to the Renaissance

1. Walters, *The Nude Male*, p. 74; illustration p. 87.

2. Gill Saunders, *The Nude* (New York: Harper, 1989), p. 71.

3. Bernard Rudofsky, *The Unfashionable Human Body* (Garden City: Doubleday, 1971), p. 154; see also Walters, *The Nude Male*, p. 82.

4. Shulamith Shahar, "The Old Body in Medieval Culture," *Framing Medieval Bodies*, eds. Sarah Kay and Miri Rubin (Manchester: University of Manchester Press, 1994), p. 178.

5. Jacques de Vitry: quoted in Shulamith Shahar, *The Fourth Estate*, trans. Chaya Galai (London: Methuen, 1983), p. 59; see also Brenda Boilton, "Vitae Matrum," *Medieval Women*, ed. Derek Baker (Oxford: Basil Blackwell, 1978), pp. 253–73; Caroline Walker Bynum, *Holy Feast and Holy Fast* (Berkeley: University of California Press, 1987).

6. Michael Camille, "The Image and the Self," *Framing Medieval Bodies*, p. 78. This assessment seems sounder than Kenneth Clark's reference to the figure as "a maiden of confident virtue"; see *The Nude* (New York: Bollingen Foundation, 1956), p. 314 and plate 252).

7. Georges Duby, *Les Trois ordres* (Paris: Gallimard, 1978).

8. Jo Ann McNamara, "The *Herrenfrage*: The Restructuring of the Gender System, 1050–1150," *Medieval Masculinities*, ed. Clare A. Lees (Minneapolis: University of Minnesota Press, 1994), p. 3.

9. Josef Fleckenstein, "Das Turnier als höfisches Fest im hochmittelalterlichen Deutschland," *Das ritterliche Turnier im Mittelalter*, ed. Josef Fleckenstein (Göttingen: Vandenhoek & Ruprecht, 1985), p. 246; see also, in the same volume, William Henry Jackson, "Das Turnier in der deutschen Dichtung des Mittelalters," pp. 257–95.

10. Max Weber, *Gesammelte Aufsätze zur Religionssoziologie*, 3 vols. (Tübingen: J. C. B. Mohr, 1920), 1:559.

11. Louise Olga Fradenburg, *City, Marriage, Tournament* (Madison: University of Wisconsin Press, 1991), pp. 212, 223.

12. Sydney Anglo, *The Great Tournament Roll of Westminster*, 2 vols. (Oxford: Clarendon Press, 1968), 1:29.

13. Jean-Michel Mehl, "Jeux, sports et divertissements au Moyen Age et à la Renaissance," *Jeux, sports et divertissements au Moyen Age et à l'Age Classique*, ed. Jean-Michel Mehl (Paris: Éditions du Comité des Travaux historiques et scientifiques, 1993), p. 21; see also my *Sports Spectators* (New York: Columbia University Press, 1986), pp. 35–47.

14. *Ulrich von Liechtenstein's "Service of Ladies,"* trans. J. W. Thomas (Chapel Hill: University of North Carolina Press, 1969).

15. These illustrations are reproduced in Lilian M. C. Randall's *Images in the Margins of Gothic Manuscripts* (Berkeley: University of California Press, 1966).

16. For examples, see Francis P. Magoun, *History of Football from the Beginnings to 1891* (Bochum-Langendreer: Kölner Anglistische Studien, 1938).

17. J. J. Jusserand, *Les Sports et jeux d'exercice dans l'ancienne France* (Paris: Plon, 1901), p. 282.

18. René Germain, "Jeux et divertissements dans le centre de la France à la fin du Moyen Age," *Jeux, sports et divertissements*, p. 50.

19. Jacques Rossiaud, *Medieval Prostitution*, trans. Lydia G. Cochrane (Oxford: Basil Blackwell, 1988), pp. 68–69.

20. Werner Körbs, *Vom Sinn der Leibesübungen zur Zeit der italienischen Renaissance*, ed. Wolfgang Decker (1938; Hildesheim: Weidmann, 1988), pp. 17–18; Klaus Zieschang, *Vom Schützenfest zum Turnfest* (Ahrensburg: Czwalina, 1977), pp. 82–83; F. K. Mathys, *Spiel und Sport im alten Basel* (Basel: Cratander, 1954), p. 19.

21. Sir Philip Sidney, "Dialogue between Two Shepherds": quoted in Percy M. Young, *A History of British Football* (London: Arrow Books, 1973), p. 74.

22. Walter Schaufelberger, *Der Wettkampf in der alten Eidgenossenschaft* (Basel: Paul Haupt, 1972), p. 90.

23. Silver: quoted in Christina Hole, *English Sports and Pastimes* (London: B. T. Batsford, 1949), p. 68.

24. On the situation in Venice, where gymnastics schools and pastry shops were also favored for homosexual trysts, see Guido Ruggiero, *The Boundaries of Eros* (New York: Oxford University Press, 1985), pp. 138–39, 159.

25. Brown: quoted in Maria Kloeren, *Sport und Rekord* (Leipzig: Tauchnitz, 1935), pp. 42–43.

26. Gilbert Andrieu, "L'Escrime et le duel à la fin du xixème siècle," *Actas del Congreso Internacional ISHPES 1991* (Madrid: Instituto Nacional de Educación Fisica de Madrid, 1993), p. 36.

27. Henning Eichberg, *Leistung, Spannung, Geschwindigkeit* (Stuttgart: Klett-Cotta, 1978), p. 66.

28. Baldisarre Castiglione, *The Book of the Courtier*, trans. Charles S. Singleton (1528; Garden City: Anchor Books, 1959), pp. 32, 36–37, 99–100. Not in that order. See also David Kuchta, "The Semiotics of Masculinity in Renaissance England," *Sexuality and Gender in Early*

Modern Europe, ed. James Grantham Turner (Cambridge: Cambridge University Press, 1993), pp. 233–46.

29. Elyot: quoted in Young, *A History of British Football*, p. 48.
30. De' Bardi: quoted in William Heywood, *Palio and Ponte* (1904; New York: Hacker Art Books, 1969), pp. 166–67; see also Theodor Mommsen, "Football in Renaissance Florence," *Yale University Library Gazette*, 16 (1941): 14–19.
31. Walters, *The Nude Male*, p. 102.
32. Ibid., p. 117.
33. Edward Lucie-Smith, *Sexuality in Western Art* (London: Thames & Hudson, 1991), p. 84.
34. Clark, *The Nude*, pp. 50–51, 56–59, 244.
35. Georges Bataille, *Les Larmes d'éros* (Paris: Jean-Jacques Pauvert, 1964), pp. 124–25.
36. Martin Warnke, *Peter Paul Rubens* (Woodbury, New York: Barron's Educational Series, 1980), pp. 176–77.
37. Clark, *The Nude*, p. 87.

4. Modern Times

1. Paul Gurk, *Berlin* (1925; Berlin, 1980), p. 303.
2. West: quoted in David D. Gilmore, "The Beauty of the Beast," *The Good Body*, eds. Mary G. Winkler and Letha B. Cole (New Haven: Yale University Press, 1994), p. 205.
3. Walters, *The Nude Male*, p. 208.
4. Johann Wolfgang Goethe, *Italienische Reise* (Munich: Hirmer Verlag, n.d.), pp. 40–41.
5. Robert M. Isherwood, *Farce and Fantasy* (New York: Oxford University Press, 1986), p. 39.
6. Pierce Egan, *Boxiana*, 5 vols. (London: Sherwood, Neely and Jones, 1829), 1:58.
7. William Rufus Chetwood, *A General History of the Stage* (London: W. Owen, 1749), p. 60n.
8. Egan, *Boxiana*, 1:219–20. The best modern histories of eighteenth-century boxing are John Ford's *Prizefighting* (Newton Abbot: David and Charles, 1971) and Dennis Brailsford's *Bareknuckles* (Cambridge: Lutterworth Press, 1988).

9. Vincent Dowling: quoted in Ford, *Prizefighting*, p. 132; see also Carl Diem, *Lord Byron als Sportsman* (Cologne: Comel, 1950), p. 86; Leslie A. Marchand, *Byron*, 3 vols. (New York: Alfred A. Knopf, 1957), pp. 110, 150, 153, 156, 158, 443, 728.
10. Ford, *Prizefighting*, p. 10.
11. Ibid., p. 163.
12. Pierce Egan, *Fistiana* (London: William Clement, Jr., 1841), pp. 1–3, 6
13. Ford, *Prizefighting*, p. 118.
14. Zacharias Conrad von Uffenbach, *London in 1710*, trans. W. H. Quarrell and Margaret Mare (London: Faber & Faber, 1934), pp. 90–91.
15. Nogüe: quoted in Kloeren, *Sport und Rekord*, p. 61.
16. James Pellor Malcolm, *Anecdotes of the Manners and Customs of London During the Eighteenth Century*, 2nd ed., 2 vols. (London: Longman, Hurst, Rees & Orne, 1810).
17. William Hickey, *Memoirs*, ed. Alfred Spenser, 4 vols. (London: Hurst & Blackett, 1913–25), 1:82–83.
18. Robert W. Malcomson, *Popular Recreations in English Society, 1700–1850* (Cambridge: Cambridge University Press, 1973), p. 77.
19. Malcolm, *Anecdotes*, 2:183.
20. *Morning Advertiser*; quoted in Shirley Heather M. Reekie, "A History of Sport and Recreation for Women in Great Britain, 1700–1850" (Ph. D. dissertation, Ohio State University, 1982), p. 63.
21. The comparison to Sparta was noted by J. B. LeBlanc during a 1747 visit to England; see Kloeren, *Sport und Rekord*, p. 264.
22. For typical French comments, see Kloeren, *Sport und Rekord*, pp. 45, 56–57.
23. Michael S. Kimmel, "The Contemporary 'Crisis' of Masculinity in Historical Perspective," *The Making of Masculinities*, ed. Harry Brod (Boston: Allen & Unwin, 1987), p. 137.
24. Fred Davis, *Fashion, Culture, and Identity* (Chicago: University of Chicago Press, 1992), p. 38.
25. Of the illustrations in medical books, Ludmilla Jordanova writes, "Most of the erect models are male, displaying muscles contracting and relaxing in athletic poses." Female models are far more likely to be shown supine. See *Sexual Visions: Images of Gender in Science*

and Medicine Between the Eighteenth and the Twentieth Centuries (Madison: University of Wisconsin Press, 1989), p. 58; see also Londa Schiebinger, "Skeletons in the Closet: Illustrations of the Female Skeleton," *The Making of the Modern Body* eds. Catherine Gallagher and Thomas Laqueur (Berkeley: University of California Press, 1987), pp. 42–82; Thomas Laqueur, *Making Sex: Body and Gender from the Greeks to Freud* (Cambridge: Harvard University Press, 1990), pp. 142–48.

26. Elliott J. Gorn, " 'Gouge and Bite, Pull Hair and Scratch!' " *American Historical Review,* 90(1) (February 1985): 18–43.

27. In addition to Peter M. Stearns, *Be a Man!* (New York: Holmes and Meier, 1979), see Joseph L. Dubbert, *A Man's Place: Masculinity in Transition* (Englewood Cliffs: Prentice-Hall, 1979); E. Anthony Rotundo, *American Manhood: Transformations in Masculinity from the Revolution to the Modern Era* (New York: Basic Books, 1993).

28. The literature on this topic is immense. Among the classic works are Barbara Welter, *Dimity Convictions* (Athens: Ohio University Press, 1976); Gerda Lerner, *The Majority Finds Its Past* (New York: Oxford University Press, 1979); Carl N. Degler, *At Odds* (New York: Oxford University Press, 1980); Alice Kessler-Harris, *Out to Work* (New York: Oxford University Press, 1982); and Carroll Smith-Rosenberg, *Disorderly Conduct* (New York: Knopf, 1985).

29. George L. Mosse, *Nationalism and Sexuality: Respectability and Abnormal Sexuality in Modern Europe* (New York: Howard Fertig, 1985).

30. For demographic estimates of Victorian sexuality, see Michael Mason, *The Making of Victorian Sexuality* (New York: Oxford University Press, 1994).

31. Stearns, *Be a Man,* p. 65.

32. Ibid., p. 81. While women symbolized purity, they were nonetheless expected to respond sexually to their husbands' sexual moves and, despite the persistent myth to the contrary, they did. See Carl Degler, "What Ought to Be and What Was: Women's Sexuality in the Nineteenth Century," *American Historical Review,* 79(5) (December 1974): 1467–90; Peter Gay, *The Bourgeois Experience: Education of the Senses* (New York: Oxford University Press, 1984).

33. Patricia A. Vertinsky, *The Eternally Wounded Woman: Women, Exercise and Doctors in the Late Nineteenth Century* (Manchester: University of Manchester Press, 1990). For an attempt to modify what sometimes seems an exaggeration of the cult of debility, see my *Women's Sports*, pp. 85–105.

34. For a brief discussion of this "minority taste," see my *Women's Sports*, pp. 85–87.

35. Théophile Gautier, *Mademoiselle de Maupin* (1835; Eugène Fasquelles, 1927), p. 215.

36. Joris-Karl Huysmans, *A Rebours* (1884; Paris: Eugène Fasquelles, 1910), pp. 137–38.

37. Clark, *The Nude*, p. 220.

38. Roy McMullen, *Degas* (Boston: Houghton Mifflin, 1984), p. 105.

39. Norma Broude, "Degas's 'Misogyny,' " *Feminism in Art History*, eds. Norma Broude and Mary D. Garrard (New York: Harper, 1982), pp. 256–57. A minor artist, Emmanuel Croisé, also exhibited a painting entitled *Les Jeunes Filles de Sparte*.

40. The tradition continued into the twentieth century; Paul Manship's helical *Diana* (1925) was his masterpiece.

41. The poem and Homer's pictures appear in David Park Curry's *Winslow Homer: The Croquet Game* (New Haven: Yale University Art Gallery, 1984).

42. For a discussion of these and many other literary and artistic images, see Bram Dijkstra, *Idols of Perversity* (New York: Oxford University Press, 1986); Elisabeth Bronfen, *Over Her Dead Body: Death, Femininity and the Aesthetic* (New York: Routledge, 1992).

43. Jean Renoir, *Renoir* (Paris: Hachette, 1962), p. 95.

44. Stearns, *Be a Man!* p. 39,

45. Stan Gray, "Sharing the Shop Floor," *Beyond Patriarchy*, ed. Michael Kaufman (Toronto: Oxford University Press, 1987), p. 225.

46. Michael S. Kimmel, "Consuming Manhood," *The Male Body*, ed. Laurence Goldstein (Ann Arbor: University of Michigan Press, 1994), p. 112.

47. Ray Raphael, *The Men from the Boys* (Lincoln: University of Nebraska Press, 1988), p. 20.

48. Stearns, *Be a Man!*, p. 49.

49. Drury Sherrod, "The Bonds of Men," *The Making of Masculinities*, ed. Harry Brod (Boston: Allen & Unwin, 1987), pp. 213–39; Dorothy Hammond and Alta Jablow, "Gilgamesh and the Sundance Kid: The Myth of Male Friendship," *The Making of Masculinities*, pp. 241–58.

50. The Abolitionists, many of whom were clerics, were also exceptional in that they expressed among themselves a kind of David-and-Jonathan brotherhood; see Donald Yacovone, "Abolitionists and the 'Language of Fraternal Love,' " *Meanings for Manhood*, eds. Mark C. Carnes and Clyde Griffen (Chicago: University of Chicago Press, 1990), pp. 85–95.

51. Oliver Wendell Holmes, Sr., "The Autocrat of the Breakfast Table—Every Man His Own Boswell," *Atlantic Monthly*, 1 (May 1858): 881; Thomas Wentworth Higginson, "Gymnastics," *Atlantic Monthly*, 7 (March 1861): 283–302.

52. Oliver Wendell Holmes, Jr.: quoted by Edmund Wilson, *Patriotic Gore: Studies in the Literature of the American Civil War* (New York: Oxford University Press, 1962), p. 753.

53. Charles Francis Adams, Jr., *Autobiography* (Boston: Houghton Mifflin, 1916), p. 129.

54. Wanda Ellen Wakefield argues, not very convincingly, that not even warfare provided sufficient assurance of masculinity; the military establishment relied on sports to buck up its recruits; see "Playing to Win: Sports and the American Military" (unpublished dissertation, SUNY-Buffalo, 1995). See also Steven A. Riess, "Sport and the Redefinition of American Middle-Class Masculinity," *International Journal of the History of Sport*, 8(1) (1991):5–27.

55. Roosevelt, *The Strenuous Life* (New York: Century Co., 1901), p. 156.

56. My attempt at explanation is *Games and Empires* (New York: Columbia University Press, 1994).

57. Brittan, *Masculinity and Power* (Oxford: Basil Blackwell), p. 77.

58. For a survey of empirical data on this counter-intuitive claim, see Allen Guttmann, Introduction to Bero Rigauer, *Sport and Work*, trans. Allen Guttmann (New York: Columbia University Press, 1981), pp. vii–xxxiv.

59. Dubbert, *A Man's Place*, p. 187.

60. Roberta J. Park, "Biological Thought, Athletics, and the Formation of a 'Man of Character,' " *Manliness and Morality: Middle-Class Masculinity in Britain and America, 1800–1940,* eds. J. A. Mangan and James Walvin (New York: St. Martin's, 1987), p. 10.

61. Patricia Vertinsky, "The 'Racial' Body and the Anatomy of Difference," *Sport Science Review,* 4(1) (1995): 47; see also George L. Mosse, *Nationalism and Sexuality*; Michael Krüger, *Leibeserziehung im 19. Jahrhundert: Turnen für das Vaterland* (Schorndorf: Karl Hofmann, 1993).

62. Richard Holt, *Sport and Society in Modern France* (London: Macmillan, 1981); Pierre Arnaud and Jean Camy, eds., *La Naissance du mouvement sportif associatif en France* (Lyon: Presses universitaires de Lyon, 1986); Gilbert Andrieu et al. *Les Athlètes de la république* (Toulouse: Éditions Privat, 1987; Georges Vigarello, *Une Histoire culturelle du sport* (Paris: R. Laffont, 1988); Pierre Arnaud, *Le Militaire, l'écolier, le gymnaste* (Lyon: Presses universitaires de Lyon, 1991); Ronald Hubscher, Jean Durry, and Bernard Jeu, *Le Sport dans la société française* (Paris: Armand Colin, 1992).

63. Walters, *The Nude Male,* p. 238.

64. Ibid.

65. Darrel Sewell, *Thomas Eakins* (Philadelphia: Philadelphia Museum of Art, 1982), p. 33.

66. *Spirit of the Times,* September 17, 1842: cited by Elliott J. Gorn, *The Manly Art* (Ithaca: Cornell University Press, 1986), p. 74.

67. George Bernard Shaw, *Cashel Byron's Profession* (1886; Carbondale: Southern Illinois University Press, 1968), p. 37; Louis Hémon, *Battling Malone: Pugiliste* (Paris: Grasset, 1925), p. 251.

68. G. Stanley Hall, *Youth* (New York: D. Appleton, 1904), pp. 3, 78, 102–3.

69. Ruth E. Hartley, "Sex-Role Pressures and the Socialization of the Male Child," *Psychological Reports,* 5 (1959): 457–68; James S. Coleman, *The Adolescent Society* (New York: Free Press, 1961); D. Stanley Eitzen, "Sport and Social Status in American Public Secondary Education," *Review of Sport and Leisure,* 1 (1976): 139–55; Andrew W. Miracle, Jr., and C. Roger Rees, *Lessons of the Locker Room* (Amherst: Prometheus Books, 1994).

70. On the overwhelming importance of high-school football in Texas, see Douglas E. Foley, "The Great American Football Ritual," *Sociology of Sport Journal*, 7(2) (June 1990): 111–35; and H. G. Bissinger, *Friday Night Lights* (Reading: Addison-Wesley, 1990).

71. Geoff Winningham, *Rites of Fall* (Austin: University of Texas Press, 1979).

72. Arto Tiihonen, "Asthma—The Construction of the Masculine Body," *International Review of Sport Sociology*, 29(1) (1994): 55.

73. On the concept, see Harold Garfinkel, "Conditions of Successful Degradation Ceremonies," *American Journal of Sociology*, 61 (1956): 420–24.

74. Marion E. P. de Ras, *Körper, Eros und weibliche Kultur* (Pfaffenweiler: Centaurus, 1988); Thomas Alkemeyer and Alfred Richartz, "Inszenierte Körperträume," *Zeitschrift für Pädagogik*, 31 (1993): 77–90.

75. Alan Dundes, "Into the Endzone for a Touchdown," *Western Folklore*, 38 (1978): 75–88.

76. John Williams, Eric Dunning, and Patrick Murphy, *Hooligans Abroad* (London: Routledge and Kegan Paul, 1984), p. 157; Patrick Murphy, John Williams, and Eric Dunning, *Football on Trial* (London: Routledge, 1990), pp. 148–50.

77. Marcelo Marió Suárez-Orozco, "A Study of Argentine Soccer," *Journal of Psychoanalytic Anthropology*, 5(1) (Winter 1982): 17. On the French and Italian fans, see Christian Bromberger, *Le match de Football* (Paris: Editions de la Maison de l'Homme), 1995.

78. Jeffrey Richards, " 'Passing the Love of Women': Manly Love and Victorian Society," *Manliness and Morality*, p. 114. Antinous was Hadrian's young lover; the statue of Hermes was, of course, unearthed at Olympia and is exhibited there.

79. Walter Pater, *Plato and Platonism* (London: Macmillan, 1910), pp. 220–22.

80. Pater: quoted by Linda Dowling, *Hellenism and Homosexuality in Victorian Oxford* (Ithaca: Cornell University Press, 1994), p. 78.

81. Ibid., pp. 138–39.

82. Synthia S. Slowikowski, "Eros and Living Statuary Tableaux" (paper delivered to the North American Society for Sport History, 1992).

83. John Addington Symonds, *Memoirs*, ed. Phyllis Grosskurth (New York: Random House, 1984), p. 94; see also John Chandos, *Boys Together* (London: Hutchinson, 1984), pp. 301–19.
84. Cyril Connolly, quoted in Mosse, *Nationalism and Sexuality*, p. 85.
85. Cyril Connolly, *Enemies of Promise and Other Essays* (Garden City, N.Y.: Doubleday, 1960), p. 187.
86. Clive Dewey, " 'Socratic Teachers,' " *International Journal of the History of Sport*, 12(1) (April 1995): 53.
87. Experimental psychologists have in fact shown that there is a significant relationship between strenuous exercise and sexual arousal; see Gregory L. White, Sanford Fishbein, Jeffrey Rutstein, "Passionate Love and the Misattribution of Arousal," *Journal of Personality and Social Psychology*, 41 (1981): 56–62; James B. Allen, et al., "Arousal and Attraction," *Journal of Personality and Social Psychology*, 57 (1989): 261–70.
88. Klaus Theweleit, *Männerphantasien*, 2 vols. (Frankfurt: Verlag Roter Stern, 1977–78), 2:368.
89. Maurice Biriotti del Burgo, "Don't Stop the Carnival," *Giving the Game Away*, ed. Stephen Wagg (London: Leicester University Press, 1995), p. 66.
90. Alfonso Lingis, "Orchids and Muscles," *Journal of the Philosophy of Sport*, 13 (1986): 20.
91. Joyce Carol Oates, *On Boxing* (Garden City: Doubleday, 1987), pp. 9, 30.
92. Alan Lloyd, *The Great Prize Fight* (New York: Coward, McCann & Geoghegan, 1977), p. 155.
93. On Sullivan's life and times, see Michael T. Isenberg, *John L. Sullivan and His America* (Urbana: University of Illinois Press, 1988).
94. Bell Hooks, "Feminism Inside: Toward a Black Body Politic," *Black Male*, ed. Thelma Golden (New York: Whitney Museum of American Art, 1994), pp. 132–33. Of the many biographies of Johnson, the best is Randy Roberts, *Papa Jack* (New York: Free Press, 1983).
95. Norman Mailer, *The Fight* (Boston: Little, Brown, 1975), p. 3.

5. Erotic Athleticism and Popular Culture

1. Wray Vamplew, "Boxing," *Sport in Australia*, eds. Wray Vamplew and Brian Stoddart (Cambridge: Cambridge University Press, 1994), p. 41.

2. David L. Chapman, *Sandow the Magnificent* (Urbana: University of Illinois Press, 1994), pp. 59, 75.
3. Richard Coleman, *Paradise of Sport* (South Melbourne: Oxford University Press, 1995), p. 79.
4. Jan Todd, "Bernarr Macfadden: Reformer of the Feminine Form," *Journal of Sport History,* 14(1) (Spring 1987): 61–75. On the nineteenth-century German body-building culture that produced Sandow, see Bernd Wedemeyer, "Body-Building or Man in the Making," *International Journal of the History of Sport,* 11(3) (December 1994): 472–84.
5. *Minneapolis Journal:* quoted in Kevin Britz, "Of Football and Frontiers: The Meaning of Bronko Nagurski," *Journal of Sport History,* 20(2) (Summer 1993): 116.
6. Kenneth R. Dutton, *The Perfectible Body* (New York: Continuum, 1995), p. 138.
7. Albert: quoted in Donald J. Mrozek, "Sport in American Life," *Fitness in American Culture,* ed. Kathryn Grover (Amherst: University of Massachusetts Press, 1989), p. 39.
8. Mike Featherstone, "The Body in Consumer Culture," *The Body,* eds. Mike Featherstone, Mike Hepworth, and Bryan S. Turner (London: Sage, 1991), p. 180.
9. Viterbo: quoted in Françoise Laget, Serge Laget, and Jean-Paul Mazot, *Le Grand Livre du sport féminin* (Belleville-sur-Saône: SIGEFA, 1982), p. 112.
10. Valerie Steele, *Fashion and Eroticism* (New York: Oxford University Press, 1985), p. 5.
11. Anne Hollander, *Sex and Suits* (New York: Knopf, 1994), p. 136.
12. Susan K. Cahn, *Coming on Strong: Gender and Sexuality in Twentieth-Century Women's Sport* (New York: Free Press, 1994), pp. 47, 50.
13. Larry Engelmann, *The Goddess and the American Girl* (New York: Oxford University Press, 1988).
14. Cahn, *Coming on Strong,* p. 79.
15. Bill Cunningham, "The Colonel's Ladies," *Colliers* 97:28 (May 23, 1936): 60–62.
16. Mabel Lee, "Sports and Games," *Recreation* 23 (July 1929): 223. Lee was, however, by no means personally insensitive to the attractive-

ness of female athletes; see Nancy B. Bouchier and Marla Steiner, "The Politics of the Physical," *International Journal of the History of Sport*, 11(1) (April 1994): 10.

17. Ethel Bowers, "Giving the Girls a Chance," *Recreation* 26 (April 1932): 15–16.

18. Richard Fotheringham, *Sport in Australian Drama* (Cambridge: Cambridge University Press, 1992), p. 181.

19. Engelmann, *The Goddess and the American Girl*, pp. 299, 305.

20. John B.Kennedy, "Little Miss Poker Face," *Collier's* 78 (September 18, 1926): 10. Cahn observes in *Coming on Strong* that the reference to whiteness was an attempt to soften the shock of a visible triceps (p. 212).

21. *Variety*: quoted in Leslie Halliwell, *Film Guide*, 8th ed. John Walker (New York: HarperCollins, 1991), p. 1092.

22. Daniel Pedersen, " 'To Finish on a High,' " *Newsweek*, 123(8) (February 21, 1994): 47.

23. Yvonne Tasker, *Spectacular Bodies: Gender, Genre and the Action Cinema* (London: Routledge, 1993), p. 73. Among the athletes to appear on the screen in feature films were Jim Brown (*The Dirty Dozen*, 1967), O. J. Simpson (*Capricorn One*, 1978), Kareem Abdul-Jabbar (*Airplane*, 1980), Bruce Jenner (*Can't Stop the Music*, 1980), and Shaquille O'Neal (*Blue Chips*, 1993).

24. Jill Neimark, "The Beefcaking of America," *Psychology Today*, 27(6) (November–December 1994): 34–35. This ideal, however, seems to be more popular among men than among women.

25. Sam Fussell, "Bodybuilder Americanus," *The Male Body*, ed. Laurence Goldstein (Ann Arbor: University of Michigan Press, 1994), p. 43.

26. Molly Merryman, "Gazing at Artemis," *Women, Media and Sport*, ed. Pamela J. Creedon (London: Sage Publications, 1994), p. 310.

27. Tasker *Spectacular Bodies*, p. 3

28. Susan Bordo, *Unbearable Weight* (Berkeley: University of California Press, 1993), p. 103.

29. John Fiske, *Television Culture* (London: Routledge, 1989), p. 219.

30. Gert Hortleder and Gunter Gebauer, "Die künstlichen Paradiese des Sports," *Sport-Eros-Tod*, eds. Gert Hortleder and Gunter Gebauer (Frankfurt: Suhrkamp, 1986), p. 12.

31. Margaret Morse, "Sport on Television," *Regarding Television*, ed. E. A. Kaplan (Los Angeles: University Publications of America, 1983), p. 45.

32. Beverley Poynton and John Hartley, "Male-Gazing," *Television and Women's Culture*, ed. Mary Ellen Brown (London: Sage Publications, 1990), p. 150. Nick Trujillo, "Machines, Missiles, and Men," *Sociology of Sport Journal*, 12 (4) (1995): 417.

33. There is a fine sequence on Macfadden in Laurie Block's documentary film, *Fit: Episodes in the History of the Body* (1991), from which the quotation is taken.

34. Anne Honer, "Beschreibung einer Lebens-Welt—Zur Empirie des Bodybuilding," *Zeitschrift für Soziologie*, 14(2) (1985): 134.

35. Mike Featherstone, "The Body in Consumer Culture," *Theory, Culture and Society*, 1(2) (1982): 18.

36. Lyon: quoted in Charles Gaines and George Butler, "Iron Sisters," *Psychology Today*, 17:11 (November 1983): 67.

37. Luc Boltanski, "Les usages sociaux du corps," *Les Annales*, 26 (1971): 224, 227–28.

38. Tournier: quoted in Claude Bérard, "L'impossible femme athlète," *Annali*, 8 (1986): 195.

39. Jennifer Hargreaves, *Sporting Females* (London: Routledge, 1994), p. 161.

40. John Updike, "The Disposable Rocket," *The Male Body*, p. 9. On the fitness craze, see Benjamin G. Rader, "The Quest for Self-Sufficiency and the New Strenuosity," *Journal of Sport History*, 18(2) (Summer 1991): 255–66.

41. Heike Egger, " 'Sportswear': Zur Geschichte der Sportkleidung," *Stadion*, 18(1) (1992): 146.

42. Germaine Greer, *The Female Eunuch* (New York: McGraw-Hill, 1971), p. 202.

43. See Block's documentary film, *Fit* (1991).

44. Janet C. Harris, *Athletes and the American Hero Dilemma* (Champaign: Human Kinetics, 1994), p. 33.

45. Susan J. Douglas, *Where the Girls Are: Growing Up Female with the Mass Media* (New York: Times Books, 1994), p. 217.

46. "Coca-Cola: 'Parrainer, c'est avoir la foi,' " *Olympic Magazine*, 4 (November 1994): 28–31.

47. Owett: quoted by Barbara Mehlman, "Changing Shapes Change Attitudes as Women Define an Image of Themselves," *Madison Avenue*, 25 (June 1983): 69.

48. Quoted in Barry Glassner, *Bodies* (New York: Putnam, 1988), p. 25.

49. Chris Laidlaw, *Mud in Your Eye* (London: Pelham Books, 1973), p.58.

50. John Fiske, *Power Plays Power Works* (London: Verso, 1993), p. 87.

51. Frederick: quoted in Janice Kaplan, *Women and Sports* (New York: Viking Press, 1979), p. 77.

52. Trix Rosen, *Strong and Sexy* (New York: Delilah, 1983), p. 47.

53. Lynda Huey, *A Running Start: An Athlete, A Woman* (New York: Quadrangle Books, 1976), pp. 204, 209.

54. Joyner: quoted by Mariah Burton Nelson, *Are We Winning Yet?* (New York: Random House, 1991), p. 87.

55. Sharon R. Guthrie and Shirley Castelnuovo, "Elite Women Body-Builders: Models of Resistance or Compliance?" *Play and Culture*, 5 (1992): 405. This result was not entirely welcome because the researchers hoped for more dedication to "feminist care-of-the-self activities" (p. 407).

56. Quoted in Judith A. DiIorio, "Feminism, Gender, and the Ethnographic Study of Sport," *Arena Review*, 13(1) (May 1989): 53.

57. Nancy Midol and Gérard Broyer, "Toward an Anthropological Analysis of New Sport Cultures," *Sociology of Sport Journal*, 12(2) (1995): 209.

58. Mariah Burton Nelson, *The Stronger Women Get, the More Men Love Football* (New York: Harcourt, Brace, 1994), pp. 36–37.

59. Kenneth R. Dutton, *The Perfectible Body* (New York: Continuum, 1995), p. 277.

60. Terri Tirapelli: quoted in Rosen, *Strong and Sexy*, p. 17.

61. Laumann: quoted in Kevin Young and Philip White, "Sport, Physical Danger, and Injury," *Journal of Sport and Social Issues*, 19(1) (February 1995): 46.

62. Heather Clarke and Susan Gwynne-Timothy, *Stroke* (Toronto: James Lorimer, 1988), pp. xiii, 12, 17.

6. Eros Imagined

1. For studies of sports in literature, see Wiley Lee Umphlett, *The Sporting Myth and the American Experience* (Lewisburg, Penn.:

Bucknell University Press, 1975); Robert J. Higgs, *Laurel and Thorn: The Athlete in American Literature* (Lexington: University Press of Kentucky, 1981); Christian K. Messenger, *Sport and the Spirit of Play in American Fiction: Hawthorne to Faulkner* (New York: Columbia University Press, 1981); Hans Lobmeyer, *Die Darstellung des Sports in der amerikanischen Erzählliteratur des 20. Jahrhunderts* (Ahrensburg: Czwalina, 1983); Christian K. Messenger, *Sport and the Spirit of Play in Contemporary American Fiction* (New York: Columbia University Press, 1990); Pierre Charreton, *Les Fêtes du corps* (St.-Étienne: Centre interdisciplinaire d'études et de recherches sur l'expression contemporaine, 1985).

2. Marcel Berger, *L'Histoire de quinze hommes* (Paris: Ferenczi, 1924), p. 97. For a brief account of these writers, see Allen Guttmann, "*Le Plaisir du Sport*: French Writers of the 1920s," *Arete*, 1(1) (Fall 1983): 113–24.
3. Jean Prévost, *Les Plaisirs des sports* (Paris: Gallimard, 1925), p. 53.
4. Gunter Gebauer and Hans Lenk, "Der erzählte Sport," *Körper- und Einbildungskraft*, ed. Gunter Gebauer (Berlin: Dietrich Reimer, 1988), p. 149.
5. Henry de Montherlant, *Les Olympiques* (1920; Paris: Gallimard, 1954), p. 23. This edition contains *Le Paradis à l'ombre des épées* and its sequel.
6. Ibid., pp. 49–50.
7. Ibid., pp. 40–42.
8. Ibid., pp. 79–81.
9. Ibid., p. 150. A similar scene opens Paul Morand's *Champions du monde* (Paris: Grasset, 1930).
10. Ibid., p. 204.
11. Montherlant, *Les Olympiques*, pp. 220–21.
12. Henry de Montherlant, *Le Songe* (Paris: Grasset, 1922), pp. 19–20.
13. Ibid., pp. 52–53, 65. Not in that order.
14. Ibid., pp. 19–20.
15. Ibid., pp. 284, 286, 332.
16. Henry de Montherlant, *Les Bestiaires* (Paris: Grasset, 1926), pp. 58, 96, 192, 260, 263, 266. Not in that order..
17. Ernest Hemingway, *The Sun Also Rises* (New York: Scribner's, 1926), pp. 225–27.

18. Peter Schwenger *Phallic Critiques* (London: Routledge and Kegan Paul, 1984), p. 133.
19. Hemingway, *The Sun Also Rises*, pp. 3, 224–25. Not in that order.
20. Ibid., p. 3.
21. Ibid. pp. 246–47, 258–59.
22. See Allen Guttmann, "Faustian Athletes? Sports as a Theme in Modern German Literature," *Modern Fiction Studies*, 33(1) (Spring 1987): 21–33.
23. Wolfgang Rothe, "Sport und Literatur in den zwanziger Jahren," *Stadion*, 7 (1981): 131–51.
24. Ibid., p. 137; Wolfgang Rothe, "When Sport Conquered the Republic," *Studies in Twentieth-Century Literature* 4 (1979): 20.
25. Kasimir Edschmid, *Der Sport um Gagaly* (Berlin: Zsolnay, 1928), p. 58.
26. Ibid., pp. 51, 65.
27. Ibid., pp. 84, 136.
28. Marinetti: quoted by John Hoberman, "The Sportive-Dynamic Body as a Symbol of Productivity," *Heterotopia*, ed. Tobin Siebers (Ann Arbor: University of Michigan Press, 1994), p. 227.
29. Edschmid, *Der Sport um Gagaly*, pp. 94, 107, 176, 204, 304.
30. Ibid., pp. 316, 354–55.
31. Eve Kosofsky Sedgwick, *Between Men: English Literature and Male Homosocial Desire* (New York: Columbia University Press, 1985).
32. Edschmid, *Der Sport um Gagaly*, p. 357.
33. Kate Chopin, *The Awakening* (1899; Garden City: Nelson Doubleday, n.d.), p. 185. (Available in several paperback editions.) D. H. Lawrence, *The Rainbow* (1915; London: William Heinemann, 1955), p. 337 The aesthetics and erotics of swimming and diving are brilliantly explored in Charles Sprawson's *Haunts of the Black Masseur: The Swimmer as Hero* (London: Jonathan Cape, 1992). See also Stephen Kern, *The Culture of Love* (Cambridge: Harvard University Press, 1992), pp. 73–75.
34. Jenifer Levin, *Water Dancer* (New York: Simon & Schuster-Pocket Books, 1982), p. 15.
35. Ibid., p. 145
36. Ibid.
37. Ibid., pp. 170, 178, 193, 233–34.

38. Ibid., pp. 363, 365, 378.

39. Pam Cook, "Masculinity in Crisis?" *Screen,* 23(3–4) (September-October 1982): 42.

40. Thelma McCormack, "Hollywood's Prizefight Films," *Journal of Sport and Social Issues,* 8(2) (1984): 19.

41. Leslie Halliwell, *Halliwell's Film Guide,* 8th ed., ed. John Walker (New York: HarperCollins, 1991), p. 897.

42. Robin Wood, "*Raging Bull*: The Homosexual Subtext in Film," *Beyond Patriarchy,* ed. Michael Kaufman (Toronto: Oxford University Press, 1987), p. 268.

43. Hitler: quoted in Leni Riefenstahl, *Memoiren,* 2 vols. (Frankfurt: Ullstein, 1990–92), 1:157.

44. Ibid., p. 158.

45. Peter Adam, *Art of the Third Reich* (New York: Abrams, 1992), p. 179. See also Thomas Alkemeyer, "Normbilder des Menschen: Der männliche Sportler-Körper in der Staatsästhetik des 'Dritten Reiches,' " *Sozial- und Zeitgeschichte des Sports,* 6(3) (November 1992): 65–80; Thomas Alkemeyer, "Images and Politics of the Body in the National Socialist Era," *Sport Science Review,* 4 (1995): 60–90.

46. Riefenstahl, *Memoiren,* 2:425.

47. Richard D. Mandell, *The Nazi Olympics,* 2nd ed. (Urbana: University of Illinois Press, 1987), pp. xvi-xvii. For Mandell's brilliant analysis of the film, see pp. 257–73.

48. Among the best analyses of the body and Fascism is John M. Hoberman, *Sport and Political Ideology* (Austin: University of Texas Press, 1984). See also his "Toward a Theory of Olympic Internationalism," *Journal of Sport History,* 22(1) (Spring 1995): 22–23.

49. In order of their appearance in the film, they were Juri Ozerov (USSR), Mai Zetterling (Sweden), Arthur Penn (USA), Michael Pfleghar (West Germany), Kon Ichikawa (Japan), Milos Forman (Hungary), Claude Lelouch (France), and John Schlesinger (UK).

50. John Fiske, *Power Plays Power Works* (London: Verso, 1993), p. 87.

51. John J. MacAloon, "Double Visions," *Kenyon Review* 4 (1982): 98–112; Richard Mandell, *The Olympics of 1972* (Chapel Hill: University of North Carolina Press, 1991), p. 123.

52. Michael Sragow, "First-Time Director Robert Towne Comes Up a Winner," *Rolling Stone*, April 15, 1982.
53. The Japanese artist Utamaro Kitagawa did a woodblock print of two prostitutes arm-wrestling: *Okita of the Naniwaya and Ohisa of the Takashimaya* (1794). Is there something especially sexy about these prone contests?
54. Greta L. Cohen, "Media Portrayal of the Female Athlete," *Women in Sport*, ed. Greta L. Cohen (London: Sage, 1993), p. 181.
55. Pauline Kael, "The Man Who Understands Women," *The New Yorker*, 58 (February 22, 1982): 112–19.
56. Laurie Stone, "*Personal Best*: What's New in Towne," *Village Voice*, March 16, 1982.
57. Spalding: quoted in Wendy Chapkis, *Beauty Secrets: Women and the Politics of Appearance* (Boston: South End Press, 1986), p. 12.
58. Veronica Geng, "Good at Games," *New York Review*, March 18, 1982.
59. Robert Hatch, "Films," *The Nation*, 223 (February 27, 1982): 252.
60. Williams: quoted in Dorothy Kidd, "Getting Physical: Compulsory Heterosexuality and Sport," *Canadian Women's Studies*, 4(3) (Spring 1983): 63–64.
61. Ironically, Hemingway disliked the body she developed for the film; she underwent surgery to have her breasts enlarged. See Kim Chernin, *The Hungry Self: Women, Eating, and Identity* (New York: Harper & Row, 1986), pp. 189–90.

7. Eros and Psyche

1. Bryan S. Turner, "Recent Developments in the Theory of the Body," *The Body*, eds. Mike Featherstone, Mike Hepworth, and Bryan S. Turner (London: Sage, 1991), p. 8. Among the exceptions to this generalization was Max Weber in the *Gesammelte Aufsätze zur Religionssoziologie*, 3 vols. (Tübingen: Mohr, 1920), 1:536–73.
2. Marcel Mauss, *Sociologie et Anthropologie* (Paris: Presses universitaires de France, 1968), p. 372.
3. Luc Boltanski, "Les usages sociaux du corps," *Les Annales*, 26 (1971): 232. Boltanski was importantly influenced by Pierre Bourdieu, whose most important contribution to the study of the body is *La Distinction* (Paris: Éditions de minuit, 1979).

4. R. W. Connell, *Gender and Power* (Stanford: Stanford University Press, 1987), p. 83. Among the other works that have influenced my thinking about the body are Nancy M. Henley, *Body Politics* (Englewood Cliffs: Prentice-Hall, 1977); Dietmar Kamper and Christoph Wulf, eds., *Die Wiederkehr des Körpers* (Frankfurt: Suhrkamp, 1982); Bryan S. Turner, *The Body and Society* (Oxford: Basil Blackwell, 1984); Scott Lash, "Genealogy and the Body," *Theory, Culture and Society*, 2(2) (1988): 1–17; Alison M. Jagger and Susan R. Bordo, eds., *Gender/Body/Knowledge* (New Brunswick: Rutgers University Press, 1989); Mary Jacobus, Evelyn Fox-Keller, and Sally Shuttleworth, eds., *Body Politics* (New York: Routledge, 1990); Mike Featherstone, Mike Hepworth, and Bryan S. Turner, eds., *The Body* (London: Sage, 1991); Jean Harvey and Robert Sparks, "The Politics of the Body in the Context of Modernity," *Quest*, 43(2) (August 1991): 164–89; Sue Scott and David Morgan, eds., *Body Matters* (London: Falmer Press, 1993; Susan Bordo, *Unbearable Weight* (Berkeley: University of California Press, 1993); John W. Loy, David L. Andrews, and Robert E. Rinehart, "The Body in Culture and Sport," *Sport Science Review*, 2(1) (1993): 69–91; Patricia Vertinsky, "The 'Racial' Body and the Anatomy of Difference," *Sport Science Review*, 4 (1995): 38–59. I have attempted to read "postmodernist discourse" about the body, e.g., Jane Gallop's *Thinking through the Body* (New York: Columbia University Press, 1988), but I find such books far less helpful than the works just cited.

5. Foucault's most relevant works are *Histoire de la folie* (Paris: Gallimard, 1972) and *Surveiller et Punir* (Paris: Gallimard, 1975). In my view, his frequently cited *Histoire de la Sexualité*, 3 vols. (Paris: Gallimard, 1976–84) has done more to obfuscate than to clarify discussions of the "techniques du corps."

6. Michael Kimmel, "After Fifteen Years: The Impact of the Sociology of Masculinity on the Masculinity of Sociology," *Men, Masculinities and Social Theory*, eds. Jeff Hearn and David Morgan (London: Unwin Hyman, 1990), p. 97.

7. In Foucault's highly theoretical work, power is a diffuse set of institutionalized practices designed to "discipline" the body. Less theoretically intoxicated sociologists still see power as the ability to achieve

individual or collective ends. Unlike Foucault, they believe that men and women have or do not have power.

8. Connell, *Gender and Power*, p. 85.
9. Eschewing the pretense of objectivity, a number of politically engaged sociologists have urged that the code defining what is socially acceptable masculine behavior be extensively rewritten to include attitudes and attributes conventionally categorized as feminine. Andrew Tolson, a British sociologist, has analyzed contemporary class differences in the expression of masculinity and concluded *The Limits of Masculinity* (1977) with an altruistic call for the end of capitalist patriarchy and the creation of an egalitarian nonsexist socialist society. Changes in conceptions of masculinity and in men's behavior have been thoughtfully described, with nuanced attention to the variations attributable to race and ethnicity, social class, sexual orientation, and political ideology, by Lynne Segal in *Slow Motion: Changing Masculinities, Changing Men* (New Brunswick: Rutgers University Press, 1990).
10. Segal, *Slow Motion: Changing Masculinities, Changing Men*, p. 319.
11. Peter G. Filene, *Him/Her/Self*, 2nd ed. (Baltimore: Johns Hopkins University Press, 1986), p. 219; see also Joseph H. Pleck and Jack Sawyer, eds., *Men and Masculinity* (Englewood Cliffs: Prentice-Hall, 1974); Joseph H. Pleck, *The Myth of Masculinity* (Cambridge: MIT Press, 1981). The bulk of popular literature on this theme is, of course, immense.
12. Mirra Komarovsky, *Dilemmas of Masculinity* (New York: Norton, 1976).
13. Ray Raphael, *The Men from the Boys: Rites of Passage in Male America* (Lincoln: University of Nebraska Press, 1988), pp. 106, 137.
14. Maarten van Bottenburg, *Verborgen Competitie: Over de Uiteenlopende Populariteit van Sporten* (Amsterdam: Bert Bakker, 1994).
15. Susan Brownmiller, *Femininity* (New York: Fawcett Columbine, 1985), pp. 195–96.
16. On the allegedly "masculine" or "androgynous" female athletes, see Anita M. Myers and Hilary M. Lips, "Participation in Competitive Amateur Sports as a Function of Psychological Androgyny," *Sex Roles* 4 (1978): 571–78; Dorothy V. Harris, "Femininity and

Athleticism," *Jock*, eds. Donald F. Sabo and Ross Runfola (Englewood Cliffs: Prentice-Hall, 1980), pp. 222–39; Sarah M. Uguccioni and Robert H. Ballantyne, "Comparison of Attitudes and Sex Roles for Female Athletic Participants and Non-Participants," *International Journal of Sport Psychology*, 11(1) (1980): 42–48; L. Chalip, J. Villiger, and P. Duignan, "Sex-Role Identity in a Select Sample of Women Field Hockey Players," *International Journal of Sport Psychology*, 11(4) (1980): 240–48; Ruth Colker and Cathy Spatz Widom, "Correlates of Female Athletic Participation," *Sex Roles*, 6 (1980): 47–58; Patricia Del Rey and Samona Sheppard, "Relationship of Psychological Androgyny in Female Athletes to Self-Esteem," *International Journal of Sport Psychology*, 12(3) (1981): 165–75; Keith P. Henschen, Steven W. Edwards, and L. Mathinos, "Achievement Motivation and Sex-Role Orientation of High School Female Track and Field Athletes versus Non-Athletes," *Perceptual and Motor Skills*, 55 (1982): 183–87; Jayne Gackenbach, "Collegiate Swimmers," *Perceptual and Motor Skills*, 55 (1982): 555–58; Steven W. Edwards, Richard D. Gardin, and Keith P. Henschen, "Sex-Role Orientations of Female NCAA Championship Gymnasts," *Perceptual and Motor Skills*, 58 (1984): 625–26; Arno F. Wittig, "Sports Competition Anxiety and Sex Role," *Sex Roles*, 10(5–6) (1984): 469–73; Ann Colley, Nigel Roberts, and Anthony Chipps, "Sex-Role Identity, Personality and Participation in Team and Individual Sports by Males and Females," *International Journal of Sport Psychology*, 16 (1985): 103–12; Evelyn G. Hall, Beverly Durborow, and Jamie L. Progen, "Self-Esteem of Female Athletes and Non-Athletes," *Sex Roles*, 15 (1986): 379–90; Herbert W. Marsh and Susan A. Jackson, "Multidimensional Self Concepts, Masculinity and Femininity as a Function of Women's Involvement in Athletics," *Sex Roles*, 15 (1986): 391–415; Craig A. Wrisberg, Vanessa M. Draper, and John J. Everett, "Sex Role Orientations of Male and Female Collegiate Athletes from Selected Individual and Team Sports," *Sex Roles*, 19(1–2) (1988): 81–90.

17. Thomas Kimlicka, Herbert Cross, and John Tarnai, "A Comparison of Androgynous, Feminine, Masculine, and Undifferentiated Women on Self-Esteem, Body Satisfaction, and Sexual Satisfaction," *Psychology*

of Women Quarterly, 7 (1983): 291–94; Linda A. Jackson, Linda A. Sullivan, and Ronald Rostker, "Gender, Gender Role, and Body Image," *Sex Roles,* 19 (1988): 429–44.

18. Sidney M. Jourard and Paul F. Secord, "Body-Cathexis and the Ideal Female Figure," *Journal of Abnormal and Social Psychology,* 50 (1955): 243–46.

19. On women's sports and body image, see Eldon E. Snyder and Joseph E. Kivlin, "Women Athletes and Aspects of Psychological Well-Being and Body Image," *Research Quarterly,* 46 (May 1975): 191–99; Linda Ho and Jon E. Walker, "Female Athletes and Nonathletes," *Journal of Sport Behavior,* 5(1) (March 1982): 12–27; V. V. Prakasa Rao and Steven J. Overman, "Psychological Well-Being and Body Image," *Journal of Sport Behavior,* 9(2) (June 1986): 79–91.

20. Ann H. Die and V. Raye Holt, "Perceptions of the 'Typical' Female, Male, Female Athlete, and Male Athlete," *International Journal of the Psychology of Sport,* 20 (1989): 143.

21. Eldon E. Snyder and Elmer Spreitzer, "Change and Variation in the Social Acceptance of Female Participation in Sports," *Journal of Sport Behavior,* 6(1) (March 1983): 3–8.

22. Robert C. Woodford and Wilbur J. Scott, "Attitudes toward the Participation of Women in Intercollegiate Sports," *Studies in the Sociology of Sports,* eds. Aidan O. Dunleavy et al. (Fort Worth: Texas Christian University Press, 1982), p. 209; see also Howard L. Nixon, Philip J. Maresca, and Marcy A. Silverman, "Sex Differences in College Students' Acceptance of Females in Sport," *Adolescence,* 14 (1979): 755–64; Susan A. Basow and Jean Spinner, "Social Acceptability of College Athletes," *International Journal of Sport Psychology,* 15 (1984): 79–87; Andrew C. Ostrow and David A. Dzewatowski, "Older Adults' Perceptions of Physical Activity Participation," *Research Quarterly,* 57(2) (1986): 167–69.

23. Maria T. Allison and Beverley Butler, "Role Conflict and the Elite Female Athlete," *International Review of Sport Sociology,* 19(2) (1984): 157–66. Eight of 19 female karate experts reported that they had been "put down" by others, but only two experienced trouble with their boyfriends; see Robert A. Smith et al., "Women, Karate, and Gender Typing," *Sociological Inquiry,* 51(2) (1981): 113–20; see

also Joseph Anthrop and Maria T. Allison, "Role Conflict and the High School Female Athletes," *Research Quarterly,* 54(2) (1974): 104–11; Mary M. Bell, "Conflict of Women as Athletes," *Arena Review,* 4(2) (May 1980): 22–31; Gaylene P. Douctre, Glenna A. Harris, and Kathryn E. Watson, "An Analysis of the Self-Image Differences of Male and Female Athletes," *Journal of Sport Behavior,* 6(2) (July 1983): 77–83.

24. Robert W. Duff and Lawrence K. Hong, "Self-Images of Women Body-Builders," *Sociology of Sport Journal,* 1(4) (December 1984): 374–80.

25. Christine Anne Holmlund, "Visible Difference and Flex Appeal: The Body, Sex, Sexuality, and Race in the *Pumping Iron* Films," *Cinema Journal,* 28 (Summer 1989): 38–51.

26. Loren Franck, "Exposure and Gender Effects in the Social Perception of Women Bodybuilders," *Journal of Sport Psychology,* 6(2) (1984): 239–45.

27. Harvey R. Freeman, "Social Perception of Bodybuilders," *Journal of Sport and Exercise Psychology,* 10 (1988): 281–93.

28. Maria T. Allison, "Role Conflict and the Female Athlete: Preoccupations with Little Grounding," *Journal of Applied Sport Psychology,* 3 (1991): 49–60.

29. Janet T. Spence and Robert Helmreich, "Who Likes Competent Women?" *Journal of Applied Social Psychology,* 2 (1972): 197–213; Kay Patterson, Robert Helmreich, and Joy Stapp, "Likability, Sex-Role Congruence of Interest, and Competence," *Journal of Applied Social Psychology,* 5 (1975): 93–109.

30. Todd W. Crosset, *Outdoors in the Clubhouse* (Albany: State University of New York Press, 1995), p. 84.

31. Donnelly: quoted in Laurie Schulze, "On the Muscle," *Fabrications: Costume and the Female Body,* eds. Jane Gaines and Charlotte Herzog (London: Routledge, 1990), p. 62.

32. Susan Bordo, *Unbearable Weight,* pp. 296–97.

33. CBS "Inside Edition," March 29, 1995.

34. Jennifer Hargreaves, *Sporting Females* (London: Routledge, 1994), p. 156.

35. Helen Lenskyj, "Measured Time: Women, Sport and Leisure," *Leisure Studies,* 7 (1988): 239.

36. Richard Green, *Sexual Identity Conflict in Children and Adults* (Baltimore: Penguin Books, 1974).
37. Saul Feinman, "Approval of Cross Sex-Role Behavior," *Psychological Reports*, 35 (1974): 646.
38. Janice M. Irvine, *Disorders of Desire* (Philadelphia: Temple University Press, 1990), p. 274.
39. B. A. Seyfriend and Clyde Hendrick, "When Do Opposites Attract? *Journal of Personality and Social Psychology*, 25(1) (1973): 20.
40. Lucia A. Gilbert, Connie J. Deutsch, Robert F. Strahan, "Feminine and Masculine Dimensions of the Typical, Desirable, and Ideal Woman and Man," *Sex Roles*, 4(5) (1978): 776.
41. Brigitte Tietzel, "Von der Frauen Schönheit, Schnelligkeit und Verführung," *Frankfurter Allgemeine Zeitung*, June 9, 1990.
42. Alessandro Salvini, *Identità Femminile e Sport* (Florence: La Nuova Italia, 1982), pp. 2, 166–214.
43. Suzanne Laberge, "Toward an Integration of Gender into Bourdieu's Concept of Cultural Capital," *Sociology of Sport Journal*, 12(2) (1995): 142.
44. Robert Bly, *Iron John* (Reading: Addison-Wesley, 1990).
45. For extensive bibliographies, see Gordon L. Patzer, *Physical Attractiveness Phenomena* (New York: Plenum Press, 1985), pp. 273–304; Linda A. Jackson, *Physical Appearance and Gender* (Albany: SUNY Press, 1992), pp. 225–95.
46. Rita Freedman, *Beauty Bound* (Lexington: Lexington Books, 1986), p. 6.
47. Since there are no objective criteria for physical attractiveness, psychologists usually commission a set of evaluators to decide which of the "stimulus persons" is attractive and which is not.
48. Freedman, *Beauty Bound*, p. 115.
49. Elaine Walster, et al., "Importance of Physical Attractiveness in Dating Behavior," *Journal of Personality and Social Psychology*, 4(5) (1966): 513; R. W. Brislin and S. A. Lewis, "Dating and Physical Attractiveness," *Psychological Reports*, 22 (1968): 976; Albert A. Harrison and Laila Saeed, "Let's Make a Deal," *Journal of Personality and Social Psychology*, 35(4) (1977): 257–64; see also Robert H. Coombs and William F. Kendel, "Sex Differences in Dating

Aspirations and Satisfaction with Computer-Selected Partners,"
Journal of Marriage and the Family, 28 (1966): 62–66; Donn Byrne,
Charles R. Ervin, and John Lamberth, "Continuity Between the
Experimental Study of Attraction and 'Real-Life' Computer Dating,"
Journal of Personality and Social Psychology, 16(1) (1970): 157–65;
Bernard I Murstein, "Physical Attractiveness and Marital Choice,"
Journal of Personality and Social Psychology, 22(1) (1972): 8–12.

50. J. Richard Udry, "The Importance of Being Beautiful," *American
Journal of Sociology*, 83 (1977): 154–60; J. Richard Udry and Bruce K.
Eckland, "Benefits of Being Attractive: Differential Payoffs for Men
and Women," *Psychological Reports*, 54 (1984): 47–56.

51. My sources for this paragraph in include Victoria M. Esses and
Christopher D. Webster, "Physical Attractiveness, Dangerousness,
and the Canadian Criminal Code," *Journal of Applied Social
Psychology*, 18(12) (September 1988): 1014–31; Chris A. Downs and
Phillip M. Lyons, "Natural Observations of the Links Between
Attractiveness and Initial Legal Judgments," *Personality and Social
Psychology Bulletin*, 17(5) (October 1991): 541–47; Karen Dion,
Ellen Berscheid, and Elaine Walster, "What Is Beautiful Is Good,"
Journal of Personality and Social Psychology, 24(3) (1972): 285–90;
see also G. William Lucker, William E. Beane, and Robert L.
Helmreich, "The Strength of the Halo Effect in Physical
Attractiveness Research," *Journal of Psychology*, 107 (1981): 69–75;
David Landy and Harold Sigall, "Beauty Is Talent," *Journal of
Personality and Social Psychology*, 29(3) (1974): 299–304; Robert L.
Dipboye, Howard L. Fromkin, and Kent Wiback, "Relative
Importance of Applicant Sex, Attractiveness, and Scholastic Standing
in Evaluation of Job Applicant Résumés," *Journal of Applied
Psychology*, 60(1) (1975): 39–43; Thomas F. Cash, Barry Gillen, and
D. Steven Burns, "Sexism and 'Beautyism' in Personnel Consultant
Decision Making," *Journal of Applied Psychology*, 62(3) (1977):
301–10; see also Glen H. Elder, Jr., "Appearance and Education in
Marriage Mobility," *American Sociological Review*, 34(1) (February
1969): 519–33; Murray Webster and James E. Driskell, "Beauty as
Status," *American Journal of Sociology*, 89 (1983): 140–65; Thomas
F. Cash and Claire A. Trimer, "Sexism and Beautyism in Women's

Evaluations of Peer Performance," *Sex Roles,* 10 (1984): 87–98; Elaine Hatfield and Susan Sprecher, *Mirror, Mirror* (Albany: State University of New York Press, 1986), pp. 62–63; Irene Hanson Frieze, Josephine E. Olson, and June Russell, "Attractiveness and Income for Men and Women in Management," *Journal of Applied Social Psychology,* 21 (1991): 1039–57; Michael S. Kalick, "Physical Attractiveness as a Status Clue," *Journal of Experimental Social Psychology,* 24 (1988): 469–89; Thomas F. Cash and Louis H. Janda, "The Eye of the Beholder," *Psychology Today,* 18:12 (December 1984): 46–52; Madeline E. Heilman and Melanie H. Stopeck, "Attractiveness and Corporate Success," *Journal of Applied Psychology,* 70(2) (1985): 379–88; Marshall Dermer and Derrel I. Thiel, "When Beauty May Fail," *Journal of Personality and Social Psychology,* 31 (1975): 1168–76. Studies of high school students suggest that these stereotypes may be on the way out: "Today's high school girls and boys associate professional career orientation with attractiveness for women"; see Hope B. Lanier and Joan Byrne, "How High School Students View Women: The Relationship Between Perceived Attractiveness, Occupation and Education," *Sex Roles,* 7(2) (1981): 148.

52. John F. and Jane Cross, "Age, Sex, Race, and the Perception of Facial Beauty," *Developmental Psychology,* 5 (1971): 433–39; Richard M. Lerner, Stuart A. Karabenick, and Joyce L. Stuart, "Relations Among Physical Attractiveness, Body Attitudes, and Self-Concept in Male and Female College Students," *Journal of Pyschology,* 85 (1973): 119–29; Richard M. Lerner and Stuart A. Karabenick, "Physical Attractiveness, Body Attitudes, and Self-Concept in Late Adolescents," *Journal of Youth and Adolescence,* 3 (1974): 307–16; Patzer, *The Physical Attractiveness Phenomena,* p. 142.

53. Erving Goffman, an unusually innovative sociologist, pioneered the field with *The Presentation of Self in Everyday Life* (New York: Doubleday-Anchor Books, 1959), *Relations in Public* (New York: Basic Books, 1971), and *Gender Advertisements* (New York: Harper, 1979). Nancy M. Henley summarized the first decades of American and British research in *Body Politics* (Englewood Cliffs: Prentice-Hall, 1977).

54. Ellen Berscheid, Elaine Walster, George Bohrnstedt, "The Happy American Body," *Psychology Today*, 7 (November 1973): 119–31.

55. Ibid., p. 123. To set the record straight: the authors reported that 15% of the men worried about penis size and 25% of the women worried about the size or shape of their breasts. A more recent study of 238 male and 307 female students at Hofstra University found that "Build/Figure" was a key to romantic attraction, but neither men nor women rated "Chest/Breasts" as particularly important; see T. Horvath, "Physical Attractiveness," *Archives of Sexual Behavior*, 10(1) (1981): 21–24; see also Stephen L. Franzoi and Stephanie A. Shields, "The Body Esteem Scale," *Journal of Personality Assessment*, 48(2) (April 1984): 173–78; Jeffrey S. Nevid, "Sex Differences in Factors of Romantic Attraction," *Sex Roles*, 11(5–6) (1984): 401–11; Stephen L. Franzoi and Mary E. Herzog, "Judging Physical Attractiveness," *Personality and Social Psychology Bulletin*, 13 (1987): 19–33.

56. Edmond and Jules Goncourt, *Journal* (October 13, 1855): quoted in Valerie Steele, *Fashion and Eroticism* (New York: Oxford University Press, 1985), p. 103. My emphasis.

57. Wendy Chapkis, *Beauty Secrets: Women and the Politics of Appearance* (Boston: South End Press, 1986); Kim Chernin, *The Obsession: Reflections on the Tyranny of Slenderness* (New York: Harper & Row, 1981).

58. Seymour Fisher, *Development and Structure of the Body Image*, 2 vols. (Hillsdale, New Jersey: Lawrence Erlbaum, 1986), 1: 68. The terms "endomorph," "ectomorph," and "mesomorph" were popularized by William Herbert Sheldon in *The Varieties of Human Physique* (New York: Harper, 1940).

59. Rebecca F. Guy, Beverly A. Rankin, and Melissa J. Norvell, "The Relation of Sex Role Stereotyping to Body Image," *Journal of Psychology*, 105 (1980): 167–73.

60. William D. Wells and Bertram Siegel, "Stereotyped Somatypes," *Psychological Reports*, 8 (1961): 77–78; Richard M. Lerner, "Some Female Stereotypes of Male Body Build-Behavior Relations," *Perceptual and Motor Skills*, 28 (1969): 363–66; Richard M. Lerner, John R. Knapp, and Kenneth B. Pool, "Structure of Body-Build

Stereotypes," *Perceptual and Motor Skills*, 39 (1974): 719–29; Sari A. Gacsaly and Cheryl A. Borges, "The Male Physique and Behavioral Expectancies," *Journal of Psychology*, 101 (1979): 97–102; Marc E. Mishkind, et al., "The Embodiment of Masculinity," *Changing Men*, ed. Michael S. Kimmel (London: Sage Publications, 1987), pp. 137–52.

61. Carroll H. Brodsky, "A Study of Norms for Body Form-Behavior Relationships," *Anthropological Quarterly*, 27 (1954): 97.
62. Marc Mishkind, et al., "The Embodiment of Masculinity," *American Behavioral Scientist*, 29 (1986): 549.
63. J. Robert Staffieri, "A Study of Social Stereotypes of Body Image in Children," *Journal of Personality and Social Psychology*, 7 (1967): 101–4; Richard M. Lerner, "The Development of Stereotyped Expectancies of Body Build-Behavior Relations," *Child Development*, 40 (1969): 137–41; Richard M. Lerner and Sam J. Korn, "The Development of Body Build Stereotypes in Males," *Child Development*, 43 (1972): 908–20; Richard M. Lerner and Elizabeth Gellert, "Body Build Identification, Preference, and Aversion in Children," *Developmental Psychology*, 1(5) (1969): 456–62; Richard M. Lerner and Christine Schroeder, "Physique Identification, Preference, and Aversion in Kindergarten Children," *Developmental Psychology*, 5 (1971): 538. Marcia Millman's *Such a Pretty Face* (New York: Norton, 1980) is the classic sociological study of this aversion and its consequences for the obese; 70. Richard M. Lerner, Stuart A. Karabenick, and Murray Meisels, "Effects of Age and Sex on the Development of Personal Space Schemata Towards Body Build," *Journal of Genetic Psychology*, 127 (1975): 91–101.
64. Naomi Wolf, *The Beauty Myth* (1991; New York: Anchor Books, 1992).
65. J. Kevin Thompson, "Larger Than Life," *Psychology Today*, 20 (April 1986): 38–44.
66. On misperceptions, see Paul Rozin and April Fallon, "Body Image, Attitudes to Weight, and Misperceptions of Figure Preferences of the Opposite Sex," *Journal of Abnormal Psychology*, 97 (1988): 342–45; Thomas F. Cash and Lora Jacobi, "Looks Aren't Everything (to Everybody)," *Journal of Social Behavior and Personality*, 7(4) (1992): 621–30; Lora Jacobi and Thomas F. Cash, "In Pursuit of the

Perfect Appearance," *Journal of Applied Social Psychology*, 24 (1994): 379–96.

67. April E. Fallon and Paul Rozin, "Sex Differences in Perception of Desirable Body Shape," *Journal of Abnormal Psychology*, 94(1) (1985): 102–5; see also John P. Mckee and Alex C. Sherriffs, "Men's and Women's Beliefs, Ideals, and Self-Concepts," *American Journal of Sociology*, 64 (1959): 356–63. The same seems to be true for British women; see Adrian Furnham, Catherine Hester, and Catherine Weir, "Sex Differences in the Preferences for Specific Female Body Shapes," *Sex Roles*, 22 (1990): 743–54.

68. Freedman, *Beauty Bound*, p. x. An exception to Freedman's generalization is James B. Weaver, Jonathan L. Masland, and Dolf Zillmann, "Effect of Erotica on Young Men's Aesthetic Perception of Their Female Sexual Partners," *Perceptual and Motor Skills*, 58 (1984): 929–30. Is it a coincidence that Zillmann has done sports-related research? For other studies relating sexuality and body image, see Fisher, *Development and Structure of the Body Image*, 1:27–32.

69. Berscheid, Walster, and Bohrnstedt, "The Happy American Body," p. 126.

70. Fisher, *Development and Structure of the Body Image*, 1:139.

71. Allen Guttmann, "Body Image and Sports Participation of the Intellectual Elite," *International Review of Sport Sociology*, 24(4) (1989): 335–43.

72. Michael Balint, "Philobatism and Ocnophilia," *Motivations in Play, Games, and Sports*, eds. Ralph Slovenko and James A. Knight (Springfield: Charles C. Thomas, 1967), p. 245.

73. Leonard L. Glass, "Man's Man, Ladies' Man: Motifs of Hypermasculinity," *Psychiatry*, 47 (1984): 261–62.

74. Gill Saunders, *The Nude* (New York: Harper & Row, 1989), p. 26.

75. Samuel Fussell, "Bodybuilder Americanus," *The Male Body*, ed. Laurence Goldstein (Ann Arbor: University of Michigan Press, 1994), p. 46

76. Rosalind Miles, *The Rites of Man* (London: Grafton Books, 1991), p.111. See also Kenneth R. Dutton, *The Perfectible Body* (New York: Continuum, 1995), pp. 229–71.

77. Ned Polsky, *Hustlers, Beats, and Others* (Chicago: Aldine, 1967), p. 37.

78. Michel Leiris, *Manhood*, trans. Richard Howard (1946; San Francisco: North Point Press, 1984), p. 27.

79. Michel Leiris, *Miroir de la Tauromachie* (1938: Paris: Éditions Fata Morgana, 1981), pp. 48–50 (text), 7, 23, 46–47, 69 (illustrations).

80. Helen Deutsch, "A Contribution to the Psychology of Sport," *International Journal of Psychoanalysis*, 7 (1926): 225–27.

81. Adrien Stokes, "Psycho-Analytic Reflections on the Development of Ball Games," *Sport and Society*, ed. Alex Natan (London: Bowes and Bowes, 1958), p. 175; originally published in the *International Journal of Psychoanalysis* in 1955.

82. Alan Dundes, "Into the Endzone for a Touchdown: A Psychoanalytic Consideration of American Football," *Western Folklore*, 37 (1978): 81.

83. Marcelo Marió Suárez-Orozco, "A Study of Argentine Soccer," *Journal of Psychoanalytic Anthropology*, 5(1) (Winter 1982): 23–24.

84. Otto Fenichel, *Collected Papers: Second Series* (New York: Norton, 1954), pp. 167, 172.

85. Heinz Kohut, *The Analysis of the Self* (New York: International Universities Press, 1971), pp. 113, 259 (in reverse order).

86. Freud, *Drei Abhandlungen, Werkausgabe*, 1:287, 289n (in reverse order).

87. Arnold Plack, *Die Gesellschaft und das Böse* (Munich: List Verlag, 1969), p. 224.

88. Mariah Burton Nelson, *The Stronger Women Get, the More Men Love Football* (New York: Harcourt, Brace, 1994), p. 37.

89. Freud, *Drei Abhandlungen, Werkausgabe*, 1:288–89.

90. Alphonso Lingis, *Foreign Bodies* (New York: Routledge, 1994), p. 221.

91. D. H. Lawrence, *Women in Love* (1921; London: William Heinemann, 1954), pp. 262–63.

92. Wood: quoted in Brian Pronger, *The Arena of Masculinity* (New York: St. Martin's, 1990), p. 184.

93. M. Ann Hall, "Women and the Lawrentian Wrestle," *Arena Review*, 3(2) (May 1979): 25.

94. Elliott J. Gorn, *The Manly Art* (Ithaca: Cornell University Press, 1986), p. 75.

95. Mark Harris, *Bang the Drum Slowly* (1956; reprint ed. New York: Anchor Books, 1962), pp. 196–97.

96. Nelson, *The Stronger Women Get*, p. 116.

8. *Concluding Arguments*

1. Andrew Doyle, " 'Foolish and Useless Sport': The Southern Evangelical Crusade against College Football, 1892–1920" (unpublished paper, 1994).
2. Apologies to my friend Melvin Adelman, who thinks I have wasted too much time on the neo-Marxists; see his review of *Essays on Sport History and Sport Mythology*, ed. Donald G. Kyle and Gary D. Stark (College Station: Texas A&M Press, 1990), *Journal of Sport History*, 20(2) (Summer 1993): 193.
3. Linda Singer, "Bodies-Pleasures-Power," *Differences*, 1 (1989): 56.
4. Gerhard Vinnai, *Fussballsport als Ideologie* (Frankfurt: Europäische Verlagsanstalt, 1970), p. 65.
5. Paul Hoch, *Rip Off the Big Game* (New York: Doubleday-Anchor Books, 1972), p. 154.
6. The practice begins with boys still young enough for Little League Baseball; see Gary Alan Fine, *With the Boys* (Chicago: University of Chicago Press, 1987).
7. Richard Gruneau and David Whitson, *Hockey Night in Canada* (Toronto: Garamond Press, 1993), pp. 121–22.
8. Mariah Burton Nelson, *The Stronger Women Get, the More Men Love Football* (New York: Harcourt Brace, 1994), p. 87.
9. Nelson, *The Stronger Women Get*, pp. 100–101.
10. Tim Edwards, "Beyond Sex and Gender: Masculinity, Homosexuality and Social Theory," *Men, Masculinities and Social Theory*, eds. Jeff Hearn and David Morgan (London: Unwin Hyman, 1990), pp. 114, 116.
11. Thomas Sari, "Gender and Social-Class Coding in Popular Photographic Erotica," *Communication Quarterly*, 34 (Spring 1986): 110.
12. Brian Pronger, *The Arena of Masculinity: Sports, Homosexuality, and the Meaning of Sex* (New York: St. Martin's, 1990), pp. 11, 193, 276.
13. Susan K. Cahn, *Coming on Strong: Gender and Sexuality in Twentieth-Century Women's Sport* (New York: Free Press, 1994), p. 206.
14. Muriel Wilson Perkins, "Female Homosexuality and Body Build," *Archives of Sexual Behavior*, 10(4) (1981): 337–45.

15. Birgit Palzkill, *Zwischen Turnschuh und Stöckelschuh* (Bielefeld: AJZ-Verlag, 1990), pp. 6, 30, 36, 86, 94.

16. Helen Jefferson Lenskyj, "Sexuality and Femininity in Sport Contexts," *Journal of Sport and Social Issues*, 18(4) (November 1994): 357, 367.

17. Fuller: in William Rose's documentary film, *The Combat Sport* (1989).

18. Carlin A. Barton, *The Sorrows of the Ancient Romans* (Princeton: Princeton University Press, 1993), pp. 24, 80n139.

19. Gerd Hortleder and Gunter Gebauer, "Die künstlichen Paradiese des Sports," *Sport-Eros-Tod*, eds. Gerd Hortleder and Gunter Gebauer (Frankfurt: Suhrkamp, 1986), p. 13.

20. Sigmund Freud, "Triebe und Triebschicksale" (1915), *Werkausgabe*, 1:167–85.

21. Nelson, *The Stronger Women Get*, p. 110.

22. Elizabeth E. Wheatley, " 'Stylistic Ensembles' on a Different Pitch: A Comparative Analysis of Men's and Women's Rugby Songs," *Women and Language*, 13(1) (1990): 21–26.

23. Pronger, *The Arena of Masculinity*, p. 23.

24. Alan M. Klein, *Little Big Men: Bodybuilding Subculture and Gender Construction* (Albany: State University of New York Press, 1993), p. 260.

25. Frankfurt: quoted in Susan Bordo, *Unbearable Weight* (Berkeley: University of California Press, 1993), p. 150.

26. Jean Baudrillard, *Amérique* (Paris: Bernard Grasset, 1986), p. 46.

27. Ulrich Dix, *Sport und Sexualität* (Frankfurt: März Verlag, 1972).

28. Klein, *Little Big Men* , p. 20.

29. Ibid., p. 210; see also Anne Honer, "Beschreibung einer Lebens-Welt," *Zeitschrift für Soziologie*, 14(2) (1985): 134.

30. Alphonso Lingis, "Orchids and Muscles," *Philosophic Inquiry in Sport*, eds. William J. Morgan and Klaus V. Meier (Champaign: Human Kinetics, 1988), p. 125.

31. Klaus Theweleit, *Männerphantasien: Frauen, Fluten, Körper, Geschichte*, 2 vols. (Frankfurt: Verlag Roter Stern, 1977).

32. Yukio Mishima, *Confessions of a Mask*, trans. Meredith Weatherby (New York: New Directions, 1958), pp. 38–40. Mishima's obsessions

are also spelled out in his *Sun and Steel*, trans. John Bester (New York: Grove Press, 1976).

33. Philip G. White and James Gillette, "Reading the Muscular Body," *Sociology of Sport Journal*, 11(1) (March 1994): 19, 33.

34. J. J. Courtine, "Les stakhanovites du narcissisme," *Communications*, ed. Georges Vigarello (Paris: Editions du Seuil, 1993), pp. 225–51. See also Geneviève Rail and Jean Harvey, "Body at Work: Michel Foucault and the Sociology of Sport," *Sociology of Sport Journal*, 12(2) (1995): 164–79.

35. Gregory Stone was the first sociologist to explore the play-display pun; see "American Sports: Play and Display," *Chicago Review*, 9 (1955): 83–100.

36. Mariah Burton Nelson, *Are We Winning Yet?* (New York: Random House, 1991), p. 87.

37. American and European motivations seem remarkably similar. See Kerstin Behm, "Women in Fitness-Centres" (unpublished paper, XIIIth World Congress of Sociology, Bielefeld, 1994).

38. Daniel Dervin, "A Psychoanalysis of Sports," *The Psychoanalytic Review*, 72(2) (Summer 1985): 288.

39. John Berger, *Ways of Seeing* (London: BBC, 1972), pp. 47, 54

40. Doane: quoted in Ruth Waterhouse, "The Inverted Gaze," *Body Matters*, eds. Sue Scott and David Morgan (London: Falmer Press, 1993), p. 114.

41. Gaylyn Studlar, "Masochism, Masquerade, and the Erotic Metamorphoses of Marlene Dietrich," *Fabrications*, eds. Jane Gaines and Charlotte Herzog (London: Routledge, 1990), p.230.

42. Laura Mulvey, "Visual Pleasure and Narrative Cinema," *Screen*, 16(3) (Autumn 1975): 6.

43. Jane Gaines, "Fabricating the Female Body," *Fabrications*, p. 21. See also E. Ann Kaplan, *Women and Film* (New York: Methuen, 1983), pp. 23–35; Annette Kuhn, "The Body and Cinema," *Grafts: Feminist Cultural Criticism*, ed. Susan Sheridan (London: Verso, 1988), pp. 11–23.

44. Griselda Pollock, "What's Wrong with Images of Women?" *Looking On*, ed. Rosemary Betterton (London: Pandora, 1987), pp. 44, 46.

45. Margaret Morse, "Artemis Aging," *Discourse*, 10(1) (Fall–Winter 1992): 39.

46. Suzanne Moore, "Here's Looking at You, Kid!" *The Female Gaze*, eds. Lorraine Gamman and Margaret Marshment (Seattle: The Real Comet Press, 1989), pp. 45, 49.

47. Jennifer Hargreaves, *Sporting Females* (London: Routledge, 1994), p. 167.

48. Margaret Carlisle Duncan and Barry Brummett, "Types and Sources of Spectating Pleasure in Televised Sports," *Sport Sociology Journal*, 6(3) (September 1989): 195–211; Margaret Carlisle Duncan, "Sports Photographs and Sexual Difference," *Sport Sociology Journal*, 7(1) (March 1990): 22–43.

49. Margaret Carlisle Duncan, "The Politics of Women's Body Images and Practices," *Journal of Sport and Social Issues*, 18(1) (February 1994): 50.

50. Frigga Haug et al., *Female Sexualization*, trans. Erica Carter (London: Verso, 1987), pp. 176, 183.

51. Marie-Luise Klein and Gertrud Pfister, *Goldmädel, Rennmiezen und Turnküken* (Berlin: Bartels & Wernitz, 1985), pp. 73, 102.

52. Marie-Luise Klein, *Frauensport in der Tagespresse* (Bochum: Brockmeyer, 1986), pp. 249, 271.

53. Margaret McNeill, "Active Women, Media Representations, and Ideology," *Not Just a Game*, eds. Jean Harvey / Hart Cantelon (Ottawa: University of Ottawa Press, 1988), p. 209.

54. Ted Vincent, *Mudville's Revenge* (New York: Seaview Books, 1981), p. 322.

55. Mariah Burton Nelson, *The Stronger Women Get, the More Men Love Football* (New York: Harcourt, Brace, 1994), p. 97.

56. Brian Stoddart, *Saturday Afternoon Fever* (North Ryde, N.S.W.: Angus and Robertson, 1986), p. 155.

57. Adrianne Blue, *Grace Under Pressure* (London: Sidgwick and Jackson, 1987), p. 110; see also Jaime Diaz, "Find the Golf Here?" *Sports Illustrated*, 70 (February 13, 1989): 158–64.

58. Provost: quoted in Jennifer Hargreaves, *Sporting Females*, p. 207.

59. Alexander Wolff, "Oh La La, Steffi!" *Sports Illustrated*, 72:17 (April 23, 1990): 45.

60. Elizabeth Dempster, "Women Writing the Body: Let's Watch a Little How She Dances," *Grafts*, p. 40.

61. Terry Todd, "The Athletic Physique," *Strength Training for Beauty*, 1(5) (September 1984): 55.

62. Margaret Hunt, "The De-Eroticization of Women's Liberation," *Feminist Review*, 34 (Spring 1990): 23–46.

63. Kathy Myers, "Toward a Feminist Erotica," *Looking On*, pp. 198, 200.

64. For a recent survey of eighty-one studies relevant to this issue, see John S. Lyons, Rachel L. Anderson, and David B. Larson, "A Systematic Review of the Effects of Aggressive and Nonaggressive Pornography," *Media, Children, and the Family*, eds. Dolf Zillmann, Jennings Bryant, and Aletha C. Huston (Hillsdale, New Jersey: Lawrence Erlbaum, 1994), pp. 271–310

65. Dolf Zillmann, "Excitation Transfer in Communication-Mediate Aggressive Behavior," *Journal of Experimental Social Psychology*, 7 (1971): 419–34; Dolf Zillmann and Barry B. Sapolsky, "What Mediates the Effect of Mild Erotica on Annoyance and Hostile Behavior in Males?" *Journal of Personality and Social Psychology*, 35 (1977): 587–96; Joanne R. Cantor, Dolf Zillmann, and Edna Einsiedel, "Female Responses to Provocation after Exposure to Aggressive and Erotic Films," *Communication Research*, 5 (1978): 395–412; Barry S. Sapolsky and Dolf Zillmann, "The Effect of Soft-Core and Hard-Core Erotica on Provoked and Unprovoked Hostile Behavior," *Journal of Sex Research*, 17 (1981): 319–43.

66. Neil N. Malamuth and James V. P. Check, "Penile Tumescence and Perceptual Responses to Rape as a Function of A Victim's Perceived Reactions," *Journal of Applied Social Psychology*, 10 (1980): 528–47; Neil M. Malamuth and James V. P. Check, "Sexual Arousal to Rape and Consenting Depictions," *Journal of Abnormal Psychology*, 89 (1980): 763–66; Neil M. Malamuth and James V. P. Check, "The Effects of Mass Media Exposure on Acceptance of Violence against Women," *Journal of Research in Personality*, 15 (1981): 436–46; Edward Donnerstein and Leonard Berkowitz, "Victim Reactions in Aggressive Erotic Films as a Factor in Violence Against Women," *Journal of Personality and Social Psychology*, 41 (1981): 710–24; Dolf Zillmann and Jennings Bryant, "Pornography, Sexual Callousness,

and the Trivialization of Rape," *Journal of Communication,* 32
(1982): 10–21; Neil N. Malamuth and James V. P. Check, "Sexual
Arousal to Rape Depictions," *Journal of Abnormal Psychology,* 92
(1983): 55–67; Daniel Linz, Edward Donnerstein, Steven Penrod, "The
Effects of Multiple Exposure to Filmed Violence against Women,"
Journal of Communication, 34 (1984): 130–47; Neil M. Malamuth
and James V. P. Check, "The Effects of Aggressive Pornography on
Beliefs in Rape Myths," *Journal of Research in Personality,* 19
(1985): 299–320; Dolf Zillmann and James B. Weaver, "Pornography
and Men's Sexual Callousness toward Women," *Pornography,* eds.
Dolf Zillmann and Jennings Bryant (Hillsdale, New Jersey: Lawrence
Erlbaum, 1989), pp. 95–125; Dolf Zillmann, "Effects of Prolonged
Consumption of Pornography," *Pornography,* pp. 127–57. At least
one experiment failed to detect the effects of violent and nonviolent
erotica on reported likelihood to rape; see George Smeaton and Donn
Byrne, "The Effects of R-Rated Violence and Erotica, Individual
Differences, and Victim Characteristics on Acquaintance Rape
Proclivity," *Journal of Research in Personality,* 21 (1987): 171–84.
67. Neil M. Malamuth and Joseph Ceniti, "Repeated Exposure to Violent
and Nonviolent Pornography," *Aggressive Behavior,* 12 (1986): 135.
68. Edward Donnerstein, Marcia Donnerstein, and Ronald Evans, "Erotic
Stimuli and Aggression," *Journal of Personality and Social
Psychology,* 32 (1975): 237–44; Robert A. Baron and Paul A. Bell,
"Sexual Arousal and Aggression by Males," *Journal of Personality
and Social Psychology,* 35 (1977): 79–87; Robert A. Baron, "Height-
ened Sexual Arousal and Physical Aggression," *Journal of Research
in Personality,* 13 (1979): 91–102; Leonard A. White, "Erotica and
Aggression," *Journal of Personality and Social Psychology,* 37
(1979): 591–401; Edward Donnerstein, "Aggressive Erotica and
Violence Against Women," *Journal of Personality and Social
Psychology,* 39 (1980): 269–77; Yoram Jaffe, "Sexual Stimulation,"
Psychological Reports, 48 (1981): 75–81.
69. Dolf Zillmann, James H. Hoyt, and Kenneth D. Day, "Strength and
Duration of the Effect of Aggressive, Violent, and Erotic
Communications on Subsequent Aggressive Behavior,"
Communication Research, 1 (1974): 303.

70. Dolf Zillmann, Jennings Byrant, Paul W. Comisky, and Norman J. Medoff, "Excitation and Hedonic Valence in the Effect of Erotica on Motivated Intermale Aggression," *European Journal of Social Psychology*, 11 (1981): 233–52.

71. John Ramirez, Jennings Bryant, and Dolf Zillmann, "Effects of Erotica on Retaliatory Behavior as a Function of Level of Prior Provocation," *Journal of Personality and Social Psychology*, 43 (1982): 971–78.

72. Edward Donnerstein and Daniel Linz, "Mass Media Sexual Violence and Male Viewers," *American Behavioral Scientist*, 29 (1986): 601–18.

73. Daniel Linz, Edward Donnerstein, Dolf Zillmann, and Jennings Bryant, "The Methods and Merits of Pornography Research," *Journal of Communication*, 38(2) (1988): 180–92.

74. Edward Donnerstein and Daniel Linz, "Mass-Media Sexual Violence and Male Viewers," *Changing Men*, ed. Michael S. Kimmel (London: Sage Publications, 1987), p. 212. See also James V. P. Check and Ted H. Guloien, "Reported Proclivity for Coercive Sex Following Repeated Exposure to Sexual Violent Pornography, Nonviolent Dehumanizing Pornography, and Erotica," *Pornography*, pp. 154–84.

75. Athletic participation explained only 1% of the variance, less than the use of nicotine and alcohol; see Mary P. Koss and John A. Gaines, "The Prediction of Sexual Aggression by Alcohol Use, Athletic Participation, and Fraternity Affiliation," *Journal of Interpersonal Violence*, 8(1) (March 1993): 94–108. See also Thomas L. Jackson, "A University Athletic Department's Rape and Assault Experiences," *Journal of College Student Development*, 32 (January 1991): 77–78. This study of 114 athletes at the University of Arkansas discovered that 11% of them admitted they had physically assaulted a woman and 4% admitted to rape, but the study's lack of data on nonathletes makes it impossible to draw conclusions about sports as a factor in sexual violence. See also Todd W. Crosset, Jeffrey R. Benedict, and Mark A. McDonald, "Male Student-Athletes Reported for Sexual Assault," *Journal of Sport and Social Issues*, 19(2) (May 1995): 126–40. According to this study, athletes, especially those playing football and basketball, are much more likely than other students to be accused of sexual assault.

76. Kim Chernin, *The Obsession: Reflections on the Tyranny of Slenderness* (New York: Harper, 1981), pp. 17–18, 55. Chernin argues, implausibly, that men dislike fat women because they are reminded of their infantile dependence on their mothers. In *The Hungry Self* (New York: Harper, 1986), Chernin sees the love-hate relationship between mothers and daughters as a principal source of anorexia and bulimia.

77. Student: quoted in Susan Bordo, *Unbearable Weight* (Berkeley: University of California Press, 1993), p. 155.

78. Susan J. Douglas, *Where the Girls Are: Growing Up Female with the Mass Media* (New York: Times Books, 1994), p. 16.

79. Susan Birrell and Nancy Theberge, "Ideological Control of Women in Sport," *Women and Sport*, eds. D. Margaret Costa and Sharon R. Guthrie (Champaign: Human Kinetics, 1994), p. 352. On the immediate impact of fitness advertisements, see Alexis S. Tan, "TV Beauty Ads and Role Expectations of Adolescent Female Viewers," *Journalism Quarterly*, 56 (1979): 283–88.

80. Bordo, *Unbearable Weight*, pp. 47, 141, 187, 273 (not in that order) See also Susan Bordo, "Reading the Slender Body," *Body/Politics: Women and the Discourses of Science*, eds. Mary Jacobus, Evelyn Fox Keller, and Sally Shuttleworth (New York: Routledge, 1990), pp. 83–112. Although Monroe may have been the dominant "love goddess" of the decade, she was rivaled by Brigitte Bardot, whose very different body (and cinematic characterizations) attracted the admiration of Simone de Beauvoir: "Seen from behind, her slender, muscular, dancer's body is almost androgynous. Femininity triumphs in her delightful bosom"; quoted by Mandy Merck, *Perversions* (London: Routledge, 1993), p. 77.

81. Linda A. Jackson, *Physical Appearance and Gender* (Albany: State University of New York Press, 1992), p. 158. The explanation may be simply that women are now taller.

82. Ibid., pp. 160–62.

83. Bordo, *Unbearable Weight*, p. 57. The depredations of anorexia are real, but, according to Christina Hoff Sommers, they have been drastically exaggerated; see *Who Stole Feminism?* (New York: Simon & Schuster, 1994), pp. 11–12.

84. Gaines, "Fabricating the Female Body," p. 9.

85. Lenskyj, *Out of Bounds* (Toronto: The Women's Press, 1986), p. 56.

86. Rita Freedman, *Beauty Bound* (Lexington: Lexington Books, 1986), p. 147. Although the assault on "the beauty myth" tends to draw little ammunition from the stores of experimental psychology, feminists might also arm themselves with the research indicating that exposure to unusually attractive bodies, such as those featured in *Playboy* or *Playgirl*, causes men and—to a lesser degree—women to become dissatisfied with their sexual partners. See Douglas T. Kenrick and Sara E. Gutierres, "Contrast Effects and Judgments of Physical Attractiveness," *Journal of Personality and Social Pyschology*, 38 (1980): 131–40; Thomas F. Cash, Diane Walker Cash, and Jonathan W. Butters, " 'Mirror, Mirror on the Wall . . . ?' Contrast Effects and Self-Evaluations of Physical Attractiveness," *Personality and Social Psychology Bulletin*, 9 (1983): 351–58; James B. Weaver, Jonathan L. Masland, and Dolf Zillmann, "Effect of Erotica on Young Men's Aesthetic Perceptions of their Female Sexual Partners," *Perceptual and Motor Skills*, 58 (1984): 929–30; Dolf Zillmann and Jennings Bryant, "Pornography's Impact on Sexual Satisfaction," *Journal of Applied Social Psychology*, 18 (1988): 438–53; Douglas T. Kenrick, Sara E. Gutierres, and Laurie L. Goldberg, "Influence of Popular Erotica on Judgments of Strangers and Mates," *Journal of Experimental Social Psychology*, 25 (1989): 159–67; Bill Thornton and Scott Moore, "Physical Attractiveness Contrast Effect," *Personality and Social Psychology Bulletin*, 19 (August 1993): 474–80.

87. Mary Jo Kane and Susan L. Greendorfer, "The Media's Role in Accommodating and Resisting Stereotyped Images of Women in Sport," *Women, Media and Sport*, ed. Pamela J. Creedon (London: Sage Publications, 1994), p. 30.

88. Eldon E. Snyder and Joseph E. Kivlin, "Women Athletes and Aspects of Psychological Well-Being and Body Image," *Research Quarterly*, 46 (May 1975): 191–99; Linda Ho and Jon E. Walker, "Female Athletes and Nonathletes," *Journal of Sport Behavior*, 5(1) (March 1982): 12–27; V. V. Prakasa Rao and Steven J. Overman, "Psychological Well-Being and Body Image," *Journal of Sport Behavior*, 9(2) (June 1986): 79–91.

89. Maryse H. Richards, et al, "Relation of Weight to Body Image in Pubertal Boys and Girls from Two Communities," *Developmental Psychology*, 26 (1990): 313–21.

90. Nelson, *The Stronger Women Get*, pp. 39, 214.

91. Anne Bolin, "Vandalized Vanity: Feminine Physiques Betrayed and Portrayed," *Tattoo, Torture, Mutilation, and Adornment*, eds. Frances E. Mascia-Lees and Patricia Sharpe (Albany: SUNY Press, 1992), p. 89.

92. Laurie Schulze, "On the Muscle," *Fabrications*, pp. 59, 261, n.65.

93. Douglas, *Where the Girls Are*, p. 262.

94. Philip N. Myers, Jr., and Frank A. Biocca, "The Elastic Body Image," *Journal of Communication*, 42(3) (Summer 1992): 127. Mood was measured by the Multiple Affect Adjective Check List.

95. Susan Bordo, "Reading the Male Body," *The Male Body*, ed. Laurence Goldstein (Ann Arbor: University of Michigan Press, 1994), p. 266.

96. Myers and Biocca, "The Elastic Body Image," p. 111.

97. Marc E. Mishkind, Judith Rodin, Lisa R. Silberstein, and Ruth H. Striegel-Moore, "The Embodiment of Masculinity," *Changing Men*, ed. Michael S. Kimmel (London: Sage Publications, 1987), p. 37.

98. On the concept, see Harold Garfinkel, "Conditions of Successful Degradation Ceremonies," *American Journal of Sociology*, 61 (1956): 420–24.

99. F. Scott Fitzgerald, *Tender Is the Night* (New York: Scribner's, 1934), p. 367.

100. Larry A. Tucker, "Relationship Between Perceived Somatotype and Body Cathexis of College Males," *Psychological Reports*, 50 (1982): 986.

101. Lora Jacobi and Thomas F. Cash, "In Pursuit of the Perfect Appearance," *Journal of Applied Social Psychology*, 24 (1994): 383.

102. Barry Glassner, *Bodies* (New York: Putnam, 1988), p. 118.

103. Laurie B. Mintz and Nancy E. Betz, "Sex Differences in the Nature, Realism, and Correlates of Body Image," *Sex Roles*, 15 (1986): 185–95; Linda A. Jackson, Linda A. Sullivan, and Janet S. Hymes, "Gender, Gender Role, and Physical Appearance," *Journal of Psychology*, 121 (1987): 51–56.

104. Glassner, *Bodies*, p. 134; Thomas F. Cash, Barbara A. Winstead, Louis H. Janda, "The Great American Shape-Up," *Psychology Today*, 20 (April 1986): 30–37.

105. Sally Bell Beck, Christine I. Ward-Hull, and Paul M. McClear, "Variables Related to Women's Somatic Preferences of the Male and Female Body," *Journal of Personality and Social Psychology*, 34 (1976): 1200–1210.

106. Willam E. Buckley et al., "Estimated Prevalence of Anabolic Steroid Use Among Male High School Seniors," *Journal of the American Medical Association*, 260:23 (1988): 3441–45: cited in Andrew W. Miracle, Jr., and C. Roger Rees, *Lessons of the Locker Room* (Amherst: Prometheus Books, 1994), pp. 113–14.

107. On the ravages of steroids, see John Hoberman, *Mortal Engines* (New York: Free Press, 1994).

108. The untranslatable term *jouissance*, which French feminists oppose to the more restrictive "phallic" term, *plaisir*, was popularized by Roland Barthes in *Le Plaisir du texte* (Paris: Seuil, 1973); see Jane Gallop, *Thinking Through the Body* (New York: Columbia University Press, 1988), pp. 119–24.

Appendix A

1. Allen Guttmann, *From Ritual to Record* (New York: Columbia University Press, 1978), pp. 1–14; for the extended development of a quite similar conception of sports, see Bernard Suits, *The Grasshopper: Games, Life, and Utopia* (Toronto: University of Toronto Press, 1978).

2. Sigmund Freud, *Jenseits des Lustprinzips* (1920), *Werkausgabe*, eds. Anna Freud and Ilse Grubrich-Simitis (Frankfurt: Fischer, 1978), 1:217.

3. Sigmund Freud, *Massenpsychologie und Ich-Analyse* (1921), *Werkausgabe*, 2:444.

4. Sigmund Freud, "Die Wiederstände gegen die Psychoanalyse" (1925), *Werkausgabe*, 2:56.

5. Christoph Wulf, "Körper und Tod," *Die Wiederkehr des Körpers*, eds. Dietmar Kamper and Christoph Wulf (Frankfurt: Suhrkamp,

1982), p. 270. Michael Richardson's *Georges Bataille* (London: Routledge, 1994) is a useful introduction to Bataille's important but frequently gnomic work.
6. Freud, *Das Ich und das Es* (1923), *Werkausgabe,* 1:393.
7. Freud, *Massenpsychologie und Ich-Analyse* (1921), *Werkausgabe,* 2:444.

Appendix B
1. Catharine A. MacKinnon, *Only Words* (Cambridge: Harvard University Press, 1993); for a similar view, see Andrea Dworkin, *Pornography: Men Possessing Women* (New York: Putnam, 1981).
2. Rosalind Coward and the WAVAW, "What Is Pornography?" *Looking On,* ed. Rosemary Betterton (London: Pandora, 1987), p. 175.
3. Harry Brod, "Pornography and the Alienation of Male Sexuality," *Men, Masculinities and Social Theory,* eds. Jeff Hearn and David Morgan (London: Unwin Hyman, 1990), p. 136.
4. Examples of this approach can be found in Neil M. Malamuth and Edward Donnerstein, eds., *Pornography as Sexual Aggression* (Orlando: Academic Press, 1984); Dolf Zillmann and Jennings Bryant, eds., *Pornography* (Hillsdale, New Jersey: Lawrence Erlbaum, 1989).
5. John S. Lyons, Rachel L. Anderson, and David B. Larson, "A Systematic Review of the Effects of Aggressive and Nonaggressive Pronography," *Media, Children, and the Family,* eds. Dolf Zillmann, Jennings Bryant, and Aletha C. Huston (Hillsdale, New Jersey: Lawrence Erlbaum, 1994), p. 272.
6. Gilman, *Sexuality,* p. 6.

INDEX

246   INDEX

Text: 10/13 Aldus
Compositor: Columbia University Press
Printer: Edwards Brothers
Binder: Edwards Brothers

RISE *and* FALL

of the

LESSER SUN GODS

Bruce Bond

www.elixirpress.com

Book design by Steven Seighman
Cover art: "Cast a Shadow" by Kathy Jones

The author would like to thank the editors of *The American Journal of Poetry*, *The Dialogist*, *The Laurel Review*, *Painted Bride Quarterly*, and *Plume* in which parts of this book previously appeared.

Library of Congress Cataloging-in-Publication DataNames: Bond, Bruce, 1954- author.Title: Rise and fall of the lesser sun gods / Bruce Bond.Description: Denver Colorado : Elixir Press, [2018] Identifiers: LCCN 2017050694 | ISBN 9781932418668 (alk. paper)Classification: LCC PS3552. O5943 A6 2018 | DDC 811/.54—dc23 LC recordavailable at https://lccn.loc.gov/2017050694

10   9   8   7   6   5   4   3   2   1

Right above the surface of the Sun, something strange happens.
The Sun becomes extremely hot again, this time it is 1. 5 to 2 million
degrees. Cooler than the center of the Sun, but not by very much!
The reason for the extremely hot outer layer (called the "corona")
is a mystery that hasn't been solved.

—STANFORD SOLAR CENTER

The least touchable object in the world is the eye.

—RUDOLF ARNHEIM, "PARABLES OF SUN LIGHT"

RISE *and* FALL

of the

LESSER SUN GODS

1.

    The way they dragged us out of bed,
tore us from the roots of one night's growth,

the incorrigible muck of dread and wishes.
How they lit each furnace, each cold eye

drawn to the mirrors and coffee machines,
to news that crackled open with the voice

of news on fire. Something in our caution,
the genuflections of our looking up

as one might look at a steeple of flame
above the courthouse before both crown

and chamber crumble as one. It felt like fate.
The heat that oils the keyhole of the eye.

Needs that follow suns and sun gods still
who fall, like us, and, in their falling, rise.

2.

A lamp then is a thing at prayer, an homage
to the slow immolation of stars turned

monstrous as they age. A lamp is one
part sun, another an elegy to sunlight.

An acolyte made of what it worships,
flames that fall to earth and just keep falling.

Light smolders through the flesh at dawn.
Another day, another obit for a stranger.

Each visual breath of print gone dry.
Each sentence cinched with small black hole.

If you look deep enough, you see a sun,
a temple, a temple on fire. I see myself,

a child, who followed a father who followed
the news as some follow rules, and others

bitterness, doubt, or any of the small-boned
uncertainties that make us us, gods gods.

3.

Long ago the one and only Father
and Son said, some things must be unclear

to appear. They must be campfire-clear
among the lords and branches of the pines.

They must be clear as dark between the stars
to camouflage the gods. Long ago

I ate the bread, and I was hungry still.
I was a kid caught in the crossfire

between day and night, day as day
and night as the harvest of daylight.

My father taught me dreams were mine alone,
and there we were. Eating the daylight.

The new dead were everywhere. Alive
in us, in every unclear kid who thinks,

isn't it a little cruel and lovely to say,
drink of this, my blood. And so, I did.

4.

It takes a full eclipse to see the deep-
red flash of the chromosphere, the hidden

sun inside the sunlight. It takes the black
plate of the moon to see what bodies see

when they open both vein and eye to give
to each an image. What I do not see

longs to speak the language of the seen,
as a child's hurt longs for lips that bind,

or a killing field for an April harvest.
The many mothers of the savior look up

to bear witness to the cross, to Christ
as mother, lifted above whatever history

and its dispensations. What remains
remains eclipsed, crowned in thorns and blossoms.

5.

Suns rise and fall and with them bodies
in the laps of mothers whose blood is stone.

Some images of kindness are neither
cruel nor kind, but sepulcher marble,

cold to the touch, if the warden lets you.
My grandfather died in a chair because

beds were painful, and he had no faith
in medicine and angels of this world.

He died of faith, which was his choice,
all of us in different chromospheres

beneath a sun that travelled one direction.
One plow to cut the sky into flower.

It takes an eclipse of the particular
sky to see the rose in it as mirror

of our own. Alone and cast out west,
each in the fate of all. The many gods

in one killing field, one believer dying
in a chair. One shadow chair pinned below.

My grandfather's house was a mansion,
its many doors laid open in the bones.

6.

Say paradise floats above our stories.
Does it take a story to get there still.

A mother unveils her face before the child
with a *boo*. One word. The speed of angels.

Somewhere the carver blows a puff of air.
It just might be his final gesture, his *boo*

over the names and dates laid in stone.
It just might blow the invisible candle

to clear the stone of flame, the flame of smoke.
To make the cut appear. More deep, more clear.

7.

They came here long ago, the great observers
who watched the many suns rise and fall

into images they made, papyrus scrolls
that went the way of the pillager's torch.

They came and rose as did their monoliths
whose faces crumbled in the desert wind.

And what they watched watched them on the altar
as the widow who talks talks to no one

at the grave. The great observers of night
read there a story full of gods because

the spirits of dead fathers and mothers rose
through their eyes and pinned them to the heavens.

Even the horror brought with it the comfort
of pins. Like talk. They came here long ago,

those who saw in the conquistador an angel
fallen to earth. And he just kept falling.

And over his grave, they laid the shield he came with.
The bright bronze cross on fire in the night.

8.

I know the loneliness of being two
who cannot find each other in the dark.

They cannot find the dark, the lone ghost
who would carry their abandoned parts

from the killing field to a widow's door
a great pillar of smoke, the wind that sweeps

Always somewhere a war between the gods,
a great pillar of smoke the wind sweeps

the remnants of a home across the border.
Is it any wonder god gets personal.

Our Mother of Perpetual Abandon,
I pray this finds you with the other spirits

whose solitary god is one part man,
the other the figure of a man in flames.

One part eye. The other the light that falls
and just keeps falling. And not a god at all.

9.

Apprenticed to his chemistry set, a boy
does the trick that turns water into wine.

His holy spirit is one part vinegar,
one the rebel science that loves to pretend.

And ammonia. All three ingredients.
Clear as water and the word that holds it.

His jars of toxins, salts, gas-blue cobalt,
the wounded russet of his ferrous metal,

they fit neatly in a box. Each a key
to open yet another box of keys

and boxes. I know that child, that stranger.
He taught me how to laugh. Being apart.

Me here, the illusion there, the gods
of rebel chemistry longing to be seen.

10.

God without the cold beauty of logic
is no god. Method no method that lives

for merely the cold methodical reasons.
What the blood versus wine debate asks

is this: is there a god of stone that is
not stone, that is a boy with a stone in hand.

Science cannot fall in love with science.
Kids will tell you. It takes a scientist. A kid.

11.

Show me the machine that powders winter
across the killing fields, and I will show you

a statue's face beneath the fallen snow.
Still this choir loft of small glass jars,

specimens that, when separate, have names
I read, when fused, names inside of names.

I have a body that a child gave me.
And before that a missing child, a trick.

Is the one world so lonely for illusion
always, and so no sooner for a witness.

When a child goes missing, there is no god
to take her place. Snow melts. Eyes emerge.

12.

Water turns to wine, and we look harder.
Wine into blood. And then, harder still.

If what we cannot explain we must pass
over in silence, tell me. Why. Explain.

Tell the mother who talks softly to her
self. Tell the no one there who answers.

The great observers look so hard sometimes,
they see their stars shatter into tears.

The killing fields into blossoms that say,
look, look hard, and no sooner, look away.

I love that. The unturned keys of flowers.
Question everything is a scripture

whose angel hovers over the testament.
What the blood versus wine debate asks

is this: when a child goes missing, what does
a mother pray for first: evidence or faith

13.

How quick we are to hang a human face
over the cold dark basement of the well.

Hello, says the child in us. *Hello*,
the hole in earth with an older voice.

So what do you see, asks the therapist
with his gallery made of accidents.

Ink, loneliness, more ink. Dear ink,
I want to talk to you about these dreams

that wake me up, the way they disappear
into the dark that made them. Is it true,

where there is chaos, there is the iconoclast
who made the world that way, just so.

Where there is sun, there are many eyes
with tiny suns in them, days that lift

and dip their pens, to pull them from the well.
How quick I am to hang a human face

over the killing fields. Dear ink, if you
are listening, I want to talk about a dream.

14.

What do you see, asks the sun, rising,
and the pen lays its figure over nature.

One of nature's own and yet a thing
apart. Which is why it writes. Lonely

beyond words or, if not words, design.
Dear something, someone, dear echo, zero, o.

15.

When my father returned from the Pacific
theater, his sentences kept trailing off.

If he was a stranger to my mother,
imagine what she, in panic, was to him.

How little she knew of the dark margins
his gunship shelled to soften up the shore.

Where there is design, there is a surge
of wild water to move it through storm.

There is the war no one can understand
though, in time, it floats to the surface

of the widowed face. Lined in ink.
There is a man talking to no one in his sleep.

16.

The core is brighter, the deeper you go,
and thrashes its iron for none to see.

Only at best to measure, number, know
as the chalk-white exponential quotient

of horrors I have seen. Take this bomb
and go, multiply, multiply again.

Take this father whose unremembered
dream seals its monument in stone.

I too am quick to hang the face of one
earth's blunders over the god-sized figures

in the mind. I too undo the old designs
to open the abyss for a new world order.

17.

War killed all fear in him. Or so he said.
And so his memoir was a skeleton

of names, dates, facts to keep him company,
to draft a fearless contract with the future.

I kept him company by asking for stories
I do not recall, though talking cheered him

in his final days. Where there is a hole
in earth, there is the softer earth nearby.

Or so it was under the black umbrellas,
our box of ash a thing we talked to, knowing

there are objects, here, and what they mean
over there. There are suns. We follow.

There is dirt, displaced, like love, or fear,
then shoveled back on what we leave there.

The seed must be buried in the earth and die in darkness in order
that the lovelier creature of light should rise.... following some dark,
uncertain law, incapable of forming anything that can endure.
—FRIEDRICH SHELLING, *PHILOSOPHICAL INQUIRIES INTO*
THE NATURE OF HUMAN FREEDOM

Black is the true face of light, only we do not see this.
—NICOLAI TESLA

18.

If the head were the lord of the body,
it would never rest. But rise and fall,

as suns fall, only to crown the night
with want, loss, words that are the children of loss.

It would stare at suicide letters, heavy
in our hands, or close our eyes in prayer

to the dark of ink that brought us to it.
Death and I, we dreamed of being here

together, but our names broke down before us.
I apologize to those whose names I forget,

whose deaths are one death now. What did I
expect. And who. What lord of the lord

brain that longs to be a servant of mind.
Last night I left a dead man in a vault.

And then I woke. And he was nowhere.
The door to the vault untouched by hands.

19.

The empty safe became my name for him.
Our shared frailty made me lighter, weaker.

I do not pretend I loved him enough
or love saves us from something other

than one such love. You and I were listening
to Leonard Bernstein once—to *God is*

the simplest of them all—and I saw
there a particle so small it was the stuff

of every other. Like desire at the root
of dread and sacrifice. Or an instinct

in the thinking core. Is it true: stars
lie down, with us, in the names of friends.

20.

One and one are still one, if you believe
the music. The language that believes in nothing.

One and one are eleven, says the logic
of chisels. They cannot make them one mark.

21.

The praise of simple things is a breath.
Go ask the uncut grasses of the common.

Must one god be our particle, our root.
Language beyond language longs to lie

in the common. To die in empathy
for death since we cannot understand it.

I never understood the friend who drank
himself blind. Easy to condemn.

Stars are cold. As nails in December.
But sky is neither simple. Nor equation.

If the head were the god of the body,
power would flow in one direction. Like light

over moons and stones and our talk
with stones, when we become the half that listens.

22.

The memorial made of black rock,
of men's names laid in a deeper shade,

recruits no child here. My language is
more a thing of stone each time I visit.

Eclipses have a history of people
going mad. Giant frogs devour them.

Villagers miscarry. Peasants bang
pots and spoons to scare the beast away.

A certain madness explains. Here lies
the one that will not, cannot. Everywhere,

the nothing that reveals. I know less
and less, when I stand before a monument.

23.

The star-hard crest of a deeper burden.
Fifty-eight thousand names. You can read

them with your hands. Imagine that
and then a rock seventy times the size.

Numbers matter. I cannot tell you why,
not in the way numbers can. Imagine

the heavier monument, the absent cry
for a nation that gave our war its name.

24.

Sun arcs the yard in one direction. It falls,
gods fall, and children, and our conflicts

in the childhood era. And the new child
works out his issues in violent avatars.

Tunes that beat the enemy unconscious.
A bored kid knows something about the power

of nothing. He has seen the black poppy
of a soldier's eye. The book opened wide

for none to read. However large the flower.
Take this black mirror, the children looking in.

Take these names that would be one nation
under God. Among the stones of millions.

25.

If you walk this way, just far enough,
alone, you see what our ancestors saw

in the twitching of reeds and sleepy limbs
of the vaguely remembered. *Are you there,*

says the literal tree that was a god once,
when the lords of bodies walked with us,

alone, and we felt connected as sleepers
are, who lie all night and speak to no one.

Are you there, says the hard evidence
of children, abandoned, intimately observed

by none. The dispossessed are echoes now
that left here long ago. Say a bird,

unseen, troubles a limb, a hidden space.
It leaves behind the shape we call *bird,*

hollow as the mouth that sings its name.
Walk with me into the open throat.

Hollow as mothers are who pulled us through
the lost angelic poverties of silence.

26.

Then the goddess in the laurel says,
the world begins in trepidation and flight,

however rooted to the unseen ground.
We are going to need a better word

for *life*, more capable of mistakes.
More attuned to words, their swift departures,

rustling the evidence of leaves in flight.
The new laurels are dead and all machine:

smart phones that shudder from a space,
a pocket, and reason beyond reckoning

makes an autumn of our ancient music.
The other face of fall is science, dear science,

vaulted in life's devices like a voice
made beautiful by what it has to learn.

27.

Tell me, if what the goddess fears is rape,
does she escape into the laurel life

with her will to choose. You who walk
this way, alone, tell me, what is science

to a will like this. What is a laurel.
What to do with the question whose answers

are dilemmas. Long ago a goddess
became a tree because a man longed

to seize her, own her. She entered a season
more inexplicable because she saw

no other way. She escaped, alive
with leaves the season cast to the river.

28.

A white ice fells the trees of November
made beautiful by what we have to learn.

We are going to need a better word
for a goddess we love and have no faith in.

The one we talk to still. And for the faith
whose repressed understandings emerge

in nightmares of poison water we give
to children. We have crossed that threshold

a child crosses into the science that makes
our pantheon a novelty. A toy.

Our gods displaced among the fetishes
of champions on club house walls, dream

boats, fast machines. When a tree-god dies,
it leaves behind a skeleton of attentions

in the pattern of trees that asks our science,
are you there. If I call, will you pick up.

29.

Will you answer the cell of each live thing,
because it is lonely, specific, afraid.

Longing might be friendship to a child
who carves a loveless letter in a tree.

As if names were spirits, lives that ask,
will you cradle my phone-call in the wild

and say, hello, in the form of a question.
As doors do, or the mouth in agony

or song. When a sun dies, will you give
the news its voice. When the darkness opens.

30.

Out of the body of the paramour,
the spouse. Out the body of the spouse,

the older spouse Out of the star charts
of the zodiac, the skeletal attentions

of a science whose telescopes look up,
apprenticed to a sky clarified of idols.

Science cannot fall in love with science.
Dear alchemy, thank you for your book

in tatters, your skeletons, your fascinations.
Out of the dark ages: the godless sun

whose distance from the rapture spawns zero
after zero. Out of the zero, the table

of elements, its step by step that grows
more heavy as we go. Out of the known,

the isotopes we engineer to nature.
No sooner born than blazing to extinction.

31.

Out of the body of the beloved: the love
that bears one name as it sheds the older

younger body, the way a god sheds
the blood of characters in books we love.

Out of our mistakes over dinner,
listening poorly: a better, kinder mistake.

Could it be our idolatries have less
to do with the fallen world of objects.

More with the fall, a failure to listen
to the silence there, in the names

and images whose spirit is not theirs.
Not ours. Where a mother was, the word

mother. And the voice that was hers
laid into the silence she needs to speak.

When my mother died, I had no words.
She was always interrupting that way.

(Out of the black car, the child in black.)
And it took letting go to hear her again.

(Out of the updraft: the leaves of birds.)
A give in the wind to absolve the branches.

Out of the younger face: a father's chin,
a mother's nervous tic, a newborn stranger.

32.

Sometimes I need a kinder, funnier savior.
As if an idea might become an idol,

and forgiveness is always elsewhere.
Out of the idea of love, nothing perhaps.

You and I, we are always partly something
coming from nothing. I love that. I do.

Out of the marriage bed comes the marriage.
Out of the marriage, the older younger marriage.

Somewhere back there we agreed, I guess.
The first to rise feeds the cats. *Hello,*

I say in my own tongue. And they come running.
Hello, dear cats, I say. Speaking cat.

33.

Hello, dear world, says the sky at dawn
as if *world* meant *earth*, and *earth* a place,

our place on the whole we never see.
A sphere that, turning toward us, turns away,

Like a song. Or an effigy of song
that fades behind the fiery horizon.

I never hear the part of me that sings
or speaks on behalf of those who listen.

Just another reason I sing again:
to turn the music over like a planet.

Long ago I lived in the center
of the world because I was a child

who died into an older child, a me
afraid of one and not the one I was.

Every child a pin in the wheel
of the sun's passage, its sacred curve

closed, with no beginning, no end,
surviving the ash of circular things.

34.

Giordano Bruno burned alive less
because earth, as he saw it, circled the sun,

than because he saw beyond the sun
the civilized planets no myth before had seen.

Only a theory, he knew, but the one
he would not take back. He never will.

Hello, dear world, says the holy city,
and the evangelical tourist bus

smokes and idles at the wailing wall.
and someone raises a hand, and the questions

have answers, and answers no question in return.
Around here a story means the world

to those afraid of burning, with their books.
And the rooftops spread their rugs in the sun.

35.

Evangelicals from the new age
keep pouring from their buses to see the basin

where their story ends. Half of seeing
is believing, the other the small sad

plain where no one lives. For all we know.
A lady asks, what happens to the Jews

who help the Christian fight the infidel.
She feels the small sad horror of a girl

or two, though the billions are more
difficult to imagine, to frighten, to mourn.

Half of believing is the empty flatland,
the other the stars that burn into focus,

and food is scarce, and birds miracles
of survival who scatter from our path.

36.

Half of believing is a story afraid
to end. And yet afraid to never end

the way some fear silence. Some release.
When a tower roars to pieces, the ground

burns with a billion scattered narratives.
What history would not give to needle

the flesh together with a mother's hand.
What a mother would not give. *Dear god,*

says the silence on TV in the mall.
A fire in the woods, and we its children.

Sometimes silence is the better story.
Everything is holy. Or nothing at all.

37.

Go ask the cities where the sirens rise
and fall so daily now they turn to suns.

When Oppenheimer saw what he made,
its wind blown through their goggles on the plains,

he thought of Shiva: *If the radiance
of a thousand suns were to burst at once.*

Not the paramour with glacial skin
no creation's drum in one hand,

the iron of the trident in the other.
What Oppenheimer saw was horror thrown

in one direction, hymen broken, beauty
crossed, fire's axis driven into earth.

38.

I knew so little of a cross like that,
when, years later, we hid beneath our desks.

The world was full of Shivas. I was told,
make yourself safe, small. *You will be fine,*

they said. You who were no one before
a you, before your father led you down

the basement stairs. Welcome to your new home
beneath the fallout of Los Angeles.

When I thought of Russia, I felt cold.
I am become death, said Shiva. Becoming

Shiva. Becoming a day when heaven goes
to paradise. Or hell. When god starts over.

39.

Hell I understand. But do you want
the man with the finger on the button

believing in paradise. In a failed
ecology of choices. I tell my stories,'

you are not alone. A father leads you
to the basement still. He pulls the handle

on the freezer, dips his hands in light.
In the ah of winter. Every December,

a light snow christens Los Angeles still.
And it is not real snow. And so it lasts.

If we separate God or the Ideas from the temporal world, "both are dead"....
like those many rays of the sun which are dissipated in space, not being
by chance reflected or absorbed.

—GEORGE SANTAYANA

His flaming robes stream'd out beyond his heels,
And gave a roar, as if of earthly fire,
That scared away the meek ethereal hours
And made their dove wings tremble. On he flared.

—JOHN KEATS, "THE FALL OF HYPERION"

40.

The city of angels is buried in exhaust
at the edge of the ocean where starlets live.

Some of them worship the sun with oil
and mirrors to turn them dark, the blood

stirred beneath an image of health, youth,
and finally, corruption. Another winter,

another rose. And *I was born there*,
I write on my retirement application,

though *there* is so much smolder, long ago,
and once it clears the homes are full of strangers.

41.

Always another Hollywood marriage,
another star slipping through the arms

of starlets, with all the stress of living
on the set and pretending as lovers do

in the movies. As a boy, I loved ideas
I thought were girls, and movies shot nearby,

with sets I recognized and girls I didn't.
Even my town was a place far away,

like sun on your skin, a radio in the sand.
A disc of fire enlarged against the skyline.

42.

As a boy, I saw Raquel Welsh
in some talk show where the ice of her

composure broke. *And if you are good,*
she said, *I just might give you a kiss.*

Her host paused, failing to respond,
and you could see in her face the scared

awkward beauty of a childhood need
stripped down to television silence.

Pity the angels, it would say. They give
to love a face and take it down again.

On a starlet's vanity: a rose, a script,
a bald mannequin waiting for its hair.

43.

The stars of Los Angeles are fading
against the ambient smoke of light.

Sleep has no illusions. You are ready
or not. No man of means can buy his way.

No fabricated comma to slip into
at will. And out. Sleep with its illusions.

And sometimes you see a celebrity
biography, a *Vogue,* a script of pills.

And sometimes it gets so bad, sleep
so far away, the pill that works works

too well. And you ask yourself what.
What did I dream. Or did I dream at all.

44.

If a body displaces the water it enters,
what of the sun that breaks the sea horizon.

What groundswell of confusion comes our way.
Like the time my friend lost his power

of speech. All except the word *shit*
spirited above the mess of language.

I see still: tears that never come and so
continue to find us, speechless, over dinner.

In a passage he wrote long ago, a movie
lodges in its projector, shudders, blackens,

and peels back in a malignancy of light.
The *uncoveredness* of being. That

is how my friend described it in a poem.
A word made of fire that burns and never

quite burns through: flower whose reverie
and license obscure whatever dread.

45.

Beauty is always larger than the form
it takes. I see that. I see light spill over

the frame of the movie. Over the man
whose holding back gives the heart a thing

to burn. If the song ends in violence,
you know it has touched something dreadful

and survived. When the soprano dies
on stage, when she swoons into the small

black pool on the surface of the eye,
you know her as real and unreal. Both.

She who suffers at the hand of music
a death made large and thereby distant, small.

46.

An act of kindness is no less *beautiful*,
which makes the word feel a little hopeless.

Whatever the story, it is always too small.
It could be heaven, our white light of erasure,

that grazes us in a moment of panic.
Or the way light falls on this and that.

My language has no word for the power
of speech returning to a man who can't say

where he has been. He has no word to show you.
And the closed eye continues to burn.

47.

Why Keats never found a way to end
his farewell to the gods, no one knew.

Our speaker, the dreamer, barely speaks.
But we do know this. As the poet wrote,

somewhere in a nearby room his brother
was dying. A tumbler tipped over and chimed.

The scent of blood had a metal in it.
No doubt a bit of insomniac confusion

explains some of the tedious weeping
of the poem's shore and gorgeous depressives.

Gods of suns and planets die and still
skies move. Planets follow the laws of seasons.

Still an April sky floats across the ocean,
buckets overflowing with black milk.

All gods the gods of beauty now, carved
of wood and stone in these, our dying postures.

48.

We remember Daphne not as this laurel
or that, but as a dream of one in all.

Not unlike a sick man whom we recall
in words that are a stranger to his sickness.

We say difference makes us memorial,
but as a god it eats us, its children. It forgets.

The way our common nature forgets the details,
or the details forget the way they felt.

The sun-god is swallowed in his own mane,
his fire roared like blood into a pillow.

What good are voices with no listener in them.
Sometimes the wind-borne anxieties—

the pillow startled red, the oblique signature
of clouds seen from the roof where a medic

smokes alone—they give themselves to one wind,
bound by a common emptiness, a cloud.

49.

If those on stage take on the fire
of the footlights, their faces pinned as suns

to the unseen gazes of the crowd,
if they become memorial by character

difficulties under the stagecraft laurels,
they are not alone. Nor seen entirely.

They are just gods after all, and so
neither suns nor separate from all that fire.

I learned how to sleep from my father
who repeated the word *one* in his head.

The weight of it would slacken on its stem.
It dreamt, I trust. He did not remember.

His silence on defenseless matters spoke
to certain strengths. Sleep came easily,

then not at all. Finally speechless,
he kissed the son he kissed last as a child.

50.

I carry my memory like a suitcase
I can't unlatch for fear the smoke would take me.

Lust or dread or the kinder dispensations,
I carry them. To love a god is lonely.

51.

I too want to believe every face at birth
is a rock on fire, falling earthward,

and the flash of arrival, the shock of milk,
burns each former life, if not at once

then slowly, over years, throwing back
the ash of what we said, how we said it.

If I'm a fool for the unbreakable
cyphers of stars, opening their designs

to the smoke of prayers and fathers' bodies,
I admit, I have my own expectations

I pinned up there like a child's drawing
full of anger: all that fire approaching.

What is a soul that it should leave in pieces,
the way an apple leaves the hand it feeds.

Here on the shore of the great forgetting,
who wouldn't look under each drowned word.

Revive, revive. Dying is a fuel that way.
Who would not tell the story that takes us

there and back, flaming into ourselves,
fighting heaven with heaven, until nothing

too would be our birthright: the closing palms
of a book, welling up with white light.

Photo by Nicki Cohen

BRUCE BOND is the author of twenty books including, most recently, *Immanent Distance: Poetry and the Metaphysics of the Near at Hand* (U of MI, 2015), *Black Anthem* (Tampa Review Prize, U of Tampa, 2016), *Gold Bee* (Helen C. Smith Award, Crab Orchard Award, Southern Illinois University Press, 2016), *Sacrum* (Four Way Books, 2017), and *Blackout Starlight: New and Selected Poems 1997-2015* (E. Phillabaum Award, LSU, 2017). Presently he is Regents Professor at University of North Texas.

TITLES FROM ELIXIR PRESS

POETRY

Circassian Girl by Michelle Mitchell-Foust

Imago Mundi by Michelle Mitchell-Foust

Distance From Birth by Tracy Philpot

Original White Animals by Tracy Philpot

Flow Blue by Sarah Kennedy

A Witch's Dictionary by Sarah Kennedy

The Gold Thread by Sarah Kennedy

Rapture by Sarah Kennedy

Monster Zero by Jay Snodgrass

Drag by Duriel E. Harris

Running the Voodoo Down by Jim McGarrah

Assignation at Vanishing Point by Jane Satterfield

Her Familiars by Jane Satterfield

The Jewish Fake Book by Sima Rabinowitz

Recital by Samn Stockwell

Murder Ballads by Jake Adam York

Floating Girl (Angel of War) by Robert Randolph

Puritan Spectacle by Robert Strong

X-testaments by Karen Zealand

Keeping the Tigers Behind Us by Glenn J. Freeman

Bonneville by Jenny Mueller

State Park by Jenny Mueller

Cities of Flesh and the Dead by Diann Blakely

Green Ink Wings by Sherre Myers

Orange Reminds You Of Listening by Kristin Abraham

In What I Have Done & What I Have Failed To Do by Joseph P. Wood

Bray by Paul Gibbons

The Halo Rule by Teresa Leo

Perpetual Care by Katie Cappello

The Raindrop's Gospel: The Trials of St. Jerome and St. Paula by Maurya Simon

Prelude to Air from Water by Sandy Florian

Let Me Open You A Swan by Deborah Bogen

Cargo by Kristin Kelly

Spit by Esther Lee

Rag & Bone by Kathryn Nuernberger

Kingdom of Throat-stuck Luck by George Kalamaras

Mormon Boy by Seth Brady Tucker

Nostalgia for the Criminal Past by Kathleen Winter

Little Oblivion by Susan Allspaw

Quelled Communiqués by Chloe Joan Lopez

Stupor by David Ray Vance

Curio by John A. Nieves

The Rub by Ariana-Sophia Kartsonis

Visiting Indira Gandhi's Palmist by Kirun Kapur

Freaked by Liz Robbins

Looming by Jennifer Franklin

Flammable Matter by Jacob Victorine

Prayer Book of the Anxious by Josephine Yu

flicker by Lisa Bickmore

Sure Extinction by John Estes

Selected Proverbs by Michael Cryer

Rise and Fall of the Lesser Sun Gods by Bruce Bond

I will not kick my friends by Kathleen Winter

Barnburner by Erin Hoover

FICTION

How Things Break by Kerala Goodkin

Juju by Judy Moffat

Grass by Sean Aden Lovelace

Hymn of Ash by George Looney

Nine Ten Again by Phil Condon

Memory Sickness by Phong Nguyen

Troglodyte by Tracy DeBrincat

The Loss of All Lost Things by Amina Gautier

The Killer's Dog by Gary Fincke

Everyone Was There by Anthony Varallo

The Wolf Tone by Christy Stillwell